David Vizard's
HOW TO PORT &
FLOW TEST
Cylinder Heads

David Vizard

S-A DESIGN

CarTech®

CarTech®

CarTech®, Inc.
6118 Main Street
North Branch, MN 55056
Phone: 651-277-1200 or 800-551-4754
Fax: 651-277-1203
www.cartechbooks.com

Edit by Paul Johnson
Layout by Monica Seiberlich

ISBN 978-1-934709-64-1
Item No. SA215

Library of Congress Cataloging-in-Publication Data

Vizard, David.
David Vizard's how to port & flow test cylinder heads / by David Vizard.
p. cm.
ISBN 978-1-934709-64-1
1. Automobiles–Motors–Cylinder heads–Maintenance and repair. I. Title. II. Title: David Vizard's how to port and flow test cylinder heads. III. Title: How to port and flow test cylinder heads.
TL214.C93V59 2012
629.25'2–dc23
2011034289

Written, edited, and designed in the U.S.A.
Printed in China
10 9

Front Cover: *Cleaning up the intake and exhaust bowls is one of the first steps you can take to improve airflow. You must choose the right grinding tip for the material of the head, select the correct speed for the rotary tool, and use a delicate touch. With experience, you can achieve some very impressive results.*

Title Page: *The moment of truth arrives at the flow bench. The data verifies the effectiveness of porting work. Glyn (left) and Nick (right) Swift are not just Swift in name. They build some of England's fastest Mini Coopers, and it all starts here on the flow bench. This particular unit is a highly instrumented Superflow 110.*

Back Cover Photos

Top Left: *A big-block Chevy Dart Iron Eagle done by a first-time porter using the guidelines laid out in this book. The resultant flow and power curves demonstrate the success of these heads.*

Top Right: *The port bowl is highlighted in red so the white background stands out. You can see that a fair portion of the back of the intake valve on this TFS Ford Mod motor head would be visible. On the stock heads, none of the valve is even close to being visible.*

Middle Left: *Changes to the chamber of the Ultra Pro-modified 427 Corvette head were minimal. In this instance the hard work was in the form of the fuel shear ramp. Getting this to work and improving flow was not an easy task.*

Middle Right: *When a standard 45-degree seat is used, back cutting the intake valve with a 30-degree angle helps form a venturi-like shape between the head and valve seat at low lift. Though usually only a minor aid to high-lift flow, it usually aids low-lift flow measurably.*

Bottom Left: *The form used for this finished seat job on both the intake and exhaust was a radius joining a 45-degree seat at 15 degrees.*

Bottom Right: *This Computational Fluid Dynamics illustration shows a prototype port for one of Edelbrock's high-performance heads and illustrates the flow pattern.*

DISTRIBUTION BY:

Europe
PGUK
63 Hatton Garden
London EC1N 8LE, England
Phone: 020 7061 1980 • Fax: 020 7242 3725
www.pguk.co.uk

Australia
Renniks Publications Ltd.
3/37-39 Green Street
Banksmeadow, NSW 2109, Australia
Phone: 2 9695 7055 • Fax: 2 9695 7355
www.renniks.com

Canada
Login Canada
300 Saulteaux Crescent
Winnipeg, MB, R3J-3T2 Canada
Phone: 800 665 1148 • Fax: 800 665 0103
www.lb.ca

CONTENTS

DEDICATION

To my loving and caring wife, Josephine

ABOUT THE AUTHOR

It is a little difficult to list David Vizard's accomplishments on a single page but we will at least give you a taste of who he is. The first thing you might want to know is that he is a workaholic; and that should more than explain the 80 to 100 hours per week he puts into a career that is his passion.

He started porting heads with the aid of a flow bench in 1958 and since then has run near countless tests. The first engine he tested for power output was in 1960 using a hill with a constant gradient as the retarding force. This gave the output at one particular RPM that happened to be near peak. The following attempts to measure his engine's output were by means of a homemade accelerometer and a lot of math.

His first chassis dyno test was in 1963 and his first engine dyno test was in 1964. To date he has run well over 500,000 dyno tests, most using the latest high-tech dynos of the day. Currently most of his dyno work is on a 2000 Dynamic Test Systems' hybrid.

As a race engine builder his best year in competition netted a combined 169 first places, track records, pole positions, and championship wins—with just eight engines. Of those eight, five powered the drivers to national championship wins. On four occasions his engines or engines built to his specs have won four championships by winning every race in the series contended.

Four different times he has entered a race series with vehicles he was unfamiliar with at the start of the season. In each case by less than halfway through the season his car was not just competitive but truly dominant.

As an inventor David has been responsible for numerous patents. At last count this was about 40 but the number of his patentable designs is probably five times that. Patents range from fuels to F1 cylinder heads. But some of his work is not really patentable. An example here was the Ford Anglia ground-effect "Tunnel" car he built in 1971. That was six years before the first Indy Car sported such technology.

As a driver David has, in the U.K., set lap records on every track he has raced on but one with cars he has built himself. The driving feats he most likes to remember were the beating of all the F1 cars on a slightly wet Prescott hill climb in his super-fast 1293 mini and at the British

Grand Prix event in the supporting British Touring Car Championship race at Brands Hatch where he went from 28th on the grid to joint 1st into the first bend. Passing some 26 cars before the first corner must be some kind of record. As a driver he has finished everywhere from 1st to 7th in championships and has had two seasons when he won every race he competed in.

As a tech writer David is truly prolific. It is the long hours put into building and modifying engines and the subsequent testing of them that produces the mountain of info from which to draw to fill the pages of a book such as this. At present he has authored 32 books.

In the magazine article department he has produced almost 4,000 major feature articles, which makes him one of, if not the most, published automotive tech writer in the world. At one time he was writing for no less than eight magazines and producing no less than a dozen major features per month. All this while designing and building race

engines for high-end clients including a championship winning factory team.

As a reader of David's work you will get the benefit of the first-hand info accumulated over a colorful career so far spanning 50-plus years. If you want more information on his career, you can Google "David Vizard" for a hit count that puts him with some of the performance industry's best know names including the late Smokey Yunick. There is also a ton of videos on Youtube.com

Of course all these and all his other accomplishments did not happen without the help of his many friends, who he is quick to give credit to, be it for moral support or a tech breakthrough on whatever project was being worked on at the time. Spend some time around David Vizard and you will hear him tell how lucky he is to have a wife that is 100-percent supportive of his efforts in all his fields of endeavor, come hail or sunshine. That is almost certainly why this book is dedicated to her.

ACKNOWLEDGMENTS

Writing a book, such as this, is never easy but this one, in terms of challenges, topped everything else I have taken on. I had to rely on the people around me to give me the support and that extra nudge to get me through some tough times. Having said that, it would have been impossible for me to write this book without the love, care, and understanding of my wife Josephine, who gave me the help when I needed it the most. During the course of writing the manuscript, I had support from friends, family, and well-wishers who were coming out of the woodwork from all directions. Without the seemingly unending support of all these good people, this book would not have become a reality.

When the deadline for the manuscript was looming and I had not made the progress that I had expected, I received the timely advice of my editor at CarTech, Paul Johnson. Let me say that I am a big worrier when it comes to copy dates and it took 4,000 or so magazine articles and 32 books before I had missed one. But all through the anxiety of missing a copy date, he handed out the necessary support, telling me not to push the envelope to get the book done and to take care of myself. I have to say that Paul's support here was near priceless.

When I needed the help of a colleague and trusted friend, I had an ace in the hole—David Baker. David is one of my true high-tech friends but with a difference. Many people who are inordinately smart are not very capable communicators. But David Baker is not only technically astute but also has great command of the English language. Many times when my health had truly pulled me down, intriguing tech conversations with David would not only pull me out of the mire but also lead to inspirations on how to better explain or illustrate whatever part of the book I was working on at that moment. Then there is David McCoig, my racing partner. We have built our race cars mostly in the 1,300 square feet of workshop under my house in North Carolina. Other than race weekends, David is in the shop about four afternoons and evenings a week, and he always manages to buoy my spirits to the point I felt I could face the next few days. Thanks go to both Davids here because I would have not fared too well without their support.

But the two Davids were far from the only support I had. Other than my now-90-year-old hot rod mom, I got calls almost daily from my best friends Mike Lane and Gary "is it break time yet?" Collander. Then there is the original inspiration for this book. That came from my good friend Roger "Dr. Air" Helgesen. Fifteen to twenty years ago, he saw my original 1969 performance cylinder head book. He would tell me that was good, but that I should update it in light of constant developments in this field. Well, here it is! The information in this book is the culmination of 50 years of research and hands-on experience. Over this period, I have been determined to minimize flow impediments and maximize effective cylinder filling and combustion. I have made many practical discoveries and have found that many intakes and heads require a vastly different approach due to design parameters and equipment packages. While reading this book, you need to keep an open mind and recognize the possibilities because one of the biggest obstacles to achieving more horsepower is preconceived notions.

The list of people to thank goes on greatly, and I have only this space for what really requires a chapter. So let me round up by saying thanks to all who helped me through a difficult time—you know who you are.

As is usual, when this book comes off the printing press, my now 26-year-old daughter Daniel will get copy number-1 and Jacque, my 15 year old (who wants to be a pro race driver and is currently building her second race engine), gets number-2. My final thanks go to my wife. Josephine, thank you for everything.

INTRODUCTION

So why am I writing this book? In a word—vindication. That's why. As a youngster, growing up in England at a time when the aftermath of World War II was part of our everyday life, I recall that motor racing and race cars was way more than just a preoccupation of mine. Preoccupation, in fact, didn't come close to describing the situation; it was a passion, one that I was literally driven to indulge almost at the expense of all else.

All through my early teens I was regarded by performance engine builders as a young brat too inquisitive for his own good and loaded with just way too many radical ideas. It seemed to me that I lived in a motorsport vacuum. That is not to say that there was not any number of performance enthusiasts in and around my hometown of Cheltenham, England. The problem was, for whatever reason, I seemed to move in entirely different circles from those who could have possibly helped me toward my goal of deep involvement in racing and the performance world in general. Looking back, I suspect that the problem was trying to integrate with people who were reasonably wealthy (that's what it took to go racing back then) and coming from a very working-class family. There were a couple of local guys, probably about 25 years my senior, who built race engines for the local and wealthier hot shots, but they were not about to tell me anything. I remember ask-ing Bill something-or-other (can't remember his last name) a question on a subject that now eludes me. What I do remember was his answer, "If I told you that you would know as much as I do then, wouldn't you?" I later found out that the gentleman concerned felt I was a bratty youngster who thought he knew it all.

I have to admit there was some truth to what he said. I could well have been bratty although I suspect that was just a term he used for convenience. It was also true that I was a youngster, but the next point is where he made his really big mistake. I was not someone who thought they knew it all, but rather someone who wanted to know it all and was prepared to do almost anything to get that knowledge.

I came away from that conversation having learned three valuable things. First, people with that kind of attitude tend not to know as much about the subject as they like you to believe. Second, time also was to tell me that very often people with that response are a little insecure. But I was concerned by the third and most

Figure 1. Here I am putting a full-service home-built flow bench through its paces. This computer-supported bench can deliver professional-style report sheets and head-analysis figures for about three weekends of work and less than $1,000.

important thing I learned or, more accurately, realized. If I were going to learn anything significant about engineering big horsepower numbers from engines, I was going to have to do a substantial amount of original research. Sure, there are plenty of books on the general design of internal combustion engines. Heck—I have most of them in my library. But back then, trying to find an engineering book that focused on the real nitty-gritty of boosting engine power left you with a very short list of books to choose from.

It has taken me more than 50 years to accumulate the knowledge I present within these pages. I know how hard I struggled to get meaningful go-fast tech and the time it took to do so. Here I am making it one of my missions to pass that on to the younger generation so they can benefit from my experience long before it's time to retire.

But didn't I start by saying that the reason for writing this book was vindication? Well, yes, it's also that. Almost all of the ideas that the "know-it-all young brat" put forward in 1956 to 1958 turned out to be right. Unfortunately, those to whom I would have liked to have said, "I told you so," are no longer with us. I may not have seen eye to eye with them, but I hope they made it to the big race track in the sky.

The tech area in which I was most often at odds with the established engine builders of the day was flow benches. All of the guys I knew that were doing okay with their race engines argued that a flow bench was of little use because the flow was steady-state on the bench but pulsing in the engine so was therefore of little use. This line of reasoning led them to believe building or even

using a flow bench was a waste of time. Over the years, I have found that the people who argue most vehemently against the need or use of a flow bench are those who have never used one. That kind of reminds me of an old Guinness ad: "I don't like Guinness because I have never tried it."

So what did I do about this? Same as always: I went out on a limb and built a flow bench, of sorts.

Bench Number-1

In 1958, at the tender age of 15, I made my first attempt to modify a cylinder head, along with the aid of what could loosely be described as a flow bench. It did not test for the cubic feet per minute (CFM) produced, but it did show whether or not a modification produced more or less flow. Back then, anyone serious about getting more power from an engine talked of owning a dyno with about the same degree of reverence as the subject of winning the lottery. In England in 1958, owning a dyno was about the ultimate race-engine tool you could imagine. It was something that was high on a wish list,

but unlikely to happen. For the few who could afford it, suspecting that it was very advantageous, owning a flow bench was just one rung down from owning a dyno.

At the time, I was far from knowing or understanding what it took to build a bench that read out in CFM and conformed to British Standards Institute (BSI) specifications. Not only did I not know what the specifications might be, I did not even know that they existed, which in hindsight actually turned out to be a good thing. So, unfettered by the complexity that BSI would have me put into the measurement of gas flow, I just went ahead and built something that completely conformed to the VRCB standards—that's Vizard's Really Cheap Bench—and time was to show that it really got the job done.

Not realizing that I was seriously bucking convention in the process, the VRCB was completed for just peanuts. But what it taught me proved ultimately to be nearly priceless. At the time it also put me in conflict with local tuners/racers who knew of the VRCB and whose engines made a lot more power than I was making from mine, and that was not so good.

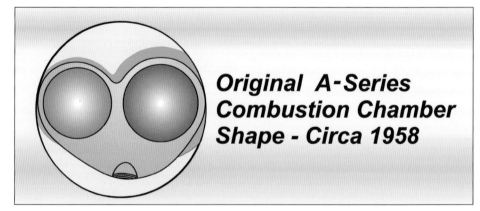

Figure 2. This Weslake-designed, heart-shaped combustion chamber was touted as a technical marvel, when in fact it was one of the worst of the era. To make this chamber work, the areas in green need to be cut away, and that is how it should have been done in the first place.

This was taken to be proof that I was a know-it-all brat whose engines were slower than theirs. This was all the evidence these guys needed to prove their point.

Always the optimist, I did not get too despondent about this. I felt that the head work I was doing might actually be a little better than the typical professionally modified head. However, as a teenage aerospace engineering apprentice, I lacked the finances to buy hot cams, intake/exhaust manifolds, Weber carbs, and the like.

The many readers who know of my deep involvement with the original Minis and Mini Coopers powered by the A-Series Leyland engine are not surprised that the first head I developed from my so-called flow bench was from one of these engines. The head, originally designed around 1953 by Harry Weslake, was also used on the A35 and Morris Minor, and in 1959 it equipped the newly introduced 850 Mini.

This head had a heart-shaped chamber that had, according to the automotive technical press of the time, near magical (and consequently unexplained) combustion properties. In hindsight, I wonder if those magazine writers had any clue about the reality of the situation. At the time, I was equally guilty of being sucked into this belief because I had reasoned no one was likely to make such a complex chamber form unless there was some merit to it (and if there was I never found it). So with all the mods done to improve port flow, I conscientiously avoided any radical alterations to the combustion chamber. That meant those chambers that I was led to believe where magic just got a clean-up and a polish job.

Although I had little time to spend on them (due to college and piles of homework, etc.), my efforts with these heads seemed to produce results as good as those guys who had already been doing heads for some years, so I stuck to a near-production combustion-chamber shape.

By late 1959 I began to comprehend the existence of a power-robbing factor now commonly known as valve shrouding, and that the supposedly magic Weslake combustion chamber design suffered greatly from it.

So the question here was: What is the tradeoff risk in de-shrouding the valves for more flow and yet possibly reducing combustion efficiency from what might turn out to be some radical chamber re-reshaping. Because my primitive, but none-the-less highly effective flow bench showed de-shrouding bumped airflow by a big margin, I thought I would give it a try.

To de-shroud the valves, I reshaped the original chamber form by cutting away the green section in Figure 2. The flow increased dramatically, indicating the chamber shape was off the mark by at least the amount shown in green! What is a little difficult to understand is that Weslake was supposedly a pioneer of the use of a flow bench. Therefore, how could the chamber be so far off optimal? That, I think, is a question for which I will never get the answer.

With the same compression ratio (CR), the head with the heavily reshaped chamber delivered no less than a 50-percent-bigger increase than the head that largely preserved the original form. That is, it delivered a 12-hp increase at the wheels instead of 8! (We are talking about an 850-cc engine with five ports for four cylinders.) Since the horsepower in my 850s had increased from 20 to 30-plus (at the wheels) with little more than a cylinder head swap, I was beginning to seriously question the integrity of the original Weslake design that had been heralded as the product of a genius. Who knows, Weslake may have been a genius (check out his autobiography, *Lucky All My Life*), but that early A-Series head was beginning to look a lot less like the genius design it had so often been touted as.

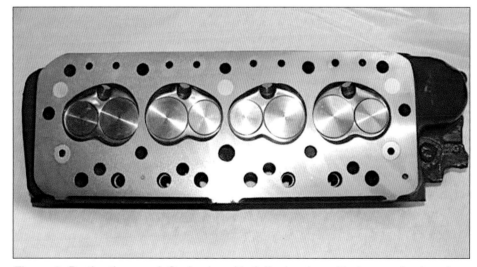

Figure 3. By the time an A-Series head is fully developed in terms of valve sizes and de-shrouding, the chamber looks more like you see here. That is a long way from the original chamber form.

The CFM Chase

After my first success with my homemade flow bench, I began to chase airflow at the expense of almost every other factor, including compression ratio. So, was the flow bench any advantage here? I thought so because I could find out what did or did not work in significantly less time than with the traditional means of the day. And by traditional I mean "look at the head—try to reason what was needed, then cut the head and try it." But as an apprentice also working for my engineering qualifications at night school, the amount of time I had to experiment was strictly limited. Because I had one, the road to really positive results via a flow bench looked wide open to me. And did my escapades with a flow bench convert any established engine builder to the same thought process? If it did, I never heard of it.

Working on those five-port A-Series heads really clouded arguments for or against the need for a flow bench to get results. In the late 1960s, I was told time and time again by A-Series head specialists that, in so many words, a flow bench was not really necessary to get results—only to quantify them after they had been achieved. A dyno could better quantify the results. I have to admit, from an observer's point of view, things really did appear that way. But time proved otherwise. Here's how it all played out.

Not as Good as They Think

The bottom ends of the engines that the A-Series heads are used on were/are starved for air by the heads they are typically equipped with. Any airflow increase resulting from good guesswork (or otherwise) made a very positive difference to total output, even if there was a negative impact or two elsewhere. These engines responded well to all flow improvements, even if quite minor in nature. In other words, the Weslake design was so poor, but with a reputation for being so good, that half of the UK's head porters figured they were brilliant because they could, with seemingly little effort, improve on something that was already a supposedly brilliant design. And because they got such good results they saw no pressing need for a flow bench.

The day of reckoning was to come. For most, it came in the form of a devastating reality check when they attempted to port heads that were intrinsically better to start with, which gave the non-flow-bench-equipped head porter much more leeway to screw up. Only those who applied real-world engineering logic and/or some kind of flow check on results managed to stay ahead of the game. And this was mostly the way it was in England until probably the mid 1970s.

But the A-Series tuning community was slow to turn to flow bench technology as an aid to find power in a shorter time frame. Why? I say that because of the wealth of knowledge already accumulated by decades of trial and error in the search for power. The UK's renowned ace Mini Cooper driver and tuner Richard Longman achieved race-winning power by virtue of a strong working knowledge of what it takes to make power from an engine, and with a lot more time spent on an engine dyno than most of his competition.

Mostly by virtue of effort, Richard was ekeing his race engines power up by a couple of horsepower per year and was driving his own Mini to race-conquering performances. So the argument here was, based on what Richard was doing, the indications were that a flow bench was far from essential for race-winning performances. This looks fine in theory, but it overlooks one major point that might just be the nail in the coffin for such an argument. Having raced against Richard Longman's fast 1,300-cc Mini in my own equally fast Mini, I can tell you for absolute certain he was one of the most gifted Mini drivers ever to have walked the face of the planet. If he had 10 hp less than most of his opposition, he still would have won a bunch of races!

But a slowing of the yearly power gains appeared to have been a prime factor for not only Richard Longman, but also a number of other top A-Series tuners, to start seriously looking at flow testing with a view to establishing where they were and where they might be with the aid of a flow bench. Rumor has it that within one month of acquiring a flow bench, the Longman 1,300-cc race engines were up by 7 hp! I asked myself if this was the beginning of the end of the "I don't believe in flow benches" era.

As you may imagine, in my business I get to talk to the industry movers—the well-known names in the field of Mini (A-Series) performance. Long ago (and I mean really long ago) I remember talking to cylinder-head ace Brian Slarke. At the time, I don't think Brian had a flow bench, but I could tell from our conversation that he was going in that direction. You may wonder why I thought Brian didn't have a flow bench; that should be an easy thing to establish, right? Well not always. Back in the 1970s, I dealt with several international race-engine companies whose bosses would, without batting an eyelid, tell you that a flow bench was a waste of time. Why? Because they had one and used the heck out of it, recognized its worth, and did not want their competition to also latch onto its substantial worth. In a recent conversation about times past, Brian commented that a cylinder head company that is willfully without a bench is "out of touch with reality." That's the mood of the industry these days.

So that's my story on flow benches. And to all those critics who loved to put down my efforts in the 1960s, let's hear what your story is now!

Building a Flow Bench

By about 1969, I wanted to have my flow bench read out in CFM just like the pros did at Weslake. By then I was more than familiar with what it took to build a bench to BSI standards, so I built one. What a deal; by the time I had made all the parts it took up the best part of 15 feet of one garage wall and severely ate into

the 330 square feet I had to work in. Not only was this an undertaking in terms of manufacture, but the math involved to get it to read out accurately in CFM was really heavy-duty stuff. That bench got a lot of use—even the McLaren guys made use of it. In 1974, I used that bench to develop heads for my British Touring Car Championship (BTCC) entry. This was a 1,600-cc Chrysler Avenger. It was an all-iron pushrod two-valve-per-cylinder, short-stroke engine with very strong parts. At the time, Chrysler used two suppliers for their race heads. Both were internationally known F1 engine manufacturers.

I spent a lot of time on my bench, refining the heads' flow capability. So how did this work out compared to my F1 competition? Well, it's a good story. During a test session at Mallory Park, the factory Avengers were slower by almost a second per lap than the Alfa Romeos. In desperation, the factory tried one of my heads. Swapping heads resulted in a lap time reduction of 1.1 seconds

without any further adjustments. Some timing and carb adjustments improved a little more on that. I throw this in not to show off, but to demonstrate that the little guy can win against big odds. However, it's unlikely to happen unless you are willing to embrace new technology.

Move to America

In 1976 I relocated to the United States to do a series of books for a publisher based in Tucson, Arizona. It was impractical to move my BSI bench from the U.K. because of its size, so I made it my mission to equip the shop I was working in with commercially available flow-test equipment. This led me to talk to the guys at SuperFlow.

My move to Tucson also dropped me fair and square right into a motor-racing community that extended north to Phoenix and west to Southern California. I was moving within a very substantial performance community. Some of the folks I worked with were very smart and some... well, not quite so. Almost all of the companies and people I dealt with had at least a working knowledge of the worth of a flow bench. Here, I was going fairly much with the flow instead of against it.

About the time I saw my first in-cylinder pressure diagram (about 1978) is when I realized that measuring the flow at a fixed pressure drop as with a BSI-type flow bench (which most are) was absolutely not the best way to do things. The super-cheap bench that I used as a kid was in fact the better way to go. And that is where I am going to start this book for real. I explain how to build a floating pressure drop bench and give you the justification for it.

Figure 4. My BTCC Avenger. Even with two vertical valves per cylinder and an all-iron pushrod engine, this grocery getter had more legs than any twin-cam sports sedan from any competing factory team.

I should point out, however, that a flow bench is only a tool, much like a painter's brush, if you will. Without the knowledge of how to best use it and the data it can supply, it is a tool largely wasted. So the purpose of this book (other than vindication) is to show you how to build a flow bench (if you do not already have one) and how to use the data it delivers. And the good news here is that it is all, for the most part, a lot simpler than you and several otherwise learned publications may have thought. By stat-ing that it is "all" a lot simpler, I do actually mean "all."

You might think that in this day and age of commercial CNC port-ing that there is no point or even no room for success by porting your own heads. That could not be further from the truth. If you are looking to port the heads for a popular V-8, there is performance potential that is well supported by aftermarket head castings. This is because almost all such castings are already flow-bench developed as far as possible, while still retaining a 90-percent cast sur-face finish. The implication here is that the home porter does not spend an inordinate amount of time carv-ing out large volumes of metal. In essence, that is already done on the as-received casting. What you, as a home porter, can do is to finesse the port to more nearly optimize what is, for the most part, already there. You are putting the frosting on the cake.

Can the CNC versions of cur-rent commercially available heads be beaten by the home porter? As I show, they sure can. Becoming an expert at this takes time, but if you follow what I have to say in these pages, you can start well and go on from there.

As far as four- and five-valve heads go, I also show that in most cases these heads need very little work done to them to make the most of what is already there. However, moving on from basic porting on such heads to more high-tech stuff may be a little more than you want to tackle. But learning the how and why still won't hurt your porting educa-tion. Just remember, race-winning porting is not the black magic some pro head porters want you to believe. It's pure tech know-how. And that is what you find within these pages.

What This Book Is and Is Not About

This book is about the practicali-ties of porting heads to a high level of proficiency without the weighty complexities of heavy-duty math-ematics and the like. It is intended to be a strong support mechanism toward a primary goal of winning races. Although cylinder heads are very much about fluid dynamics, it is not my intention to educate to the

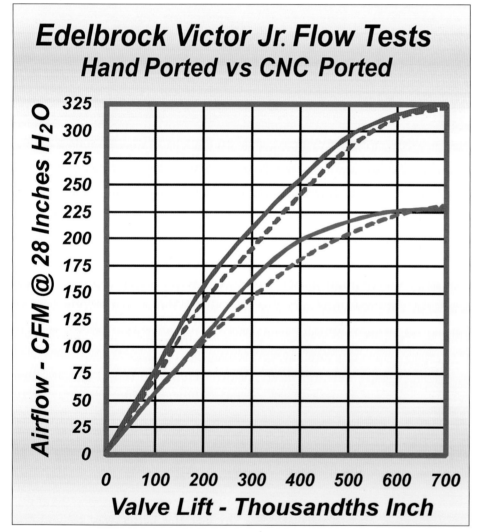

Figure 5. The difference between a novice-ported (dotted curves) and CNC-ported Edelbrock Victor Jr. (solid curves) can be seen here. The lower mid-range figures of the hand-ported head can almost certainly be attributed to less effective valve seat forms.

point where you can comfortably get a Ph.D. on the subject. What I attempt to do here is give you what you need to know to prepare heads that are, from the start, at very high levels of competition. The idea is not to chase flow and flow-bench tech to a super-fine degree and consequently use up a mass of time and make that the primary goal, but rather to chase down race wins in a reasonably short time span.

Throughout my career, my goal was to win races, not to win flow-bench contests. If fluid dynamics is your end goal, you may well need to know about such things as Navier-Stokes equations, and those of Fleigner, Euler, Bernoulli, Darcy-Weisbach, and Reynolds to name a few. However, if the intent is to pass the finish line first, I can tell you it can be done without resorting to most of the normally complex equations that these learned minds have come up with. Sure you may see mention of Bernoulli and Reynolds in places and maybe even the mention of Navier-Stokes, but they are only referred to where needed and not as a means to pound out some mathematical result.

As the author of this book, I have not spent hours talking to cylinder head specialists to find out what they know and do to produce heads that win races; instead, I have spent thousands of hours on the flow bench and dyno to produce head designs that have won many championships, ranging from local club events to international events. Sure, I have learned much from others (some of the best in the industry) but my heads and head technology have been on everything from stock to Pro Stock and from Formula 3 to Formula 1. I am going to pass on a lifetime (52 years as of the time of writing) of winning tech knowledge from firsthand experience of *doing* the work, not secondhand from watching or researching results gained by a third party.

WHAT IT TAKES TO MAKE POWER

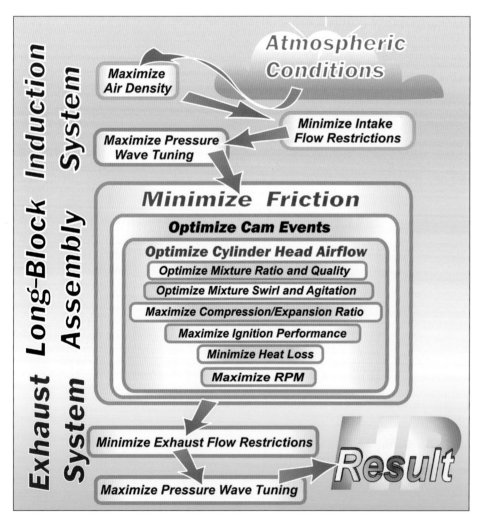

Fig. 1.1. This is my power box. So called because it contains all the elements you need to address to build a high-performance engine. If all these facets are optimized and we add high RPM to the concoction, the result is high output.

Before going any further, I want to make a point about this chapter. Usually the front end of a tech book starts with stuff that is easily assimilated. Although this chapter may at first seem a little more complex than might be expected, bare with me because here I set and simplify what comes later. Take a look at my "power box" (Figure 1.1). Right in the middle of everything, you see in large red letters "Optimize Cylinder Head Airflow." That is our focal point. If we don't get good results in terms of airflow here, the horsepower output per cubic inch (or liter) suffers, and there is nothing we can do to compensate.

In Chapter 7, I talk about what I loosely describe as "Five Golden Rules to Successful Porting." To make my point here, I need to jump the gun and introduce you to Rule Number-1: Locate the point of greatest restriction and attempt to improve it as far as is possible. Applying this rule means identifying the point of greatest restriction and minimizing it. So without any Alfred Hitchcock suspense, I can tell you that the ultimate roadblock to making super-high horsepower per cube is the intake valve. The path on which the air has to flow to make it around the intake valve is tortuous at best. As you can see from Figure 1.2, flow is valve-limited to such an extent that it is only a couple of steps removed from having a leaky cork in the system. The bottom line is: Everything we do is directly influenced by the valve seats and valve form in close proximity to the seat.

Point of Maximum Flow

Initially, it might seem that having flow-efficient valve seats is of only minor consequence because the piston motion on the induction stroke is very slow when the valve is at low lift. But it also seems that the high-lift flow must be important because, when the valve is at high-lift, demand by a piston that is now rapidly moving down the bore is high. I go into the subject of cylinder demand versus valve lift in detail in Chapter 10. Suffice to say at this point, a well-developed high-performance engine actually has two induction phases. The first is caused by the scavenging of the tuned exhaust and takes place during the overlap period, and the second is the suction caused by the piston going down the bore. For engines with cams of about 280

degrees or more of seat-to-seat opening period, the scavenging brought about by the exhaust is greater than the suction caused by the piston on its way down the bore.

Valve-and-seat combinations that flow poorly during the overlap period can cost dearly in terms of high-RPM power. To demonstrate the point, in Figures 1.3, 1.4, and 1.5 I have used a single-pattern cam of 285 degrees of off-the-seat duration (which from here on I refer to as "seat-to-seat duration") as an example. Figure 1.3 shows where in the valve opening events the overlap occurs. Figure 1.4 shows the overlap period on a typical card as issued with the cam when purchased from the cam manufacturer. In this diagram, we can easily see the shared time (overlap), in terms of degrees, that the intake and exhaust are both open. What is not apparent from such a diagram is how far off the seats the valves are. To better appreciate this, refer to Figure 1.5.

Using a hydraulic cam for a pushrod motor, we can see from Figure 1.5 that the tappet lift at the top dead center (TDC) point of the overlap phase is approximately 0.060 above the lash point. Selecting a typical 1.6:1 rocker ratio means (assuming split overlap) that the intake and exhaust valves are both open

by some 0.096 inch. That is close to 1/10 inch, and here we are considering nothing more than a fairly hot street cam. If this were an all-out race engine, the amount of lift seen at the valves at TDC on the commencement of the induction stroke could exceed 1/4 inch!

For the record, cam manufacturers are always striving for faster lift rates off the seat. This provides the cylinders with as much flow as possible in an attempt to keep pace with air demand at increasingly higher RPM. The reality is that the cylinder does not actually see lift; it sees flow. This means the more efficient the valves are throughout the lift range, the less we need to rely on aggressive and, consequently, wear-prone valvetrains to get the job done.

Seat and Port Priorities

At low valve lift, we can see that the flow is almost totally dependent on the forms just before and after the actual seat, and this determines the flow efficiency. If the chamber scavenging is well sorted, we find that the gas velocity between the valve and the cylinder head seats is really high. However, because the flow area between the seats is small, the velocity in the main body of the port is low. In other words, we could see 300 ft/sec at the seats and only 10 ft/sec in the main part of the port. At such low port-flow velocities, the shape of the port and its surface finish has almost zero influence on the overall flow while the seat design is all important.

This leads to the question: When does the port form become more important than the seat form? By making a study of the velocities involved, this can be determined

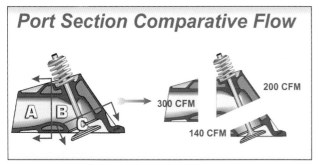

Port Section Comparative Flow

300 CFM
200 CFM
140 CFM

Fig. 1.2. Cutting a small-block Chevy into sections (designated A, B, and C), and flow testing each section, produces figures as shown here. In this instance the valve is at average lift. It is obvious that reworking the already efficient section A does little to overall flow, but improvements to C pay useful dividends. So the intake valve seat is our primary focal point.

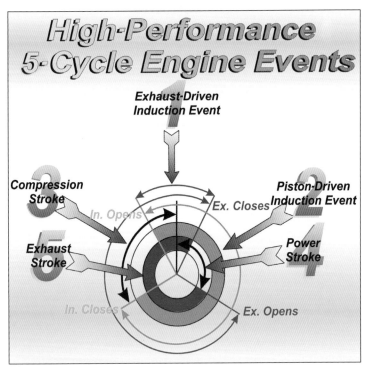

High-Performance 5-Cycle Engine Events

1 — Exhaust-Driven Induction Event

3 — Compression Stroke

In. Opens

Ex. Closes

2 — Piston-Driven Induction Event

5 — Exhaust Stroke

4 — Power Stroke

In. Closes

Ex. Opens

Fig. 1.3. Starting at cycle number-1, the exhaust-generated vacuum can aggressively start the intake charge moving into the cylinder long before the piston goes down the bore. As the crank rotates farther we get to cycle number-2, which is typically considered the charge-inducing stroke. In an ideal situation, cycle number-1 has cleared the combustion chamber and put a considerable amount of kinetic energy into the incoming charge before the piston starts down the bore. The result is an engine that can achieve a volumetric efficiency well in excess of 100 percent. The bottom line is, a good exhaust system is worth a lot of extra torque, horsepower, and, best of all, extra mileage. But to make all this work optimally, the cam must generate the right opening/closing event timing around TDC and the valves' low-lift flow must be good to take full advantage of the situation.

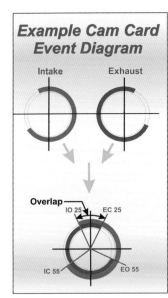

Example Cam Card Event Diagram

Intake

Exhaust

Overlap

IO 25   EC 25

IC 55   EO 55

Fig. 1.4. The intake and exhaust opening duration arcs are at the top. By melding the intake and exhaust duration arcs together we form the valve-opening event diagram at the bottom.

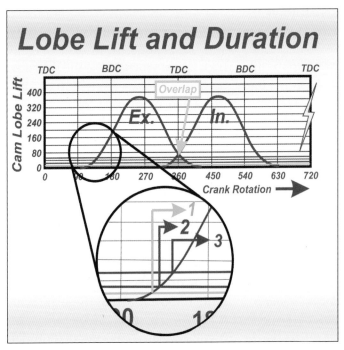

Lobe Lift and Duration

Cam Lobe Lift

TDC   BDC   TDC   BDC   TDC

400
320
240
160
80
0

0   90   180   270   360   450   540   630   720

Overlap

Ex.   In.

Crank Rotation →

1
2
3

Fig. 1.5. Arrow number-1 is the duration at a solid lifter's lash point. (The lash point at the lifter is the lash at the rocker divided by the rocker ratio.) Arrow number-2 is the so-called advertised duration and is usually 0.006 inch for hydraulic cams and 0.020 inch for solids. Arrow number-3 indicates the duration at 0.050 inch.

and such tests indicate that almost regardless of the port type, two- or four-valve layouts and the like, seat priority is the most important up to about 0.18 inch of the valve's diameter. Above that figure, the port shape starts to become the dominant factor toward good flow. For most production and even high-performance modified street motors, valve lift rarely exceeds about 0.28 inch of the valve's diameter.

What this means is that the form of the valve seat plays a dominant role for more than half the valve lift involved, and it does this twice during the open/close cycle. The only conclusion that can be drawn here is that the valve seat form is of great importance to the overall success of the port—intake or exhaust. In practice, the flow bench and dyno prove this to be the case.

Do You Need a Flow Bench?

So, I have already introduced a degree of complexity that you may not have thought of. From this, you may be thinking that having a flow bench is almost a necessity. Well, a flow bench provides important data, and therefore is a real benefit. However, you can do a basic porting job based on sound principles and expect a good return for the effort put in. As long as your aspirations don't include preparing the winning heads for a car running in a big-time international event, you are okay.

But if you want better-than-average results, a flow bench is about as necessary as the die grinders and cutters you need to do the job itself. Yes, we can port without a flow bench. But not only is a bench a valuable tool to take you well into the professional arena, it's also fun to use. Finding that extra air and trying to beat Mother Nature can become an exciting challenge. If you are concerned about the cost of an effective bench, fear not—you can, as you will see in the next few chapters, be in business with a highly functional bench for as little as $150.

How to be a Skilled Head Porter

The cylinder heads influence what combination of parts and the setup that's optimal for the rest of the engines spec. For instance, the camshaft required for a ported big-valve cylinder head usually requires, for a given set of duration figures, quite a different cam spec to achieve top performance compared to the stock head.

Also, strange as it may seem to a novice in this field, the original cam often does not deliver optimal performance, and I am not talking in terms of valve opening duration here. For a given intake opening duration and lift, there is an optimum exhaust duration and a set of valve opening and closing points that can make or break your efforts as a head porter. If you want to get the best results from your porting efforts, you need to understand how the changes you have made impact the rest of the engine's requirements, so the best possible outcome is achieved. Also if you are going to make head porting a career, you will be the first person your customer asks advice for cam selection, intake, exhaust, and the like. You have to give them astute and accurate answers, otherwise, and trust me on this, unless your price is rock bottom, it will be the last time they come to you.

If you have the best flowing head in the world for the application at hand, you must also have a good notion of how best to use it. All that you need to know to make the best of any head comes under the topic of "combinations."

For example, take an engine that was very common during my early days of engine building and cylinder head modifying: the 850 A-series-powered Mini. This engine didn't breathe well because of an intake valve only 1.06 inches in diameter. Porting this head could increase output by about 10 hp (up from 20 hp at the wheels stock to about 30). The optimal cam for the same intake/exhaust duration had a tighter lobe separation angle than the factory used. And as such, if used with the ported head with stock intake valves, the power went up to about 34 hp. If a later 1,000-cc casting replaced the stock 850 casting, you could increase power because this head could accommodate an intake valve of as much as 1.3 inches, but this engine with a stock cam did not make as much of a power increase as expected from the huge airflow increase seen.

When such a move was made, i.e., big-valve modified head and stock cam, a power increase over the small-valve modified head was only from about 4,300 rpm up. Below that, the output was actually down. With a stock cam, the peak output was only about 2 to 3 hp more than the stock-valved modified head.

When a cam of stock duration was used but with a wider and more suitable lobe centerline angle, the big-valve head made 8 wheel hp more than the small-valve head with its optimum cam. Not only that, minimal power was lost below 4,300 rpm. The reality is that a slightly shorter cam would have given back all the low-end power of the small-valve head with at least 5 hp more at the top end.

As I said above, it's the combination that counts.

Unfortunately for you, "combinations" are the least written about or taught subject within the whole realm of performance engine technology. I have made the subject of optimal engine spec combinations a lifelong study. You will find my book *How to Build Horsepower* to be of great benefit in supporting your cylinder head efforts. Plus, if you also build high-performance engines, it will help you produce a lot more power.

FLOW TESTING PROCEDURES

Before getting into the subject of physically modifying cylinder heads, let's look at the history and basic logic and techniques involved with establishing a cylinder head's number-one criteria: airflow. A working knowledge here allows a better understanding of all the head characteristics we are attempting to improve and how they may each affect the others involved. Make no mistake; in the quest for optimal head configurations, you need to make many compromises.

The information covered in this chapter will help you make many better decisions down the road. As you have probably guessed already, measuring cylinder heads' capacity to flow air is our number-one priority. After that, there are a number of secondary but none-the-less vitally important factors we need to measure and manipulate in the manner most beneficial to us. Such factors include port velocity, velocity distribution, wet-flow characteristics, swirl, and the like. All of these factors tend to start at one focal point: the standard pressure drop.

The Standard Pressure Drop

Air is an elastic medium and, as such, its rate of flow has to be measured under specific conditions. An analogy of where I am going here is to imagine you have to measure the length of several different elastic bands for comparison. Just how long these elastic bands are depends on how much tension they are experiencing. To make an

Fig. 2.1. Why the crosshairs? Simple. Getting it right means making it happen here, and by "happen" I mean cylinder pressure. To produce the highest cylinder pressure means feeding the cylinder with as much air as possible. Next, the charge has to be effectively burned and then dispelled through the exhaust port as efficiently as possible. The red dot represents a prime position for the spark plug tip; the green one is poorly positioned for a high-compression engine.

across-the-board comparison, we need to have a fixed amount of tension. In this case, we need to know how long these bands are when stretched by a tensile load of 2 pounds. In this instance, we call that our standard load.

By adopting a standard load we are eliminating the principal variable that changes its length, without actually involving any properties the band may have in the first place. Much the same situation applies when it comes to the measurement of airflow. The greater the suction on a given orifice, the greater the volume of airflow through that orifice. To make a comparison across the board for a number of different orifices, we have to fix the amount of suction, so that it is the same for each orifice tested. Figure 2.2 shows why we must, for comparative reasons, have a standard pressure drop or, at the very minimum, quote it on our test results. As of 2012, common practice when testing cylinder heads is to use a fixed "standard pressure drop" throughout the valve opening range tested. Although going this route may make the comparison of results fast and convenient, it can also, as we shall see, compromise port development.

Until the 1990s, when the International Automobile Federation (FIA) let the reigns go on naturally aspirated F1 engine development, it seemed the heyday of rapid piston engine development was during World War II. Back then, each engine manufacturer used a test pressure drop of its own choosing, so there really was no universally accepted pressure drop.

As postwar civilian companies, such as Weslake in England, got into flow testing for engine development, nothing much changed. When it came to test pressures/vacuums, it was each to its own. But then along came the ever-innovative hot rodder Henry "Smokey" Yunick. Smokey was not only something of a rascal (and, in performance-automotive circles, a famed one at that), but a rascal who was always pushing boundaries when it came to making power from piston engines. I knew Smokey personally, but since his passing in 2001, I wish I had taken advantage of numerous opportunities to spend more time with him. Smokey was one of the great performance-engine innovators of the later part of the twentieth century. He was also very vocal about his theories and findings and any other of his opinions he thought you should know about.

He was the kind of a guy who devised equipment to test theories almost at the drop of a hat, if it looked like it might bring about any kind of progress. After utilizing any possible advantages, he was ready to share what he found with the rest of the

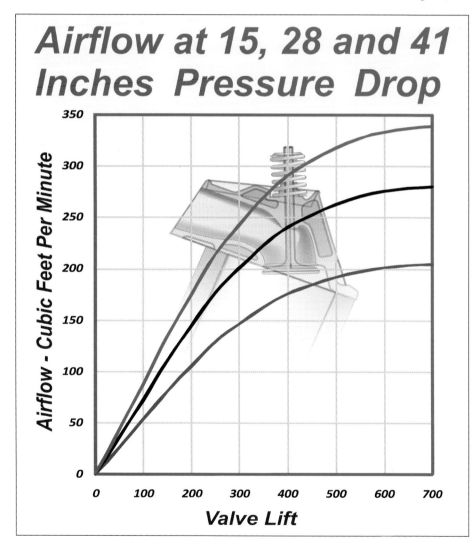

Fig. 2.2. These curves show how the airflow varies with test pressure. To make viable comparisons, we need to test at or near the same test pressures. Although corrections can be made, the bigger the correction, the greater the possible error produced.

performance community. It's worth mentioning that, apart from having a must-read autobiography, Smokey did a book for CarTech. Here, I can say with all certainty that you may want it in your auto-tech library.

Anyway, returning to the subject of the standard pressure drop, Smokey built a number of flow benches and his final one was a monster that did a whole lot more than just deliver CFM numbers. Early on, Smokey made it one of his missions to find out which standard pressure drop value, in a meaningful manner, translated observed flow improvements to possible power improvements on the dyno. Starting at a relatively low test pressure, he ran the gamut on this and declared that tests had to be done at a minimum of 28 inches of water (H_2O) depression for a flow bench improvement to consistently show up as a power improvement on the dyno.

Fig. 2.4. In 1958 this was the combustion chamber that caused me such a dilemma. Hailed as a tech wonder by the press of the time, it proved to be in error by the amount shown in green. Weslake was a pioneer in the use of a flow bench, so why the engineers made it the way they did is still a mystery today.

The majority of engine builders in the United States held Smokey in high regard, and he was also widely read, so this 28-inch measurement became an accepted standard for the performance-engine building community. So when you see airflow test results in various publications, and in my books, you find that the test pressure at which the flow is quoted (as opposed to actually being measured at) in the charts and graphs is with 28 inches H_2O pressure drop.

So was Smokey right in claiming that at least 28 inches was needed for that meaningful translation of results from the bench to the dyno? Well, although test results can be

converted from one test pressure to another, the results, when corrected from a lower to a higher test pressure, don't quite tally (for reasons I address shortly). Certainly, there was more than enough justification for Smokey's claims here, but it is still a few steps short of what we may do for optimal port development. What I want to do here is to address how relevant a steady-state flow test is as far as correlating it to the pulsing flow seen in a running engine.

Let's go back to when the other guys kept telling me a flow bench was not even worth its weight in paper because of the difference between steady and pulsing flows. The difference in flow seen on a bench versus that within a running engine is dramatic. At first sight, this makes the other guys' argument appear very valid, but the following was my counter argument on this subject:

"If we open a valve and test the flow at whatever pressure drop is chosen, we can say that in a running engine the flow will, for all practical purposes, be steady if it is considered over a short enough period of time. In other words, if we looked

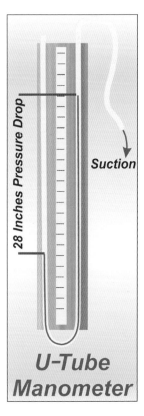

Fig. 2.3. An illustration of a simple manometer made from a hose, a tape measure, and a piece of 2x4. This shows the usual fixed pressure drop used when testing is at 28 inches, although there are good reasons for not going this route.

28 Inches Pressure Drop

Suction

U-Tube Manometer

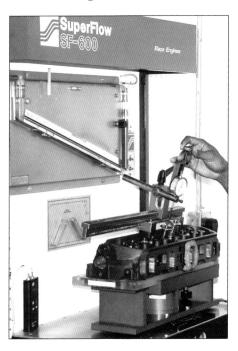

Fig. 2.5. The current standard for the industry is this SuperFlow 600. This company makes a range of flow benches; the smallest and least expensive one is the SuperFlow 110.

at the flow past the intake valve for a period of, say, one millionth of a second, the flow at the beginning of that period essentially is the same as the flow at the end of that millionth of a second. So we can say, within close limits, the flow in a running engine, when taken over a small-enough time increment, is virtually steady. The implication here then is that our flow bench, on this score, does reasonably simulate what goes on in a running engine."

In the 1980s or so, a top Japanese engineer, apparently with a large amount of funding, researched this subject right down to the bare bones. At the end of the program he proclaimed that, for all practical purposes, a steady-state flow test was a meaningful test because it substantially related to the pulsing flow seen in an engine and the dyno results produced.

So, now we have an accepted standard pressure drop from which to get fully serviceable flow figures and strong evidence that the steady flow seen with the bench still correlates well with the pulsing flow seen in a running engine.

Although we have now arrived

at what are now widely accepted practices, I am far from finished on the subject. Why? I am not finished because 28 inches can present its own set of test problems.

Real-World Test Pressures

So why can 28 inches of test pressure drop be a problem? The short answer is that it is a compromise. A higher test pressure allows the development of better ports, especially the intake, but stepping it up can present real bench-motor power problems. In an effort to overcome this, I have seen flow benches that required two 50-hp electric motors to run. The space, time, money, and effort required to build a bench like this is nearly prohibitive and, as we shall see, unnecessary. The problem is: If you want to test a typical big-block Chevy head or even a really good small-block head,

you need a lot of amps for the inevitably large electric motors needed to produce the required vacuums/pressures. This means buying a pretty stout commercial flow bench at something between $6,000 and $18,000, or building your own bench with as many as six high-powered vacuum motors. On top of that, you may have to have your shop or household electricity supply up-graded to deal with the amperage involved.

Corrections

In the early 1970s, Neil Williams, the founder and driving force behind SuperFlow, introduced the compact SuperFlow 110 flow bench. I believe this was the first commercially available flow bench and it tested heads using a 10-inch pressure drop. I had the opportunity to do a comparative check on one of these benches in

Fig. 2.6. An AFR small-block Chevy combustion chamber. This shape is the result of flow testing and then qualifying it on the dyno.

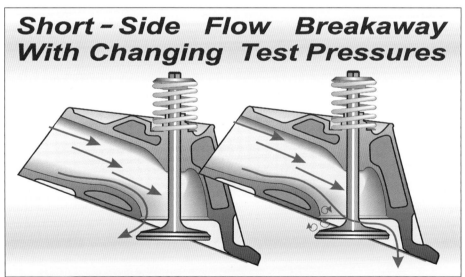

Fig. 2.7. Here is what happens as the test pressure and, consequently, the port velocity goes up. At low test pressures (left) the air has a better chance of staying attached to the port floor, and as a result the entire circumference of the valve is used to good effect. When the test pressure is increased to that more commonly seen in a running engine, the flow detaches from the short-side turn, and the higher-velocity air attempts to exit the long side, which is already busy passing air from the long side. Result? A drop in efficiency, which is otherwise unaccounted for during normal pressure-drop corrections.

late 1973 at Piper Cams in England. For all its simplicity, it did produce results that compared well with the ones I saw on my monster BSI flow bench, which tested at 20 inches for small heads and 15 or so for larger heads (such as Chevy big-blocks).

As mentioned earlier, you do have an option here to correct a, say, 10-inch pressure drop to 28 inches with a mathematical correction. The problem is that this type of correction is only satisfactorily valid when corrections are small, and you are testing a simple orifice or a straight port with absolutely no bends in it. Any time a seat and valve enters the equation, errors made in corrections from a low to a high test pressure have a greater impact on flow. Equally as bad is the fact that the corrections almost always produce artificially higher flow numbers.

But there is a fix for this problem, and it's one that has absolutely no downsides. The fix makes testing more meaningful, reduces the cost of a bench, and you are able to do it all without having to invest in any workshop electrical upgrades. To see how all this works, let's get back to test pressures.

Floating Pressure-Drop Testing

As I just mentioned, the Super-Flow 110 bench tested at 10 inches of pressure drop. When doing so, the port velocity is substantially lower than when that same port is tested at 28 inches. At 10 inches, the air could be traveling at a speed just marginally less than that needed to produce flow separation around the short-side turn (Figure 2.7).

When the flow stays attached, the air makes better use of the entire valve circumference. Under these conditions, the valve is more efficient. When that same situation is tested at 28 inches, the air in the port may not make it around the short-side turn in anything like the same way and the flow past the valve adjacent to the short-side turn is consequently disrupted to a far greater extent, thus cutting the overall flow.

However, the typical mathematical adjustments applied to correct a 10-inch measurement to a 28-inch result do not work well for this. Also it is a problem that it results in a port that may work at 10 inches but be far less effective at 28. At 28 inches, the flow separation influences the development of the final seat and port used. In other words, that higher test pressure goes toward solving a problem that did not even show up at a 10-inch test pressure.

Taking stock of the situation so far, we can say that we need higher test pressures, but the downside is the requirement for increasingly larger pump motors.

The situation looks bleak until we stop to look at the cyclic pressures that exist in the intake port of a high-performance engine. In Figure 2.8 we

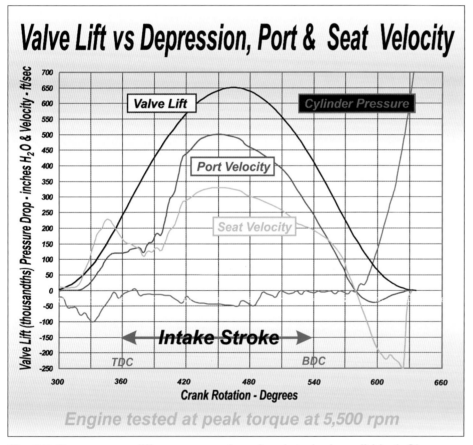

Fig. 2.8. The pressure differences on a bored and stroked small-block Chevy (final displacement: 441 ci). This was a little large for the heads involved, but the trends we need to appreciate can be seen here. When the intake valve was 0.070 off the seat, the suction from the exhaust as measured in the combustion chamber (red curve) was 100 inches H$_2$O while the suction caused by the piston never exceeded 50 inches H$_2$O. This graph also shows that the intake port velocity (blue curve), while the piston is parked at TDC, is no less than 120 ft/sec.

see the pressures that occur within an intake port of a street/strip 441-ci (7.23-liter) small-block Chevy during the induction phase are far from being a steady 28 inches. During the overlap period, where valve lift is relatively low, we can see a depression across the intake valve as high as 100 inches, and it can be much higher in an all-out-race, two-valve engine.

This low pressure is brought about by the negative pressure wave arriving at the exhaust valve and it functions as a means of extracting the combustion residuals. It does so with sufficient amplitude to pass through the chamber and act on the intake port. This high-exhaust-generated vacuum starts the intake flow into the cylinder well before the piston even starts down the bore.

Do not underestimate the value of this effect. In practice, it can make or break the degree of success seen on the development of a high-performance engine. Although at high valve lift, the pressure drop across the intake valve for our example is some 50 inches we find that for a highly developed engine with decent seat and port design, depression is more in the 15- to 20-inch range. If in-cylinder pressure measurements show anything much more than that, it's a sign of inadequate heads for the displacement/RPM involved.

Now here is where we get a break. If we hook up a typical vacuum cleaner to a cylinder head and progressively open the intake valve, we find the pressure drop at low lift is high and at high lift is low. That is exactly what we are looking for. Accepting a floating pressure drop is the key that immediately unlocks the door leading to the building of a very simple yet extremely effective flow bench. The construction of such

a bench is explained in Chapter 3, but I first want to address the relative importance of the intake versus the exhaust.

Intake Fixation?

It is patently obvious that any cylinder head has two distinctly different ports that need to be developed to produce high-flow effi-

ciencies for maximum power: intake and exhaust. The question being posed here is: Which of these two is the most influential toward the production of power? At first sight, it may seem to be the exhaust because, after the charge has been burned, the volume is so much greater. Let's assume for the moment we are dealing with a naturally aspirated (non-supercharged) engine. At the point

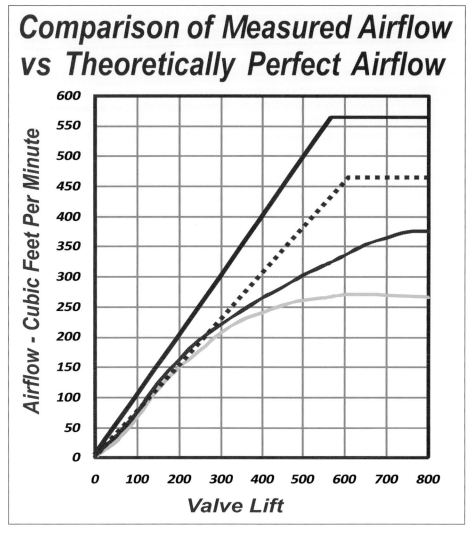

Fig. 2.9. The green curve is the intake flow of a big-block Chevy 049 casting in stock form but with a 2.250 valve. The blue curve is for the same head ported. The solid red curve is for a head having a flow efficiency of 100 percent based on the valve O.D. In practice, it is helpful to look at the flow efficiency based on the throat diameter of the port (red dotted curve). In either case, the flow efficiency of most heads is a long way from the best that can theoretically be obtained.

of exhaust valve opening, there is between 70 and 120 psi waiting to escape from the cylinder. When the exhaust valve opens, the flow velocity between the seats in the head and those on the valve momentarily exceeds the speed of sound.

For the intake valve, the situation is far different. The greatest pressure available to drive the charge into the cylinder is that of atmospheric pressure (i.e., 14.7 psi). Worse yet, of that 14.7 psi, we can't really use more than 1 or 2 psi at most. Therefore, we need to see the minimum drop across the intake valve for best breathing. From this, we can see it is going to be a lot harder to fill the cylinders than it is to empty them. In addition, if the cylinder fails to adequately fill due to poor induction efficiency, the engine's power potential is reduced no matter how good the exhaust may be. So, initially at least, we need to focus on finding intake flow from a performance cylinder head. It is not until average flow efficiencies of the intake throughout the intended valve-lift envelope have exceeded about 60 percent that we need to start considering intake-to-exhaust flow ratios and the valve sizes involved.

Flow Efficiency

For a given pressure drop, there is a relatively well-defined limit for how much air can pass through a given area available for that flow. At 28 inches pressure drop, an opening like the size of the one created between a valve and the seat in the head flows 146 cfm for every square inch of available opening area. At this level, the aperture created is 100-percent efficient. Of course, the area available to flow in or out of the cylinder varies with lift. As the aperture geometry varies, so does the flow efficiency. At very low lift (0.0 to 0.050 inch), the gap at the valve seat resembles a venturi.

At this size of gap, there can be some pressure recovery, so at these low lifts the valve seat configuration acts as a nozzle. Then the flow efficiencies appear very high and can often exceed 100 percent. However, that is more a function of how we determine what the 100-percentile figure is. In practice, a nozzle requires a different equation to compute its flow, hence the apparent anomaly here. Figure 2.9 shows the difference between a stock big-block Chevy head, a ported

one, and the 100-percent mark that we should strive for.

A similar high-efficiency situation at low intake lift can exist for a well-designed exhaust port. Not only can very high efficiencies be realized at low lift, but also at lift values exceeding about 0.28 inch of the valve diameter. At these lift values, a steeply up-drafted port can start to take on the properties of a nozzle. As a result, the flow figures can appear extremely high and in certain instances exceed the 100-percent mark.

I address flow efficiency more in Chapter 10. But it may help here to show some typical efficiency figures versus the figures seen if the valve and port were 100-percent efficient. Figure 2.9 shows this. Note how a typical stock port is usually barely more than about 50-percent efficient. If porting time is put into production two-valve heads, efficiency can be raised to 65 percent or more, depending on the casting involved. That, without resorting to bigger valves, is a 30-percent increase in airflow. What that can do for power output, especially if it is combined with a compression ratio (CR) increase, is very gratifying.

A FLOW BENCH—BUILD OR BUY

May 2008 was something of a milestone for me as far as the modification of cylinder heads for more performance was concerned. It was 50 years since I performed my first cylinder-head flow test. The technique I used was crude, to say the least, but it worked. Looking back on it many years later, I realized I should have continued flowing heads using this original method, instead of being swayed by convention. My original method employed the floating pressure-drop measuring method described in Chapter 2. This was not because I had, even at the tender age of 15, figured out that a floating pressure drop was better; it was because I had no idea how else to do the job. But as events unfolded, I flew into the face of convention for one of the first times as far as high-performance technology was concerned, but it was hardly the last!

Here is how events unfolded. The first flow bench was, in fact, my mother's vacuum cleaner. I mounted the head to be tested (an A-Series head as per the Austin/Morris Mini engine) on a bare A-Series block. The head was equipped with a way to precisely open the valves. Then, for the intake tests, the suction side of the vacuum cleaner was located in the bottom of the bore and sealed, so there were no leakages at this point.

Next, a spark plug with the middle removed and a piece of 1/4-inch-diameter copper tube glued in was installed into the spark plug hole. It was connected to a manometer, made of clear plastic tubing stapled to a 2 x 4-inch board. This was marked out in

Fig. 3.1. Glyn Swift (left) and Nick Swift (right) are not just Swift in name. They build some of England's swiftest Mini Coopers, and it all starts here on the flow bench. This particular unit is a highly instrumented SuperFlow 110.

inches from –48 inches at the bottom through zero to +48 inches at the top. The plastic tubing was looped, so that the bottom of the "U" was formed about a couple of feet or so below the bottom of the 8-foot-long 2 x 4. A section of the U-tube was filled with food-coloring-dyed water until it reached the zero mark.

As you can see from Figure 3.2, there is not much to this bench. It can be constructed in a few hours for a minimal expenditure. If you already have a shop vac, the rest of it costs probably less than $75.

Here is how it works. The more open the valve is, the lower the pressure drop is, as measured by the manometer. At low valve lift, say, 0.050, the manometer can read (depending on the vacuum cleaner's capability and the valve's ability to flow air) anywhere between 60 and about 100 inches H$_2$O. If the flow at a given lift is improved, the manometer reading at that lift drops. Let's say that the stock head at 0.050 valve lift produced a reading of 80 inches. We then do some seat blending on the valve and head casting, and on

the next test the manometer reading is 70 inches. This means the flow has gone up, so the pressure drop pulled by the vacuum cleaner is lower. To a first approximation, the flow has increased by the square root of 80 divided by 70. That works out to 1.069, or a 6.9-percent improvement.

You can see that this bench primarily tells us whether or not the port is flowing better or worse. Also we can see that it does not test the head at a standard pressure drop, as does almost every pro-built bench. This standard pressure drop, as previously stated, is considered conventional practice and allows a uniform method to be used for quoting the CFM of flow produced.

At this point, you may be thinking that not having the ability to determine the CFM is a small price to be paid to establish positive or negative trends in a head's airflow capability. After having built my bench, I spent a couple of years wondering how I could get real CFM numbers off it, so I could swap flow bench war stories with the guys at Weslake (the big name in airflow at the time) with-

out revealing both my youth and then-amateur status.

As far as CFM measurement was concerned, I saw the light some years later during a conversation with an engineer who was somewhat older and more experienced than I. During our conversation he used some key words: "standard pressure drop." Well, there we go—I realized that I could adjust the test pressure/vacuum so that it was a constant; and then I could calculate the CFM. It was not quite as easy as typing the words but that, in essence, was it.

Over the next few years, I built increasingly more sophisticated benches until finally, during the early 1970s, I built a bench that conformed to British Standards for precision gas flow measurement. It was a 15-foot-long monster. It worked just fine and cost a small fortune but the payoff was a lot of flow work that was done for those porters who didn't have a bench. In the late 1970s to early 1980, I even did some work on it for the McLaren F1 guys.

A Rethink on Matters

By the time the mid 1980s came around, I began to have second thoughts about using a standard pressure drop to test heads. The issue here was: What sort of pressure differences do we see between the port and cylinder on a live-running race engine compared with what was typically being used on a flow bench? In *Smokey Yunick's Power Secrets*, the author went to some length to make sure we understood that a seemingly magic 28-inch pressure differential should be used. That, as of 2012, is practically an industry standard. But as I have already pointed out, a race or even a high-performance street

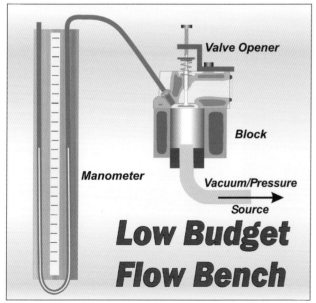

Fig. 3.2. The type of flow bench illustrated here is the floating-pressure type. Round up the minimal parts required, and you can build one like this on a Saturday morning. If you already have a block and vacuum cleaner, the rest of what is needed can usually be sourced for less than $75.

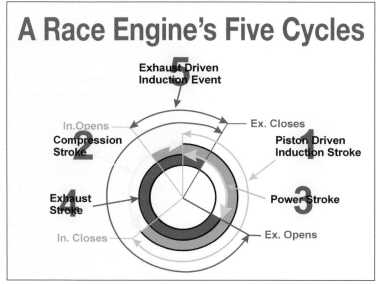

Fig. 3.3. At cycle number-1, the exhaust-generated vacuum starts the intake charge moving into the cylinder way before the piston even starts down the bore. As the crank rotates farther we get to cycle number-2. This is normally considered the charge-inducing stroke. In an ideal situation, cycle number-1 has cleared the combustion chamber and put a considerable amount of kinetic energy into the incoming charge before the piston starts down the bore. The result is an engine that can achieve a volumetric efficiency well in excess of 100 percent. The bottom line is a good exhaust system that is worth a lot of extra torque, horsepower, and, best of all, extra mileage. But to make all this work as intended, the cam must generate the right events around TDC.

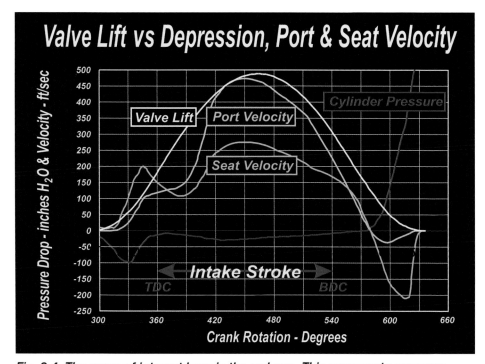

Fig. 3.4. The curve of interest here is the red one. This represents pressure seen in the cylinder. The valve lift starts at the 315-degree mark. With the valve just 0.050 inch off the seat, the suction caused by the exhaust is 100 inches H_2O, and the velocity between the seat on the valve and the head is 200 ft/sec.

engine does not see a fixed standard pressure drop. Here, we need to deal with the reality.

The induction system on a true race engine is, for the most part, exhaust driven. That means the scavenging pulse from the tuned exhaust pulls a far bigger depression in the cylinder than the piston pulls going down the bore. On something like an engine from NASCAR's Cup series, this can amount to 120 inches or more at TDC during the overlap period. The draw on the intake port at TDC can be such that, even though the piston is virtually parked, the intake charge in the port can be moving into the cylinder at as much as 90 mph!

When the valve is near wide open and the piston is traveling at peak piston speed (this is between 72 to 74 degrees after TDC), the draw is somewhat less. How much less? For a typically high-flowing two-valve head feeding about 1.2 cfm per cubic inch to the cylinder, the pressure drop is about 15 to 20 inches H_2O at peak power.

The red curve in Figure 3.4 is a smoothed curve of the pressure difference between the cylinder and the intake port throughout an induction stroke. Although the curve can vary quite substantially from one similar engine to another (due to relatively small changes in lengths, diameters, and cam characteristics), this curve is representative of a 620-hp, single 4-barrel 355-ci motor.

The first point of the graph is that the draw on the intake valve/port is greatest at low lift, in which the suction reaches 100 inches H_2O while the valve is at just 0.050 lift. This means testing at 28 inches at this low valve lift is far from representative of the real world. Therefore, your floating pressure-drop tests should use a high-pressure differential at low lift and a lower one at high lift.

Current Conclusions

All the forgoing leads to one conclusion: To more nearly simulate what happens in a running engine, intake flow tests need to be done at a high pressure drop at low valve lift and a lower one at high lift. This is exactly the situation that happens with a flow-test rig (Figure 3.2). An uncontrolled vacuum source, such as a shop vac, pulls a large vacuum when the intake valve is closed and a progressively lesser vacuum as the intake is opened. So running a floating pressure drop, as we are doing here, is actually a more realistic simulation of what happens in real life.

At this point we have, with a floating pressure-drop bench, a flow testing situation that more closely mimics the pressure differentials seen in the cylinder/intake port of a running engine. So what are the advantages? Let's quickly go through them again to be clear on the justification for adopting this procedure over the more normal fixed pressure-drop method.

If the pressure drop is too low, the flow pattern that develops in the port, especially in the more critical regions close to the valve seat, is not the same as at the higher pressure drop seen in a running engine. If we use a pressure drop that is too low, the flow attaches itself to the port wall on critical curves, such as the short-side turn, without any significant flow separation.

When these conditions exist, air is fed to the part of the valve circumference that is situated adjacent to the short-side turn, so that the flow is better than it typically is at a higher pressure drop. When the pressure drop is increased to something more nearly representing that seen in a running engine, the port velocity increases to the point where the air simply skips off the short-side turn and tries to exit the valve on the long side. As a result, a considerable section of the intake valve's circumference experiences very little flow.

If we take a low standard pressure drop test of, say, 8 inches and correct it to 28, the resulting number comes out higher than if we had flow tested at 28 inches in the first place. In practice, if pressure drops significantly below 8 inches are used, the flow in the port slows enough to stay attached even around a relatively tight turn.

Running the flow bench tests and conducting high-to-low floating pressure-drop tests creates the same pattern of flow-reducing port-to-wall separations that occur during real-world running conditions. From this, it follows that the most effective port modifications are achieved by addressing real-world flow patterns and improving the port shape to improve such patterns.

The bottom line is that our cheapo flow-test setup is actually a better tool for developing an intake port than a $10,000 commercial flow bench used in a conventional manner. At this point, the only down side is determining just how many CFM the head is flowing when each reading is corrected to the common 28-inch pressure drop. Without this number, you won't be able to make a comparison with other flow test results or be able to compare your work to others. This can be fixed relatively easily, but for now let's consider the exhaust.

Flowing the Exhaust

Without making some fancier test equipment, we are not going to be able to flow the exhaust at real-life test pressures. Typically, when an exhaust valve opens, the cylinder pressure is somewhere between 70 and 120 psi. If you are intent on having a pump that develops this kind of test pressure, even for just the low-lift tests, be aware that you need about a 200-hp motor to drive the pump. Very few flow bench setups are capable of this. Although unconfirmed, I have heard that Ford's Detroit division has a flow bench that can approach real-world pressure drops, and that it costs a mere seven-figure number to build. For the most part, we flow the exhaust at 28 inches and live with the fact that it is not the best way to do things.

However, our budget bench, with its uncontrolled floating pressure drop, actually does a better job than a commercial bench at a fixed pressure drop. I can say that there is little to prevent using a commercial fixed-pressure drop bench, such as the SuperFlow 600, in a floating pressure-drop mode, which I address in Chapter 3.

Quantifying Results

My friend Roger "Dr. Air" Helgesen built a bench that worked along the same lines as this in the early 1980s and still uses it today to flow heads and intake manifolds. As usual, Roger adopted a singularly simple way to convert the pressure drop seen on the manometer to CFM at 28 inches with nothing more than a sheet of graph paper and a few calibration orifices. Just how this is done is our next subject.

Establishing the Numbers

Okay, so you have built a budget flow bench. While this may allow you to establish whether a move has increased or decreased airflow, it does not, at this time, allow you to compare your efforts with the rest of the head porting community. Within reasonable limits, that problem can easily be taken care of.

When using my early flow bench, I never made the connection between using a floating pressure drop and actually calibrating the setup to give CFM. Instead, I invested a lot of hours building my monster British Standards bench with all the corrections then known to man. A venture like this is not the sort of job I recommend to other would-be porters/cylinder-head development engineers. Your time is better spent on developing heads and selling what you are producing. Doing otherwise means investing what is potentially a huge amount of time, effort, and money in a bench that, at the end of the day, serves you less effectively than the super-cheap floating-pressure-drop one I advocate here. However, if you want a little more than just a vacuum-cleaner-powered bench for a greater range of pressure drop, by all means build it with more powerful motors.

Fig. 3.5. The Helgesen calibration plate (foreground) I made up to check my bench. Behind it is another plate with four 160-cfm (at 28 inches) holes in it.

But let's get back to reading out our results in CFM. Here's where the revelation came in. For many years, I knew Roger Helgesen had a flow bench but the deal was we always hung out at my place (maybe that's because the Serdi seat and guide machine was there). But one day I was at his house, where he had his flow equipment, porting bench, and tools. What an eye opener that was. If ever there was a guy who could come up with ultra simple ways of doing ultra-complex jobs it was Roger (Another good friend of mine christened Roger "Dr. Air," and I always thought that to be a very appropriate moniker).

What really caught my attention was the calibration plate Roger had made and the graph he was using to simply read off the CFM at 28 inches of depression. The plate is shown in Figure 3.5, and the dimensions to produce it in Figure 3.6. It has holes sized to flow 5, 10, 20, 40, 80, and 160 cfm at 28 inches of depression across the plate. Not only can you use this plate to figure out how much flow is passing through a head on a floating depression bench, but you can also use it as a reference tool for a regular bench, such as a Superflow.

A few words about producing or acquiring a Helgesen plate: With

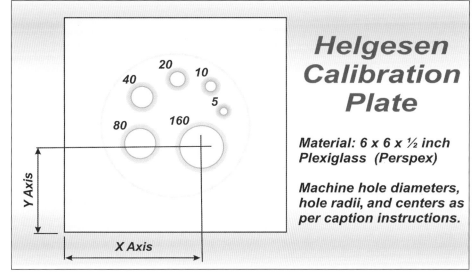

Fig. 3.6. These holes need to be machined to a very smooth surface. Make tolerances as accurate as possible (+/- 0.001 is acceptable). The hole sizes and X-Y coordinates are:

- Hole 5: 0.210 Dia. on 4.30/3.40 inches
- Hole 10: 0.296 Dia. on 3.95/4.10 inches
- Hole 20: 0.419 Dia. on 3.05/4.30 inches
- Hole 40: 0.594 Dia. on 2.10/3.80 inches
- Hole 80: 0.840 Dia. on 2.05/2.5 inches
- Hole 160: 1.185 Dia. on 3.70/2.40 inches

Radius entry for all holes is 0.25 inch. This is machined so that the edge of the radius goes out to 80 degrees, not the full 90. The back of the 5 and 10 size holes must be chamfered with a 90-degree cutter. The 5-hole chamfer should be 0.460-inch diameter and 0.546 for the 10 hole.

Roger's kind permission I have reproduced the dimensions here, so you can make your own. I trust you to not go into production with these and sell them. It is Rogers's idea and I ask you respect that. If you are not in the position to make one, you can check to see what the availability is through Dr J's Porting Supply.

Let us assume at this point you have a plate; how is it used to give CFM at 28 inches? Here is how that is done.

Step 1: Make sure your bench is sealed so no leakage takes place, except through the test piece. Position the Helgesen plate on the bench with all holes plugged with clay (or any convenient plugs).

Step 2: Start with a reading on the manometer, with the plate completely blocked off for a "zero flow" depression test, and note the pressure drop seen on the manometer. Note this stalled depression. (If you did not make your manometer tall enough, the vacuum cleaner has now drunk all the water from it!)

Step 3: Open the 5-cfm orifice and note the depression (when I was talking about machining this plate they were referred to as holes—now that we are flowing through them they are orifices).

Step 4: Plug the 5-cfm orifice and open the 10; flow test and note the depression.

Step 5: Open the 5- and 10-cfm orifices together and again note the depression. Continue in 5-cfm increments until all the orifices are open and you have recorded the depression at each 5-cfm increment.

Step 6: Get a couple of large sheets of graph paper, the larger the better. I recommend something like 20 x 20 inches. Then for the intake, make a graph as shown in Figure 3.7.

If you plot out your results, you should get a similar curve. Where it starts and finishes is totally dependent on the vacuum/pressure source you are using.

Step 7: When you have a curve for the intake, repeat the test but use the blower side of the vacuum cleaner and reverse the plate.

Step 8: Blow through all the holes in the same progression used for the intake and make a graph for the exhaust.

You can now flow a head and get some respectably accurate flow figures for comparative purposes.

Accuracy—How Good?

Although what we have done here is very basic, it can produce results comparable to benches costing $10,000 or more and considered the industry's standard. There are, however, many points at which errors can creep in and considerably

reduce the accuracy of your results.

Let's start first with leakages. For the numbers to stand even a halfway decent chance of being accurate, the bench must not leak at any point.

The voltage input to the motor influences the amount of suction a vacuum cleaner or any electric air mover can produce. You must monitor the voltage at the motor input and make sure you test at the same voltage each time. For the record, Dr. Air has a step-up transformer that increases the line voltage from whatever it may be (it varies between 110 and 115) to 130 volts, and then a rheostat device is used to adjust it to 115 volts.

The way the calibration plate is mounted on the flow bench also affects the readings. The ideal situation is to mount a box, which can be made of wood but must be airtight, about 9 inches down each side (9 x 9 x 9) with a 5-inch hole in the top,

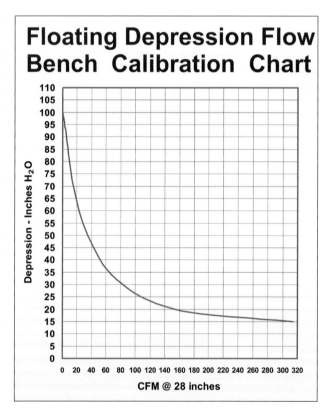

Fig. 3.7. By plotting the individual orifices against the depression, you can develop a graph like this. You can then convert the subsequent pressure drop to CFM.

and whatever size hole mates up to the block or whatever you are using to simulate a block. Place the calibration plate directly over the 5-inch hole in the box and flow test it. If the plate is mounted on top of a bore even as large as 4 inches, there is a residual effect from the downstream velocity of the air and the plate flows about 2 to 3 percent higher than if flowed into an open box.

Big changes in temperature and pressure also affect the reading, but this is only minor if the bench is in a constant indoor temperature. If there is any doubt about the figures, recheck the depression with the plate at, say, 160 cfm. Using this reading, correct the numbers up or down by whatever percentage of error is seen.

Note: When the depression falls between 160 inches and 15, the highest degree of accuracy is achieved. If the depression drops much below about 6 inches at high valve lifts, you can figure that when corrected they could read a little higher than they should. Just how much is dependent on how severe any flow separation on the short-side turn is at the higher pressure-drop readings I am advising you to use.

Summary

If you have built a bench along the lines I've suggested, then at this point, you have a bench that was cheap to build and can deliver CFM numbers. The next step for an upgrade here is to write a spreadsheet program that does the number crunching for you. I have written a relatively simple Microsoft Excel program that allows me to input the depression numbers into my computer and subsequently prints a

professional-looking set of graphs of the flow tests, complete with my business details along the top of the paper.

You may say that's all well and good, but I am not into writing my own programs. That is not really a problem. But whether you can write programs or not, I have a simple question here: How would you like to upgrade what we have built so far with an electronics package? Such a package costs about $1,000. It allows your bench to read out in corrected CFM and directly integrate with your computer, so you can do fancy printouts. Sound good? Well, in practice you have two companies that I know

of that can be of great help with this, so that's our next topic.

Budget Computerization

Okay, you have built the budget flow bench detailed so far. While this may allow you to see moves/alterations that help or hinder and to determine CFM flow, it does not necessarily allow neatly printed comparisons of your efforts with the rest of the world. Nor, without considerable programming yourself, does it produce an analysis of what has been achieved such as flow efficiencies, port velocity, velocity gradients,

Fig. 3.8. The McDonald/Vizard team (left/right) put the Audie Technology Flow Quik through a bank of rigorous tests. In a week, we had most certainly sized up the value of this piece of equipment to the budget-constrained racer/porter.

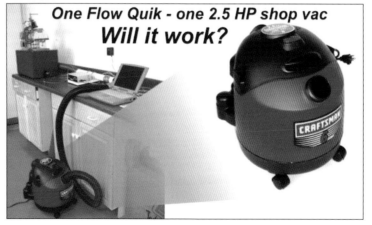

Fig. 3.9. Can a low-power shop vac be used as a pressure/vacuum source for a flow bench intended to flow typical small-block V-8 heads? You might guess this Sears 2½-hp, 6-gallon unit cleans but cannot flow a head; but with a floating pressure drop, this unit got the job done in spite of its marginal power.

and the like. Although there may be others, Audie Technology and Performance Trends are two companies I have dealt with that have very cost effective products that are professional quality but well within the reach of the home-based porter.

Budget Bench Electronics

Let's look at how to take the floating depression bench just described, and substantially upgrade it to a professional-grade piece of test equipment. This includes an electronic readout in CFM, pre-corrected to the depression of your choice (probably 28 inches), and that alone might convince most of you wanting a more up-market bench to take the plunge.

But that is far from all that is dealt with here. If you hook up your bench to a computer, you can record data with a push-to-read button that, while held down, averages the readings for as long as you do so. In addition, the system can also screen-display graphs of your porting efforts as well as print out professional-looking reports with your name on the top of the sheet (customers like this). Probably the best news is that you are only out of pocket by about $750 or so in 2012 dollars. If all this sounds appealing, let's make a start on why and how to get from here to there.

You don't need to have moved that much up the ladder from novice to realize that maximizing power means maximizing cylinder head capability. Everything else in the loop is developed simply to make the most of the cylinder head's capability.

If we further analyze the performance equation, we find that at least 70 percent of a cylinder head's performance capability is airflow related. The upgrades and accuracy tests, which I conducted with the aid of engine builder/tech writer Bob McDonald, brought our floating depression bench to full professional capability. This allowed it to meet the needs of those who port and prep high-dollar, four-valve heads for equally high-dollar clientele, as well as the more regular home-porter applications. But, in our case, meeting the needs of a high roller is maybe not quite as important as meeting the needs of the racer on a tight budget, and that probably includes most of us.

Plenty of drag and circle-track race classes limit head castings to less-expensive, production-style items. This puts a greater emphasis on even small flow differences; and if you want to win, it's important that whatever you have is better than whatever your competition has. Though it's not the only category to do so, the IMCA racer in the United States falls squarely into this group. Since the engine can be claimed for a fixed fee, it's good to get power without parting with a bunch of cash.

If you are building an engine for this or a similar class of racing, you have to ask yourself: Just how much money can I afford to give away to be competitive? Like it or not, time and money are closely linked. We may resent giving away a pair of heads with an $800 porting investment, but not feel nearly as bad parting company with similar heads we have personally spent 10 to 15 hours porting. The bottom line is: Most racers have far more surplus expendable time than surplus expendable income!

You don't have to tour many head shops to realize the most popular bench used by pros is the SuperFlow 600—possibly with electronic support. You probably also understand the reason you don't have one of these benches is because it can cost as much or more than the race car you are planning to build. So, for most racers and enthusiast engine builders, a $10,000 to $15,000 bench is simply out of the question. The electronic support system I am going to cover is not.

Audie Technology

Within pro engine/cylinder head circles, Audie Technology is well known. This company produces, among many other things, the Flow Pro data acquisition unit that is an add-on for non-computer-supported benches such as the big SuperFlow units. It also produces the cost-conscious Flow Quik, which sells for about $750, and is not a flow bench in itself but more a means of measuring flow. By adding this unit to an existing flow bench, we can achieve as much as can be done with a commercial flow bench but at a fraction of the cost.

Accuracy and the Budget

Any piece of measuring equipment that comes in at less than 1/10 of the cost of its principal competition might rouse some concern about functionality and accuracy. Since the Flow Quik is a measuring instrument, tech writer/racer Bob McDonald and I decided to put it through its paces and pass on that info to possible end users. Our plan was to check ease of use, repeatability, and, most importantly, overall accuracy. To expedite matters, Audie Thomas of Audie Technology shipped us the Flow Quik unit the company exhibits at the Performance Racing Industry show. Bob and I extensively tested it for a full week and what follows are the results.

Introducing the Flow Quik

Audie's show unit has a dummy cylinder mounted on a flow box. This is connected via a 2-inch-inside-diameter (I.D.) hose to the tube containing the measuring device. Upstream and downstream of this orifice is a pressure tap, which is connected to a box of electronics. The pressure transducers in this box convert air-pressure signals to electronic signals. These signals are transmitted to a microprocessor and the data is displayed as CFM on an LED readout.

The first tests we ran were to compare the end results of a run at 28-inch fixed-pressure drop and another run with a floating pressure drop. To do this, we ran the bench both ways and used our Helgesen calibration plate as the test piece. In the floating mode, the test pressures seen on the bench by the Flow Quik ranged from about 72 inches to less than 10. The resultant corrected numbers and the accuracy produced (compared to corrected 28-inch numbers) are shown in Figure 3.15.

A calibration tube, which is installed in the system, is supplied with the Flow Quik. The readout is adjusted to 80.9 cfm on the 28-inch scale. In this instance, the unit was calibrated with the 80-cfm orifice in our Helgesen calibration plate, hence the zero error at that point. As far as overall accuracy, it is far better than the majority of benches in the performance world. Compared with a typical commercial bench, the Flow Quik, from 40 cfm up, averages about the same error; i.e., about 2 percent.

Although overall accuracy is important for us to make comparisons from different benches, the number-one requirement for a head porter is consistency from one month to another. We were able to make a

relatively good check of that because of a dramatic weather change during our testing period. Readings taken seven days apart showed the Flow Quik's repeatability to be about 1 percent. At the end of the day, we can say that the Flow Quik's accuracy against a calibration plate was as good as a bench costing ten times as much.

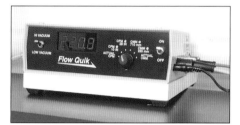

Fig. 3.10. The Flow Quik's readout. The reading shown here is corrected to 28 inches depression. The selector knob on the right of the unit allows a 10- or 28-inch correction to be shown as well as the metric equivalent.

Flow Quik CFM	Helgesen CFM	% Error
28.0	25.0	+7.2
41.00	40.0	+2.5
80.00	80.0	0.0
164.07	160.0	+3.3
311.80	315.0	-1.0

Computer Program

At this point our tests turned to determining just how well, given the floating pressure drop, the Flow Quik's performance translated into accurate and repeatable results on a real head. The LED readout on the Flow Quik box is only one function of it. This box has connections to allow

Fig. 3.11. This Ametek motor is the type used in the big Super-Flow benches. The Audie unit tested was equipped with two such motors sourced from Grainger at $85 each.

Fig. 3.12. A comparison of our Helgesen plate, flow tested on the floating depression method as used by our budget bench in conjunction with the Audie Technology Flow Quik unit. It produces creditably accurate numbers in this mode; and in terms of accuracy, compares well to fixed-depression tests done on a SuperFlow 600.

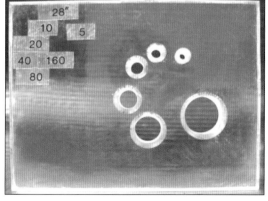

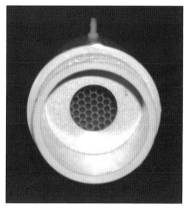

Fig. 3.13. For the tests done here, a Helgesen plate (left) was used as a reference to test the Flow Quik's overall accuracy. On the right is the flow measuring device housed in the Flow Quik's measuring tube.

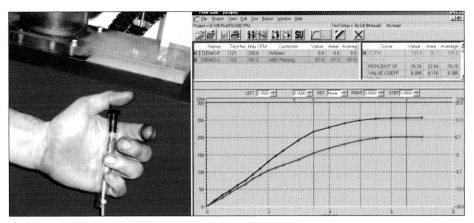

Fig. 3.14. The "take-reading" button (left) averages the readings for as long as the button is held down. A 5-second "hold down" interval produced repeatable results. The graph (right) is what comes up on the computer screen.

the output from the microprocessor to be input into a computer. Also a push-to-read or take-reading button can be used to transfer the measured CFM to a Flow Quik program.

The Flow Quik program allows the user to type in info relative to the head being tested. This head-spec info is then used to calculate many factors important to the serious head porter. Such things as valve discharge coefficient and port velocities at various pre-determined points are calculated and displayed. The take-reading button also greatly improves accuracy and repeatability by virtue of its averaging capability. For our tests, a 5-second interval was used as the averaging period.

To put the Flow Quik through its paces, we used a Holley 23-degree, high-performance street small-block Chevy head. This pushed the Flow Quik to what we perceived to be about 80 percent of its limit with a dual motor-vacuum source.

Head Setup

Although installing the test head on this bench was the same as with any other bench, there was a difference from, say, a SuperFlow

bench: The Flow Quik does not directly sense and compensate for any extraneous leakage. Although leakage at any point other than the intake valve can be deducted from manual readings, the same cannot be done in the computer-supported mode if accurate number crunching is expected. This means making sure there are no leaks in the equipment

itself. And because the test depression goes so much higher than on a regular bench, the springs holding the valves closed must be at least twice the stiffness.

Test Pressure Comparisons

Our first tests with the Holley head were made in floating pressure drop mode. This allowed the Ametek motors to pull whatever maximum test-pressure differential they were capable of. At 0.050 inch lift, 62 inches of vacuum was seen across the intake valve of the test head. As the lift increased the pressure dropped; so at 0.700, it was down to just more than 12 inches. Several tests run under identical conditions showed readings spanning less than 1 percent.

Our next test was designed to simulate a lesser pressure/vacuum source. To do this, we introduced a fixed leak prior to the measuring point, to bleed off some vacuum.

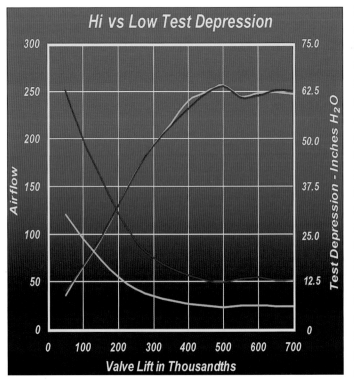

Fig. 3.15. The curves starting high on the left and dropping toward the right show the test depression used for each of the two flow tests. Regardless of the big difference between the red and green test depression curves, the Flow Quik still corrected the flow numbers to generate the nearly identical red and green flow curves seen here.

Executing the same test but with about half the vacuum, and comparing the readings with the full-vacuum source, produced the results shown in Figure 3.15. You can see the microprocessor computations compensated and corrected, to within a close margin, for the difference between the floating test pressure and the 28-inch fixed test pressure. Comparing these numbers with those achieved from a freshly calibrated SuperFlow 600 (using a fixed 28 inches) we saw a maximum difference of 2.8 percent below 0.200 lift and 2.2 percent above. The average difference from 0.050 to 0.700 was only 0.9 percent, with the Flow Quik showing slightly more flow than the SF 600. The bottom line: Our test Flow Quik unit produced figures (which could be expected to vary a little from unit to unit) that are closer than typically measured between two conventional and supposedly identical fixed-depression benches.

The Shop-Vac Test

The last and, from our point of view, the most important test was to run the Flow Quik with a regular shop vac. Since the point was to see if a typical vacuum cleaner could be used, it was not part of the plan to get the biggest one we could find. The goal was to see if we could get respectable CFM readings with an average shop vac. Figure 3.16 shows that this is possible.

Conclusions

Our first thoughts on the performance of the Audie Technology Flow Quik were that it far surpassed expectations. Ease of use, speed, and accuracy were far beyond what you normally expect of such a cost-conscious unit. In its least expensive form, the unit from Audie sets you back about $650. Add to this the cost of building the bench as detailed earlier, a dial gauge, and a means of opening valves, and you are in business. If the shop-vac

selected is about 6 hp, like a big Sears unit, I estimate a realistically accurate range of flow capability of about 330 cfm. Think about this: You can have a professional-capability floating-depression bench for under $750. Port two sets of heads, and you have more than recovered your investment!

Performance Trends

Another recognized name for flow bench testing is Performance Trends. In fact, SuperFlow resells Port Flow Analyzer software, Pitot tubes, swirl meter, and other accessories with its flow benches.

Performance Trends offers a couple of options for the DIY flow-bench builder: Port Flow Analyzer software and Black Box II electronics. These can be fitted to almost any type of DIY bench, even older SuperFlow, JKM, and FlowData benches. Their sales and tech staff ensure that you get the correct system for your DIY bench.

Performance Trends also offers calibration services for a small charge; you simply provide them flow readings from your bench with orifice plates of various sizes. Using this data, they tell you the full-scale CFM readings for your particular bench; so your bench, with their software, now matches the rest of the industry.

For those who want to start building a bench from scratch, Performance Trends offers a system called EZ Flow for about $999. This kit includes software and electronics, and plans for building a bench from PVC tubing. PVC tubing and fittings are especially suitable because they are inexpensive, easy to work with, and they do not leak. That is a good point because the major drawback of a DIY bench is air leakage. Unless multiple layers of paint are applied,

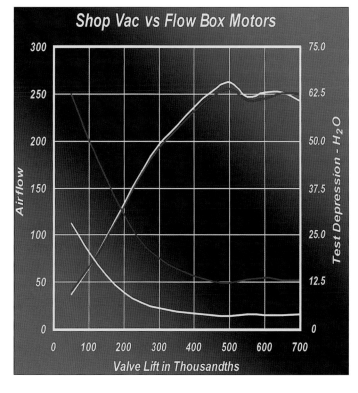

Fig. 3.16. Although about at the limit, a 2½-hp Sears shop vac is capable of sufficient pressure/vacuum to deliver the results shown by the yellow curves in this graph. Until the 220-cfm mark, the correlation between results produced by two powerful Ametek vacuum motors and the shop vac was extremely good. Above that, only a modest error of up to 1.5 percent was shown.

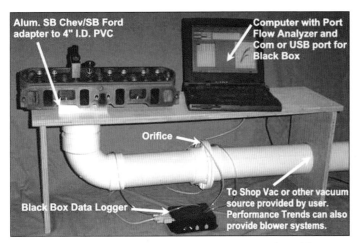

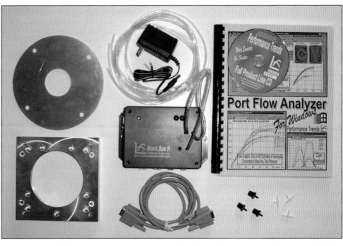

Fig. 3.17. The EZ Flow kits come in two sizes, for either 4- or 6-inch PVC. For flows up to about 150 cfm, the 4-inch system works fine. For anything greater, up to around 500 cfm, you need to build it out of 6-inch PVC.

Fig. 3.18. The components of the Performance Trends EZ Flow kit. This leaves only items such as the PVC piping to be sourced to complete the parts list required for a finished bench.

significant amounts of air can leak right through plywood if enough care is not taken during prep and assembly.

EZ Flow kits come in two sizes, for either 4- or 6-inch PVC. For flows up to about 150 cfm, the 4-inch system works fine. For anything greater, up to around 500 cfm, you need to build it out of 6-inch PVC.

The EZ Flow system also includes critical machined components, the flow orifice, and the head adapter. If you don't have a machine shop, or want to get running right away, this is a huge time and cost saver. The head adapter for the 6-inch EZ Flow allows for easy replacement of the head-bolt adapter plate and bore sleeve. This means you can quickly change your bench to flow different-style heads and engine bores in minutes.

The standard 4- and 6-inch systems come with a head adapter

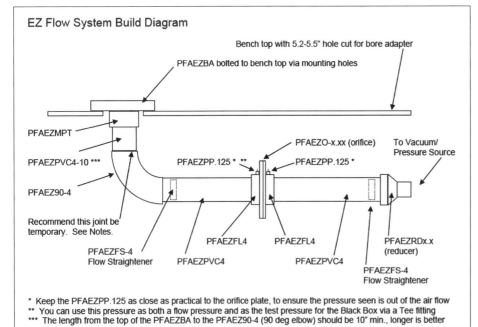

Fig. 3.19. The Performance Trends EZ Flow system comes complete with drawings for the basic components the end user needs to source. Most home improvement/hardware stores have the materials at user-friendly prices. Here is the general assembly drawing; there is not much to construct to get a working system.

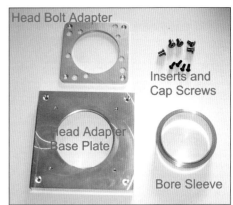

Fig. 3.20. If you are building a bench that can top 400 cfm at 28 inches, you should seriously consider building the 6-inch EZ Flow unit. Seen here are the head adapter and bore sleeve included with the 6-inch EZ Flow kit.

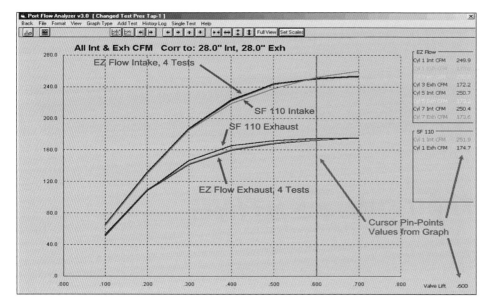

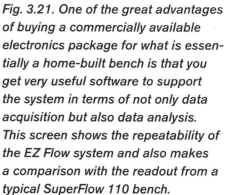

Fig. 3.21. One of the great advantages of buying a commercially available electronics package for what is essentially a home-built bench is that you get very useful software to support the system in terms of not only data acquisition but also data analysis. This screen shows the repeatability of the EZ Flow system and also makes a comparison with the readout from a typical SuperFlow 110 bench.

Fig. 3.22. A swirl meter can make important contributions toward developing heads that produce wide power curves. I have used three different types over the years, including a paddle-wheel type (from Performance Trends), a Torsional torque one (no longer available), and a honeycomb one (as seen here from Audie Technology).

and components to accommodate a small-block Chevy and small-block Ford bolt pattern with a 4.030-inch bore.

Other Bench Sources

After building my British Standards compliant monster bench and using it for several years, I moved from the UK to Tucson, Arizona. This was my second introduction to SuperFlow airflow benches. I had used a small 110 for accuracy comparison to my home-built bench while still living in the UK. But that was only a few hours of experience.

In 1976, the publisher I was writing for acquired an SF 300, which is the big bench that evolved into the SF 600. I have put literally thousands of hours on such a bench. I still, as of 2012, regularly use an SF 600 bench with all the Audie Technology add-ons. The only difference between what I do on this bench and what most others do is that I use a sliding scale of pressure drop, the same floating pressure drop I described earlier in this chapter.

Another bench I am cur-rently testing on is the Saenz J-600 bench, built in Brazil. What I can say is that this Saenz unit lends itself well to the floating-pressure-drop measurement technique because it pulls a lot of vacuum. Combine this with the fact it comes equipped with the Audie Technology flow measuring gear and software, and you get a bench that delivers results in a standard form while measuring with a sliding scale (floating) pressure drop—all good for doing the job right.

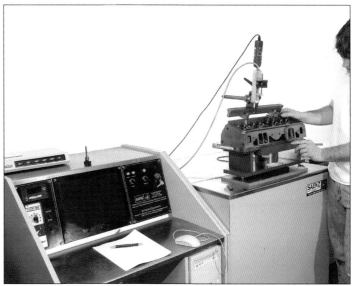

Fig. 3.23. The Saenz J-600 bench I currently use. It comes fully instrumented with the Audie Technology electronics and computer software. Also available is the automatic valve opener seen here, which speeds up testing significantly.

WET-FLOW TESTING

When you throw a lit match onto a gasoline-soaked rag, it ignites very easily. This is not an experiment I recommend or that is even needed. However, when gas so easily combusts, it's hard to imagine there ever being a problem igniting it in the cylinders of a hot, high-compression engine. The reality, though, is that we have all the time in the world to wait for a burning rag to exhaust its fuel through combustion. In a well-developed engine turning 9,000 rpm, the time for 90 percent of the charge to burn is one-and-a-half thousandths of second!

Fig. 4.1. Here is one of my hot street small-block Chevy engines. This one displaces 383 ci (6.28 liters) and dyno'd out at 609 hp (97 hp per liter) and 538 ft-lbs (85.7 ft-lbs per liter). This sort of output for a pump-gas 10.5:1 street-drivable motor of reasonable cost means covering every possible aspect of the power production chain of events. Good mixture quality and distribution are as vital as good airflow.

Wet-Flow Testing— What's it Worth?

During my Mini Cooper era in the early 1960s, I first realized that the fuel droplet size and the state of the mixture quality (or lack of it) dramatically affects power output. I learned a lot on the A-Series engine that powered this car—much of it totally contradictory to what you might expect. If the engine that powered these race-dominating roller skates was fed with fuel even a little too finely atomized, the power dropped like a rock. The valuable lesson I learned was to never take anything for granted.

This paid off handsomely a few years later (1972–1975) when, after winning a drag race championship with the same type of engine, I ended up developing a dominant four-cylinder Chrysler engine for the British Touring Car Championship series in England. With this engine the route to success was exactly the reverse of my success with the Mini Cooper's engine. Very finely atomized fuel and good dispersion, along with very low re-aggregation, were the key factors. They allowed me to produce a carb/intake manifold and head combination that substantially out-horsepowered (by about 20 hp) the two Formula 1 manufacturers also competing for the job. Not bad, I thought, for a guy who had more than a full-time job helping fill pages for eight or more magazines—each month!

In the late 1990s I was also involved in some similar work on six-cylinder Aston Martin race engines. This involved a study of mixture quality from the carb to the cylinder side of the intake valve, to ascertain how the fuel mixture behaved. Achieving certain goals here netted 20-plus hp.

About 1985, the late Ken Sperling (of Air Flow Research) got into wet-flow testing big time. The subject of his research was Chevy heads for NASCAR use. Although I did not know Ken that well at the time, we had a mutual friend, who was none other than airflow fanatic Roger "Dr. Air" Helgesen. One day, after a big wet-flow test session with Ken, he turned up at my California shop with a car half full of gear to do wet-flow testing and, he was eager to get started. This, along with some of the late (and corny as it sounds, great) Smokey Yunick's preaching was my baptism into the world of how fuel/

air mixtures react in the induction tract of a single 4-barrel-carbed, high-performance V-8 engine.

Since the Ken Sperling wet-flow-test era of the mid and late 1980s, the subject of wet flow, for all practical purposes, seemed to be dead. That changed when the late Joe Mondello, with a heap of help from some of his high-tech cronies, introduced a new and innovative wet-flow bench, which hit the speed headlines in 2002. At that point, the whole wet-flow debate re-ignited. But with Joe Mondello involved, what else could we have expected?

Since then, I've learned a lot and one thing is for sure: Whatever

you think might happen, probably doesn't happen; and what you never suspected, probably does. Actually, performing wet-flow tests is not that difficult, but it can be time consuming. All you have to do is pass a liquid/air charge through the induction system. The easiest way to do that is to blow it through, but it can also be done by suction.

Although the big Dart wet-flow bench shown in Figure 4.3 measures CFM while wet-flow testing, measuring flow at the same time is not really necessary. When wet-flow testing, what you are looking for is how the mixture reacts in terms of staying atomized, and how it may form

Fig. 4.2. Seen here is the late Joe Mondello showing off his wet-flow attachment for a conventional Super-Flow bench. This add-on is available for most of the commercially available race shop benches on the market.

Fig. 4.3. Dart's wet-flow bench is truly a monster. Unlike most of the wet-flow test systems, it combines flow capability in CFM and the ability to analyze wet-flow patterns. Note the huge pumps and electric motors needed for this bench to perform its various functions.

unwanted fuel rivulets. Still, wet-flow testing done without accounting for what is going on in the real intake tract is much less effective in power development than it could be. But for many this is a new science. So next I offer insights I have gleaned over a long time span.

Six Wet-Flow Mistakes to Avoid

It is very easy for a novice in this area to make some fundamental mistakes and, as a result, produce data that is not as applicable to a real-life induction system as you may assume. Most of the mistakes actually make what you are working with look worse than it really is; so take note as I run through the most common mistakes made.

Mistake Number-1: Less-than-Optimal Test-Pressure Differentials

A lot of wet-flow testing is done with a fixed test-pressure differential

of between 28 and 50 inches H_2O. Since our main focus here is a racing engine, what is needed is to emulate the depression curve that occurs in a running engine. This means drawing about 100 to 130 inches of depression at low lift (0.050 to 0.100 inch) and about 15 inches at high lift. A fuel wetting problem that exists at even 50 inches of depression at low lift can completely vanish at 120 inches. A problem that does not exist on the bench at 50 inches and high lift can easily show at 15 inches.

Mistake Number-2: Wrong Liquid-to-Air Ratio

If the excess liquid is put through the system, the wet-flow characteristics are bad no matter what you do. The key here is to take into account that about 15 to 20 percent of the liquid fuel vaporizes by the time it passes through the intake valve. The best fluid/air ratio to use to get meaningful results is a mixture (by volume) that represents a fuel/air ratio of about 15 to 20 percent lean.

Mistake Number-3: Wrong Surface Tension

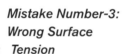

Water has a much higher surface tension as well as a density some 30 percent more than gasoline. These two factors can upset the spread and

shear patterns. Adding alcohol and small amounts of detergent can cut the surface tension to the point where water-based test fluids more closely emulate gasoline.

Mistake Number-4: Wrong Temperature

Running the test fluid and the intake valve at a hot temperature made a difference in the way the streams and shear areas reacted. This area might need more research to get a better correlation but, as of now, I recommend a fluid temperature of at least 150 degrees F.

Mistake Number-5: Incorrect Interpretation of Results

I don't quite know how to address this; there are so many aspects to consider. Many wet-flow tests reveal problems that are self evident, but some issues are regarded as a problem when, in fact, they are an asset. Fuel shearing off chamber edges and into vortices is often okay, but when they migrate to the cylinder-wall side of the widest part of the quench

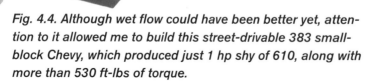

Fig. 4.4. Although wet flow could have been better yet, attention to it allowed me to build this street-drivable 383 small-block Chevy, which produced just 1 hp shy of 610, along with more than 530 ft-lbs of torque.

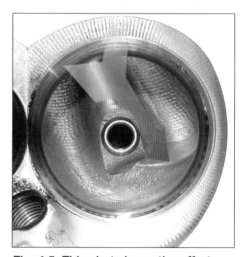

Fig. 4.5. This shot shows the effort that GM put into the development of the 427 Corvette engine's cylinder heads. The arrow indicates the fuel ramp, incorporated with apparently little flow loss.

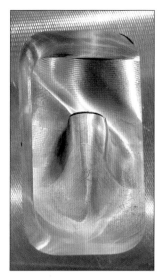

Fig. 4.6. Looking down the Ultra Pro 427 Corvette intake port clearly shows the fuel shear ramp angling off to the left of the valveguide.

Valve Lift	Stock In. Flow	Modified In. Flow	CFM Difference	Stock Ex. Flow	Modified Ex. Flow	CFM Difference
100	79.1	78.9	-0.2	55.9	56.3	0.4
200	162.2	160.1	-2.1	115.4	113.2	-2.2
250	201.1	207.2	6.1	141.5	142.6	1.1
300	248.7	252.9	4.2	167.8	172.1	4.3
400	313.9	308.5	-5.4	206.6	210.6	4
500	354.7	351.1	-3.6	218.3	228.2	9.9
550	371.4	371.1	-0.3	224.4	232.8	8.4
600	382.9	387.9	5	227.8	237.1	9.3
650	388.3	400.3	12	231.1	240.2	9.1
700	362.1	405.1	43	233.7	243.6	9.9
750	362.2	410.1	47.9	234.9	244.9	10

Fig. 4.7. The way flow numbers increase over stock at higher lifts clearly demonstrates the need for high valve lifts. However, the small improvements made in swirl and wet-flow properties also played a part. With a net valve lift of 0.670 inch, the power figures were measurably up, as shown here.

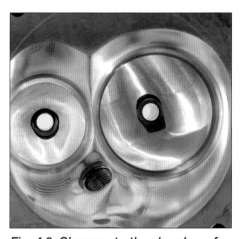

Fig. 4.8. Changes to the chamber of the Ultra Pro–modified 427 Corvette head were minimal. In this instance the really hard work was in the form of the fuel shear ramp. Getting this to work and improving flow was not an easy task.

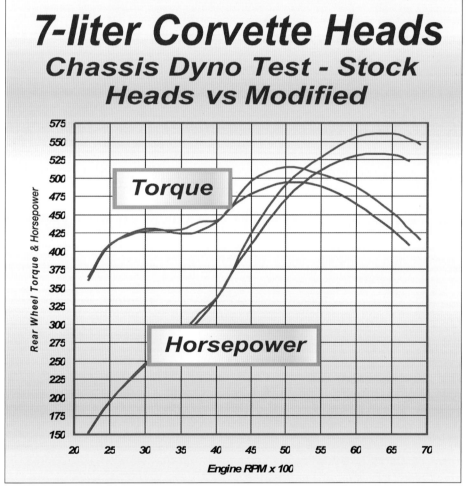

Fig. 4.9. Here is what moderate swirl and attention to wet and dry flow can do for an already well-developed cylinder head. Gains start at 3,500 rpm and amount to 20 ft-lbs and 25 hp.

pad, it is not okay. As the combustion cycle takes place, raw fuel can end up in the ring land volume and contribute absolutely nothing to the game. The obvious problems are just that—obvious. It's the more subtle issues that require an experienced eye and that just takes time.

Mistake Number-6: Incorrect Flow Model Setup

Guess what? The intake port on those heads is fed via an intake manifold and in turn by a carburetor. Each

modifies the characteristics of the air/fuel mix flowing out of the base of the carb. Sure, we can start any tests with just a bare head and valves. But from there, the quest for better wet flow needs to have an intake introduced and then a carb. As for the carb itself, it should have the same boosters as used by the end product, if you want to get real fussy about results.

Wet-flow testing something like a set of big side-draft carbs, such as Webers or the like, with each barrel on an independent runner, presents

no great test traps. This, however, is far from the case with a plenum-style manifold, such as a single-plane intake for a V-8.

It may seem easy enough to just flow one cylinder through the carb and intake and on through the cylinder head itself. This is often how manifolds are tested. Unfortunately, it's the wrong way to do it. On a single-plane intake, when the piston of the test cylinder is near maximum velocity and the valve wide open, the valve on the next cylinder to draw is as much as a 0.250 inch off the seat and (assuming a race engine) drawing air at a rate of about 20 to 25 percent of the test cylinder. If that cylinder is not hooked up to a depression that simulates this two-runner flow system, the direction and pattern of any wet flow in the intake does not simulate that of a running engine.

On intakes that utilize a plenum, I usually see some basic mistakes made. For a V-8 equipped

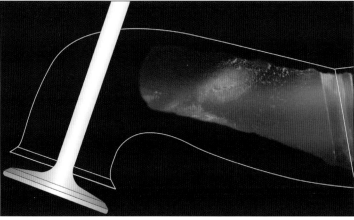

Fig. 4.10. Here, the approach angle of the manifold runner does not match the intake port, so the fuel tends to target the short-side turn more than we want to see.

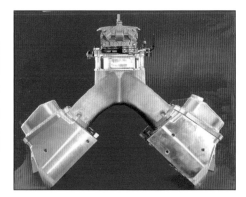

Fig. 4.12. Having a more direct line of approach to the port in the cylinder head from the manifold runner almost always helps sort out and improve wet flow. This 18-degree-style small-block Chevy head has manifold runners that, from this view, align directly with the ports. This is not so on many heads, such as the stock-style 23-degree heads.

Fig. 4.11. Dart's Tony McAfee doing the initial wet-flow tests on a 23-degree small-block Chevy head. For these tests, he is using a straight stack on the intake. After getting the port close, in terms of fuel distribution within the port and reducing fuel rivulets to a minimum, tests with a representative intake need to be done.

with a tunnel ram 2 x 4 intake, don't forget that at any particular moment there are two valves open to that plenum and all the barrels of the carb(s). That means the wet-flow tests must have air drawn through the induction system, with valves open as in a running engine. At this stage, there is one valve open to the lift value at peak piston speed, which occurs about 70 to 75 degrees after TDC on the induction stroke, and one valve in the cylinder about to draw at a lift equal to 20 percent of the flow of the fully opened valve. This compensates for the test pressure differences that are normally experienced at each valve during a running cycle of each cylinder. Going this route means we don't need to be concerned with the differing test pressures that are normally seen at each valve. I can't say

that what I have outlined here is optimal, but it is a good starting point. For a depression on the nearly fully opened intake, I use 15 to 20 inches.

If I am checking the wet flow of a valve in the low-lift position, I use as much depression as the bench can provide, right up to about 140 inches. Making sure the wet-flow properties are good at the point of valve opening and on up through the low-lift range is important because bad wet flow at low lift encourages bad wet flow at higher lifts.

At first sight, it may seem that going to all this trouble is very important for something like a Pro Stock intake. For a single 4-barrel, it may seem like overkill, but in this case it is even more important to use this multi-open-valve technique to get optimal results.

When physically modeling the system, the rule is "Be sure it flows the way it goes!"

Only if you are investigating chamber wet flow should you deal with only one valve at a time. And doing so means using the right test pressure. Fail here and your wet-flow tests lose half their value.

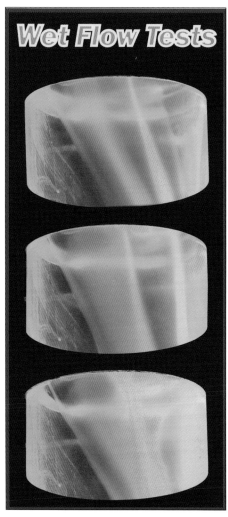

Fig. 4.15. Top to bottom, we have the wet-flow pattern of a big-block Chevy at 0.300, 0.500, and 0.700 inch of lift. Note how the "wettest" part of the stream (in blue) becomes greater and spreads wider down the cylinder wall. Any wet fuel still on the cylinder wall on the compression stroke finds its way directly into the top ring land crevice.

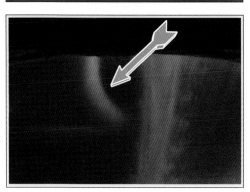

Fig. 4.13. A plane view of a single 4-barrel intake manifold reveals the fact that the ports are either turning with the swirl pattern or against it. On these Chevy heads, the outer manifold runners tend to favor the rotational direction of the swirl whereas the inner runners do the reverse. This affects the pattern of the wet flow as it approaches the cylinder head port. Under ideal circumstances, this difference in flow patterns is set up during the wet-flow development of the manifold/head combination.

Fig. 4.14. This interesting shot shows the initial rush of fuel just as the intake valve (arrow) opens. Because of the high depression caused by a strong exhaust-chamber-scavenging pressure wave, the fuel shearing at this low lift (about 0.1 inch) is very strong even with a radius approach to the seat itself.

Wet-Flow Power

As I mentioned earlier in this chapter, wet-flow testing has moved in and out of the realms of mainstream power topics many times during the past 40 years. Like many aspects of race engine development that are a step outside of normally debated subjects, wet-flow testing has minority groups of both staunch supporters and staunch detractors. That leaves a huge majority middle group just waiting to see the results supporting one or the other group's rhetoric.

The Test Engine

For a back-to-back test to produce realistic and representative results, the engine must already be a well-developed combination. A Chevy 383-ci small-block with a 9.5:1 compression ratio and equipped with a Comp Cams 288 single-pattern hydraulic flat tappet was our starting point. The plan was to test a set of as-cast Dart Pro 1 heads and then replace the heads with the wet-flow-developed Platinum Pro 1 heads (also in as-cast form). An Edelbrock Performer RPM Air Gap two-plane intake manifold was used for this test because it was a known quantity in terms of airflow and mixture distribution. An AED Holley-style 800-cfm 4-barrel carb was used. This was another deliberate choice; this company's carbs are noted for good fuel atomization, which is a priority in a test such as this.

Conventional Flow Tests

Our starting point was to use a dry bench to measure the ports' CFM capability of each head flowed. For the heads to be an effective means of determining any wet-flow advantages, the heads needed to flow nearly similar amounts of air, so that the only difference in the A-to-B test is the wet-flow characteristics. First, let's take a quick look at the heads we are dealing with. At first, an assembled 200-cc-port Pro 1 and the Platinum Pro 1 that it replaces appear little different. But closer inspection with the valves removed shows otherwise.

Looking into the combustion chamber with the valves removed reveals most of the changes made to produce the later wet-flow-developed Platinum Pro 1 head. Take a look at the original Pro 1 combustion chamber and port throats in Figure 1, then check out the differences depicted by the arrows in Figure 2.

Going through these in order, we first have the introduction of a long guide vane (Arrow 1) in front of the guide boss. This serves a number of purposes. First, it provides

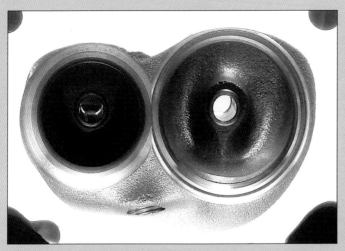

Figure 1. Here is the original Pro 1 head combustion chamber. Check the bump to the right of the spark plug and the leading edge of the guide boss and compare with the Platinum head.

Figure 2. The arrows indicate all the spots that the Platinum Pro 1 differs from its predecessor.

better streamlining of the guide boss, which proves to be beneficial in terms of a small increase in high-lift flow and a small increase in velocity throughout the lift range if this guide boss reduced port volume. Additionally, this upstream guide-boss vane can be used to change the path of wet fuel flow within the port as well as alter the swirl characteristics. The trailing guide vane (Arrow 2) also serves in much the same way. The area indicated by Arrow 3 is scalloped slightly deeper than is seen on the original Pro 1 head. This has the effect of turning the charge more as it enters the cylinder and generating a better swirl action.

The small area indicated by Arrow 4 looks seemingly unchanged, but as little as 0.020 inch of metal added to this point can benefit the swirl greatly, especially in the 0.400-inch-plus lift range. It can also eliminate the intake valve airflow tip-over so often seen at about the 0.600-inch-lift point on 23-degree small-block Chevy heads.

The area indicated by Arrow 5 has been scalloped away more than the original Pro 1 head and the bump to the right on the original has been eliminated. The spark plug has also been repositioned.

On the Bench

Visually, we now know what we are dealing with; next we look at how such differences affect flow bench results. To establish this, regular dry bench flow tests were made on examples of the original Pro 1 and new Platinum Pro 1 heads. Figure 3 shows the results. You can see there was very little difference in actual flow between the original Pro 1 (dark blue curves) and the Platinum Pro 1 (red curves) on the intake until about the 0.530-inch-lift mark had been exceeded. What we do see here is the elimination of the tip-over that so often occurs in the 0.550- to 0.600-lift range. This is due to the minor chamber reshaping at the point indicated by Arrow 4 (in Figure 2).

Other than that, a conventional flow test reveals very little difference between these heads. However, Dart's wet-flow bench revealed the difference in the swirl and mixture distribution. The wet-flow tests, as seen in Figure 4, essentially involve a marker dye in the test fluid. When the marker dye is irradiated by an ultraviolet light, it becomes lumines-

cent, which makes it much easier to see what's going on with the naked eye but difficult to photograph.

Note: So the flow differences at higher lift don't influence the results, the valve lift was limited to 0.536 in this test. Up to that lift, the flow of the test heads was virtually identical.

Dyno Time

The test engine produced the before-and-after results shown in Figure 5. Even with the original Dart Pro 1s, this 383 made more low-speed torque than the dyno could handle in the range below 3,000 rpm, hence the graph curves starting at 3,000. Although the Platinum heads produced a few ft-lbs more at the bottom end of the range

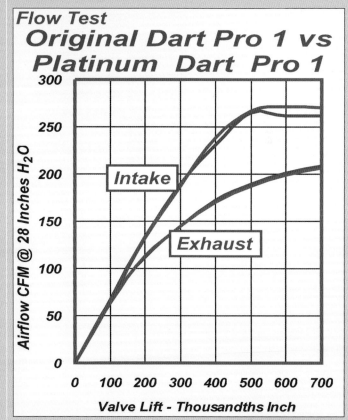

Figure 3. Conventional flow testing, such as seen here, reveals little difference between the original Pro 1 (blue curves) and the new Platinum Pro 1 (red curves).

Wet-Flow Power CONTINUED

tested, the true gains showed up from about the 3,700-rpm point. From there on up, the gains were truly outstanding. Peak torque with the original heads was already impressive at 488 ft-lbs, but the Platinum Pros bumped the figure up by 14 ft-lbs to 502 ft-lbs. Likewise, peak power rose by 22 hp, pushing peak power to 504 hp at 5,600 rpm. However, the biggest power gain, seen at 5,800 rpm, was more than 26 hp!

Remember that the flow difference between these two head styles is non-existent within the lift range we used (0.536 inch). This means that virtually all the extra output we see here is the result of air/fuel mixture management within the intake tract. From these tests, it can be seen that working toward a high-quality air/fuel mixture is a real benefit. Since wet-flow testing isn't that complex a job, I can say it is worth doing.

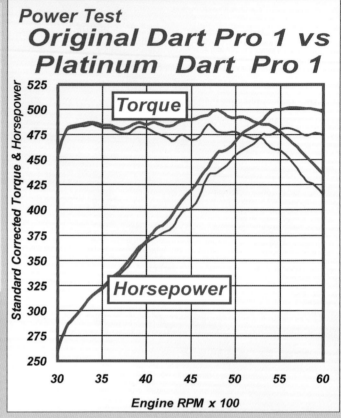

Figure 5. The new Dart heads benefited greatly from their extensive wet-flow development program. Peak torque increased by 14 ft-lbs and peak power rose by 22 hp. The biggest gain was at 5,800 rpm where more than 26 extra horses were produced.

Figure 4. Where the wet flow is going is shown to great effect when the dyed fluid is irradiated with ultraviolet light. The brighter the blue is, the more fuel the air locally contains. The trick is to even out the coloration as much as possible.

PORTING AFTERMARKET HEADS

In the late 1980s and early 1990s, production processes resulted in much more accurate castings. The result was head castings that had far more effective ports as received from the head manufacturer. This was the start of what can truly be described as the golden age of cylinder heads for the V-8 performance community and head porters alike. In this chapter, I list manufacturers that produce easy-to-port head castings. All the castings I refer to are best described as having port and chamber forms nicely roughed out, requiring little more than a finishing job.

Getting pro results from these heads is about as simple as it can get. If you have average dexterity, a cheap die grinder, and a porting kit you are in business. For the most part, you do not even need a flow bench except to check your results. Even then, if you follow my porting recommendations, a flow bench really only determines if you have done a good job or a really good job.

All of the heads I discuss here work very well in the as-cast form, but about 12 to 30 hours of porting work (depending mostly on whether it's a small- or big-block) turns them into heads that, even as recently as the mid 1990s, are considered "race-grade" hardware. Indeed, after being home ported, most of these heads can produce results close to or about as good as their much-more-expensive CNC equivalents. Throughout this book, I perform a basic porting job to the heads, which entails narrowing the guide bosses, blending the machined part of the short-side turn

Fig. 5.1. I'm heading this chapter with the TFS head for the 4.6- and 5.4-liter Ford Modular motors for one good reason. TFS took a very mediocre factory design and, with some innovative thinking, turned it into an outstanding two-valve cylinder head.

into the cast part around the main body of the port, and blending the bowls into the rest of the port and the bottom cuts of the valve seats. From here on, finishing involves blending the cast finish with a 60- or 80-grit abrasive cartridge roll.

Now that you know your role as a porter, let's look at the heads that are included in this easy porting scenario.

Air Flow Research

Air Flow Research (AFR) is a company that has been around since the early 1970s. It has been used by many of NASCAR's top teams. Among the earliest of companies outside of General Motors to produce aluminum heads, this is a brand that I have had a very long association with. AFR has, over the years, pioneered many aspects of cylinder head design and development that we tend to take for granted these days.

As an early producer of CNC-style ported heads (in the mid 1970s with tape-controlled machines) this company has experienced much change. When net porting was in its early days, AFR looked at ways to speed up CNC porting, so it could offer such

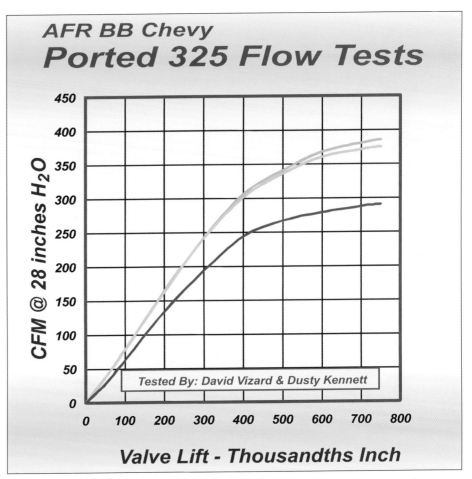

Fig. 5.3. A fat flow curve and 387 cfm at 0.750 lift (good port) produced a very strong output from a 496-ci big-block Chevy street driver.

Fig. 5.2. With the chambers already machined and the port bowls extensively machined, these big-block AFR heads port up quickly and effectively.

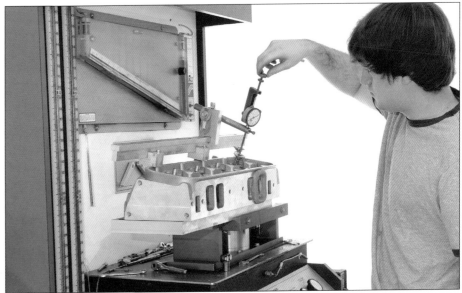

Fig. 5.4. Running the numbers on an AFR big-block Chevy head. With just very basic porting work, more than 700 hp can be expected from a true street, 10.5:1 496 big-block Chevy.

heads for little more money than as-cast heads. The company was largely successful in doing this, and the result is that small-block Ford and Chevy heads are coarse-step CNC ported. They produce excellent results right out of the box and leave little on the table for the home porter to do.

But "little" does not mean "nothing," so if you choose to use a Street Eliminator–spec AFR head as your starting point, you can pull a few more horsepower for relatively minimal effort in the porting department. I have done this in the past because the ports that AFR develop are well sorted, and some simple moves on these heads can make them more application specific without a huge investment in time. As for the full fine-feed CNC-ported AFR heads, I have had some very positive results right out of the box and can really recommend them if you don't have time to port a set of heads yourself.

AFR Big-Block Heads

If you want a set of as-cast big-block heads, the AFR offerings are really top notch. The chambers come already fully machined and the valve throats (bowls) are already cut to near-net shape. This means all you need do is finish the ports and do just the mildest amount of bowl work, and the job is done. Dyno results are outstanding.

Dart

This company produces a wide range of heads for both Chevrolet and Ford. At some time or other, I have ported at least one set of its popular-application as-cast heads. In the small-block Chevy 23-degree range of heads, Dart produces highly effective heads in both iron and aluminum. At the time of this writing, the cheapest bare Chevy Iron Eagles cost well under $300 each.

Small-Block Chevy

Iron Eagles can be had with intake port volumes of 165, 180, 200, 215, and 230 cc. All work well right out of the box, and all port up really well, such as the example shown in the following chart.

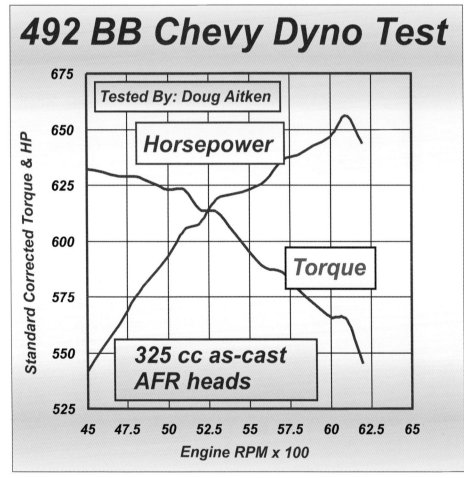

Fig. 5.5. As these figures show, the "as cast" 325-cc port AFR put on a good show. This street driver used a Comp Cams 280 street roller to get these results. A basic porting job on these heads typically nets about a 25- to 35-horse increase.

Dart Platinum Iron Eagle 215-cc Port flow test

Lift (inch)	Cast Int.	Cast Exh.	Mod Int.	Mod Exh.
0.05	33	28	34	27
0.10	64	58	66	62
0.15	99	78	104	87
0.20	131	100	146	110
0.25	167	113	173	139
0.30	179	130	192	161
0.40	220	165	242	187
0.50	253	184	260	202
0.60	274	192	281	207
0.70	277	193	290	210

I have done basic port jobs on 165- and 180-cc heads for 350s and 383s intended to make good torque right off idle. A short hydraulic flat-tappet cam of around 265 to 270 degrees at lash (0.006 tappet lift) with a high lobe lift and 1.6 rockers all around gets the job done. For the cam lobe centerline angles (LCAs): for a 350, use a 108 LCA; for the 383, a 106. For a racy spec of 350, the 200-cc heads work well; for a 383, the basic ported 215 (as shown on page 49) zips right by the 600-hp mark given a 12:1-plus CR and a cam of 250 degrees at 0.050 tappet lift.

Dart's aluminum Platinum Pro 1 heads have basically the same ports as their iron siblings. These heads cost more, but the advantages are faster porting and a finished head that is half the weight of an Iron Eagle. For what it's worth, my favorite move with Dart heads is to port

the 200-cc heads and install the 2.08 valve normally used in 230-cc Darts. This does involve having the intake seat cut by someone who knows how to cut a high-flow seat, but the results are well worth the minimal extra effort. My 383 with 10.5:1 compression with a cam of no more than 242 degrees at 0.050 (280 advertised) regularly cracked the 605-hp mark and produced torque figures in the low 530 ft-lbs. And it was still streetable.

Big-Block Chevy

Dart offers two big-block Iron Eagles, one at 308 cc for the intake port and one at 345 cc. I have worked with both. They work well as cast, but because big-block Chevys are

so starved for air I port them for any build requiring iron heads. The results are far and away worth the effort. I have used both the small- and big-port variants. On smaller engines (454 to about 500 ci), my favorite move is to port the 308 heads and install the larger 2.3 valve used in the 345-cc heads. With the small-port heads done in this fashion, it is entirely possible to approach the 700-hp mark from a relatively low-budget 482 (1/8-inch overbore on a sonic-tested thick-wall 454 block).

In much the same way as with Dart's small-block offerings, the 24-degree aluminum heads share the designs used for the Iron Eagles. The Pro 1 aluminum heads are available in 275-, 310-, 325-, and 345-cc ports. I have not used the 275-cc option but have ported the other three to good effect. My favorite combo here is the 325 with a 2.3-inch intake. I have made streetable 540s that have cracked the 800-hp mark on pump gas.

Fig. 5.6. For small-block Chevys, here is what you get in the as-cast form from Dart. Porting these heads is fast and easy and can be done by someone with little or no prior experience.

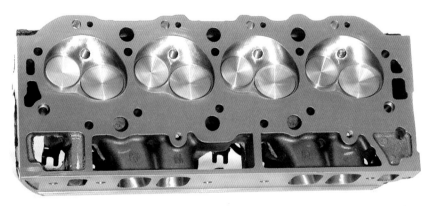

Fig. 5.7. A big-block Chevy Dart Iron Eagle done by a first-time porter using the guidelines laid out out in this book. Checking the resultant flow and power curves shown on page 51 demonstrates the success of these heads.

Small-Block Ford

Dart's Windsor small-block Ford heads can be had as an Iron Eagle (165-cc port) or as an aluminum casting with either a 170- or 195-cc port. I have had top-notch results with all of these heads. As I write this, my latest effort using the 170-cc aluminum heads, ported and equipped with a 2.08/1.6-valve combo, gave my 280-degree (advertised) cammed 347-ci stroker 5.0L with 10.5:1 compression some really respectable results. Using a Parker single-plane intake, this combo cranked out 562 hp and 472 ft-lbs on pump gas.

When I swapped the Parker race intake for an Edelbrock Performer RPM Air Gap two-plane intake, the torque below about 3,500 rpm picked up to the tune of 30 to 40 ft-lbs.

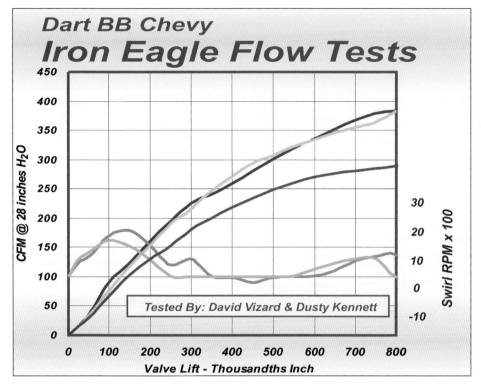

Fig. 5.8. The great results seen from a set of big-block Dart Iron Eagle heads done by a first-time porter following the porting guidelines laid out in this book.

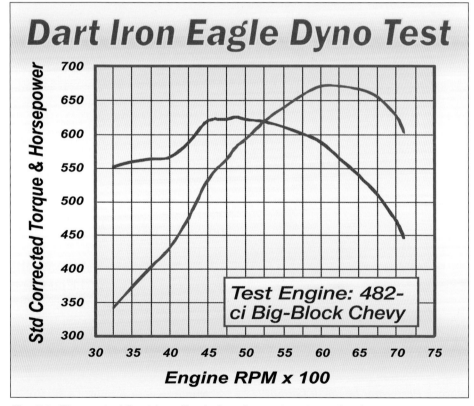

Fig. 5.9. The ported Dart Iron Eagle heads went on to make these output curves in a relatively low-dollar big-block Chevy.

Peak torque stayed about the same. At about 4,500 rpm, both manifolds produce the same output, but above that the two-plane started to show the signs of its lesser breathing capability. Even with the two-plane intake and its superior street drivability, peak power was still a very respectable 531 hp.

Edelbrock

Edelbrock offers a variety of high-tech aluminum heads for most American V-8 engines. These heads feature efficient ports and cutting-edge chamber design, but for how good these cylinder heads are out of the box, they certainly can be improved with some work.

Small-Block Chevy

Again, I begin with heads for the small-block Chevy. Edelbrock lists an extensive range of heads for this engine, which numbers almost to the point of confusion. I have heard good stuff, from reputable engine shops that dyno everything they build, about most of Edelbrock's small-block Chevy heads. But my experience is with the three least-expensive categories: the E-Street, the Performer, and the Performer RPM E-Tec range of heads.

E-Street: These are a 185-cc intake port casting and can be had with 64- or 70-cc chambers. I have only had experience with the 64-cc heads because I am a believer in compression. The main aspect favoring these heads is that, although they are American made, they rival the price of lesser-quality offshore-made heads. Although they work well right out of the box using the basic porting techniques I describe, these heads can be made to produce

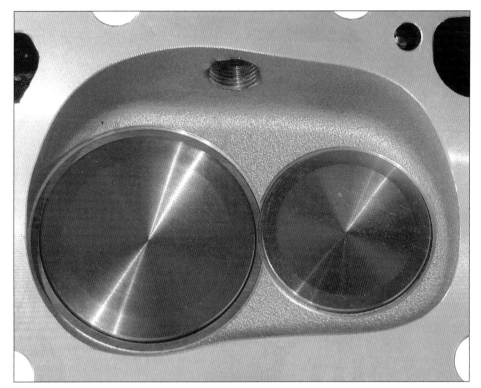

Fig. 5.10. These E-Street heads from Edelbrock are a budget saver—almost the cost of offshore heads, but with an American-quality manufacturer. Porting is also a breeze even for a first-time porter.

Fig. 5.11. I have ported several sets of Edelbrock Performer heads. If bought complete, these heads come with quality hardware. If you are going to port them, get them in disassembled form; it saves some work.

output results that are really satisfying. A nicely built 10:1-CR 350, utilizing an aggressive hydraulic flat-tappet cam of around 270 (advertised) on a 108 LCA, goes 440-plus ft-lbs and comfortably breaks the 450-hp mark.

Performer: Moving on, what I see here is heads that are close to identical and consequently port up about like the E-Street heads. The difference is that the Performers have upgraded hardware if you are buying them in complete, rather than bare, form. If you get these heads bare, figure in the cost of a valve job.

Performer RPM: These heads are available with a 170- or a 200-cc intake port. Edelbrock claims one of the design advantages of the E-Tec heads is that the spark plug is in a more favorable position than on most other heads. This may or may not be the case, but results on the dyno certainly suggest something is working for these heads. When given a basic porting job, the flow of either port-size head is good but not exceptional. The same goes for the swirl; good but not exceptional. If we add port velocity and velocity distribution, the same applies.

On the dyno, these heads deliver more than the individual numbers indicate, so what they deliver is a good working combo. For this reason, I suggest that unless you really know what you are doing do not do any major reworking of anything. Just clean up the ports, skinny the guide bosses, and blend the ports and chambers into the valve seats. With these heads that proves to be a simple recipe for some very positive results.

Big-Block Chevy

Much like Edelbrock's small-block heads, the big-block heads we are going to look at fall into the same three categories: E-Street, Performer, and Performer RPM.

E-Street: This entry-level head represents great value for the money. Not only is low cost a positive, but also the fact that this head sports a smaller-than-usual, 110-cc combustion chamber. On the negative side is the fact it has a 2.190 intake valve instead of the more normal 2.25- or 2.3-inch valve. At the time of this writing, I have only personally had one set of these heads. They were used on a 496-ci street big-block intended for a high-performance truck that still had to be capable of carrying out normal truck duties. Dyno tested on Terry Walters Precision Engines' dyno my 9.5:1 engine made 524 streetable hp and a torque curve starting right off idle and peaking at a solid 620 ft-lbs. Not bad for what was essentially a low-buck, two-bolt block and cast-steel crank (Scat) build.

I have ported only one set of E-Street heads. Even the basic porting (as detailed in my book *How to Build Max-Performance Chevy Big-Blocks on a Budget*) I did "woke up" these heads. After just about 10 hours work, they flowed 352 cfm on the intake (which is good for a port still under the 300-cc mark) and 270 on the exhaust. The bottom line is that these 290-cc-port heads are easy to rework and produce better results than Edelbrock claims.

One aspect, though, that you seriously need to take into account is the fact that these smaller valve heads need to have a cam with an LCA 1 or 2 degrees tighter than their bigger-valved counterparts. I suggest you read my book on big-block Chevys (*How to Build Max-Performance Chevy Big-Blocks on a Budget*), which goes into great detail on the matter of cam event requirements for this engine.

Performer and Performer RPM: These heads are offered in two configurations. One has combustion chambers with 110-cc volume. The other (basically the same head but called The Performer RPM series) is offered as a 290-cc oval-port version with a 110-cc combustion chamber (same as E-Street and regular Performer) or a 118-cc-chamber casting with a 315-cc runner. Both these castings port up well, but the rectangular-port head, when reworked, really deserves a bigger intake valve.

RPM Xtreme: Not originally on the list, but I want to mention them because these heads are about as fast to port as it gets. Although they cost more because the chambers and much of the ports are CNC machined, there is still a useful amount left on the table, and therefore you can gain a significant amount of performance. If you use the big-block porting guide in my big-block Chevy book, you will be in business with some 400-plus cfm on the intake and 290-plus on the exhaust. All this can be had for about 4 to 6 hours of work and the result, for a 13:1 496, is a relatively low-cost engine that easily exceeds 800 hp when used with a suitable cam and induction system.

Fig. 5.12. Heads from EQ (shown), Dart, and RHS can make big horsepower numbers right out of the box, and they don't have to cost an arm and a leg!

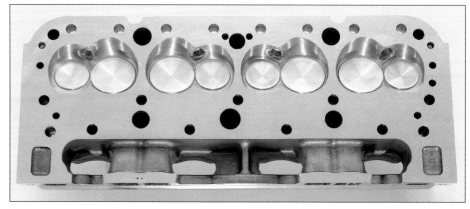

Fig. 5.13. Here's a finished EQ 23 head. If you compare this with the one in Fig. 5.12, you see how little, in the way of metal removal, has been done to it.

Small-Block Ford

Again, we have the Edelbrock identification tags of E-Street, Performer, and Performer RPM to look at. This time I am going to lump them all together because the primary difference between them seems to be the cost of the associated hardware. The E-Street castings are low cost, that's for sure. As for the performance capability of these heads—the power and torque figures Edelbrock quotes are not even close to reality.

I did a quick cleanup on a set of Performers with the 1.9-inch intake valve (fits stock valve cutouts). My then-11-year-old daughter Jacque used them to build a 0.030 overbored 302. She did all the assembly other than timing in the cam, lifting in the crank, and torqueing up the mains,

big end, and head bolts. Using an Air Gap Performer intake, a 650-cfm carb, and a flat-tappet hydraulic cam of 280 degrees at lash, that engine made 381 ft-lbs and 406 hp. A 2.02-inch-intake-valve version of this head would have gone about 10 to 15 hp more.

Any of these heads, given a serious but still straightforward porting job, flows enough air for a 10.5:1 302 to pass the 500-hp mark.

EngineQuest

EngineQuest (EQ) is primarily in business to supply the engine recon community with new parts for rebuilt engines. Part of its program was to produce new stock-replacement high-grade, cast-iron cylinder heads

at a price that made reconditioning worn-out and often fragile factory heads less than worthwhile. With this part of its business established, EQ took a look at the cast-iron performance segment and decided it could produce a head that was both performance and cost effective. The company met that goal very well and has a stack of circle-track championships as proof.

EQ's small-block Chevy heads work very well in the as-cast form and even better when given just a basic porting job. Since these heads are only available in cast iron, they do take a little longer to port than aluminum counterparts from other manufacturers. The porting, though, is about as simple as it gets and speed of porting cast iron is, in this case, partly made up for by the minimal amount of metal removal. As can be seen from the flow numbers in Figure 5.14 the EQ heads acquitted themselves very well. The flow figures delivered in test number-4 are more than enough to make a 12.5:1 350 small-block Chevy deliver in excess of 600 hp and 465 ft-lbs without requiring a massive budget. All that is needed is a good block to contain the loads generated and a strong rotating assembly.

There is not a lot else I can say about these heads other than I have used a half-dozen sets myself and have been involved in at least another four or five builds where I was called in to spec the build. In every instance the results were outstanding.

Racing Head Service

Although I have done a couple of sets of Racing Head Service's (RHS') Pro Action small-block heads in both iron and aluminum, most of

EQ 23 Flow Bench Tests

| | #1 | | #2 | | #3 | | #4 | |
| | Stock 180 cc | | Stock 200 cc | | Ported 2.02V | | Ported 2.08V | |
Lift	In	Ex	In	Ex	In	Ex	In	Ex
50	35	28	34	27	34	28	36	28
100	67	56	68	55	69	57	73	57
150	102	83	103	83	105	86	111	86
200	134	108	136	109	140	112	145	112
250	162	124	164	121	170	133	178	133
300	185	140	189	139	198	151	204	151
400	216	175	230	175	244	187	249	187
500	237	186	247	185	260	199	269	199
600	244	188	259	189	282	206	288	206
650	246	190	266	190	288	209	296	209
700	247	192	270	191	292	212	301	212

Tested By: David Vizard & Dusty Kennett

Fig. 5.14. Test number-1 was for an as-cast 180-cc-port 50-cc-chamber head. Test number-2 was the same as number-1 but with a 200-cc intake port. Number-3 was a basic rework of the ports but with the original 2.02/1.6 valves retained. Number-4 was the same as number-3 but with the valve seat machined to accept a 2.08 intake valve.

my experience is with small-block Fords and big-block Chevys. For ease of porting, the Pro Action series is really good. In most instances, it's a case of skinnying the guide bosses and blending the rest of the port to be in business grand style with any of these heads, Chevrolet or Ford and big- or small-block. As good as the small-block Chevy heads are, I want to give extra kudos to the small-block Ford and big-block Chevy heads in iron or aluminum.

Small-Block

First the Pro Action small-block Ford heads from RHS—these are an excellent choice for a first-time porter. One of my students ported a set of these when I was teaching at the university in Charlotte, North Carolina. He produced, over a weekend, a set of ported 215-cc aluminum heads. When used on a hydraulic roller-cammed 415-inch bottom end, these heads produced a very creditable 562 ft-lbs of torque and 628 hp. All this on pump gas!

At the other end of the scale, I have used several sets of 160-cc port runner small-block Ford heads on 302s, 331s, and 347s. Even ported and sporting no more than a 170-cc port, these heads crack the 300-cfm mark at less than 0.600 valve lift. All this big intake flow comes with the complementary amount of exhaust flow. In all, these RHS Ford heads get my top marks for easy porting and great results.

Big-Block

Similarly, I have found that the RHS big-block heads deliver well. A first-time porter following the basics needed for big-block heads can pass the 400-cfm mark with relative ease even on the smaller 320-cc variant. With the 360 port heads, the flow at 0.750 to 0.800 valve lift can approach 420 cfm without reference to a flow bench.

Trick Flow Specialties

Trick Flow Specialties or TFS, as they are commonly known, made a big impression in the hot rod scene when it introduced its "Twisted Wedge" small-block Chevy head in the 1980s. The company have been in the forefront ever since.

Small-Block

TFS is well known for its Twisted Wedge small-block heads for Ford and Chevrolet. The advantage of the Twisted Wedge concept is that it is possible to get a lot of compression without the need for big valve cutouts. I have experience on each of the small-block Chevy and Ford heads, and they work well. However, they take a little longer to port, but the effort-to-return ratio is still good.

TFS also sells a nice line of conventional small-block Chevy and Ford heads. However, to date, I have no hands-on experience porting them but they look like they deliver easy results.

Big-Block

For the TFS big-block heads, let me start off with a possible negative.

Fig. 5.15. Here is a chamber from a set of factory SVO Modular engine heads I ported up. The 260 cfm on the intake was a struggle.

Fig. 5.16. The factory Modular Motor heads may be easy to port. Although better than stock, the results seen are at best average for the valve sizes involved.

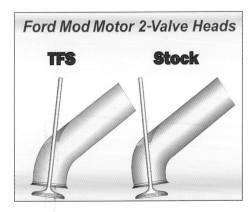

Fig. 5.17. The engineers at Trick Flow Specialties made a brilliantly simple but less-than-obvious move with their version of Ford's two-valve Mod-motor head. They inclined the intake toward the intake side of the head (left) instead of toward the exhaust (right) as the factory did. The result is a hugely successful head that for street use outperforms the factory three- and four-valve heads.

These heads come with a claimed 122-cc combustion chamber, but by the time they are cleaned up and blended into the seats they are nearer 130 cc. This means that they either need to be milled, or that you use them on a big-inch engine that does not have that high a CR.

With that out of the way, all else with these heads appears to be a plus. They are as easy to port as most of

Fig. 5.18. Whatever you do to the factory heads in the way of modifications, they still fall way short of the TFS heads by 20 to 50 hp, depending on the engine specs involved.

Fig. 5.19. I highlighted the port bowl in red so the white background stands out. You can see that a fair portion of the back of the intake valve on this TFS head would be visible. On the stock heads, none of the valve is even close to being visible.

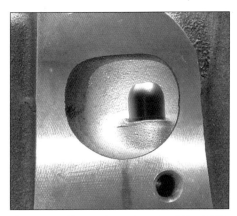

Fig. 5.20. The exhaust port of the TFS Ford Mod Motor is in keeping with the excellent intake port.

Fig. 5.21. The TFS Mod Motor chamber appears to work well. Its small volume allows high compression ratios to be easily achieved.

Fig. 5.22. Another asset of the TFS head is replaceable bearing shells for the cam.

the others I mention in this chapter. If you are intent on building a big-inch, all-street torque monster, the small 280-cc-port TFS heads work just fine and still make big horsepower numbers upstairs. The bigger-port variants (320 and 360) also port up well and produce flow numbers close to the top of my list of easy-to-port heads. I have dyno tested the 320 but not the 360 heads. The 320s I did test produced top-of-the-line results (over 800 hp and 730 ft-lbs) on a 10:1-CR 525-inch dyno mule.

Ford Mod Motor

Right from the get-go, I have never been very impressed with the two-valve heads used on Ford's 4.6- and 5.4-liter Modular (Mod) engines. In fact, I was not that impressed with the first of the four-valve heads either, but that's another story. When these externally large, small-cubic-inch engines were first introduced, I could see no endearing virtues whatsoever. They looked larger than a big-block

Fig. 5.24. The Edelbrock carb and intake used to replace the 4.6's fuel-injection induction system was worth more than 50 hp. This was the setup used to test the TFS heads for a race application.

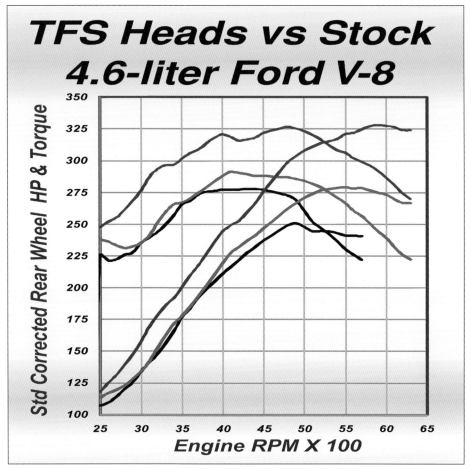

Fig. 5.23. These are figures for a 2004 4.6-liter two-valve Mustang. The black curves are for a strong-running stock engine. The blue is the result of adding a set of Edelbrock headers and mufflers and a DV spec'd (short with high lift) street cam from Crane. The red curves were produced after fitting a set of as-cast TFS Street Heat heads.

More Than Just Heads

Although having good cylinder heads is a great start to building a real powerhouse of a motor, it is only the start. If you fail in the combinations department, all your work on the heads will be for naught (or at least close to it). This means at the very least getting the carburetion, intake manifold, cam, and exhaust system such that the principal characteristics of all these components complement the head characteristics. If you have any doubts here you need my book *How to Build Horsepower.* At this point, however, I want to show that no matter how good the heads are—by not taking care of business in the other departments—output will suffer by a substantial margin.

What we see here are the results of less-than-optimal choices with cams, intakes, and exhausts. The difference is night and day. I'll start with cams first as, judging by the number of poorly spec'd cams being sold, the cam industry at large is not that good at telling their customers what their particular engine needs. So Round-1 is a cam test; a point worth noting is that an incorrectly spec'd cam costs exactly the same as an optimally spec'd one. Near-optimal cam spec'ing is a science known to, at most, a handful of specialists worldwide.

Chevy on the outside but displaced a mere 4.6 liters on the inside. Early on, I modified a set of the factory heads and I was well short of happy with the results. Then Ford introduced a few special versions that were better. But still, even after a makeover, they were nothing to shout about.

After spending quite a few hours porting a set of limited-production SVO heads, I got to take a look at the new (2009) Trick Flow Mod Motor heads. Somebody thought this one through really well. The intake valve was inclined at the opposite angle from vertical that was used on the stock head. This had the effect of straightening the port by more than 30 degrees. This resulted in a down-draft angle about as steep as a serious race head and its effect on flow was dramatic.

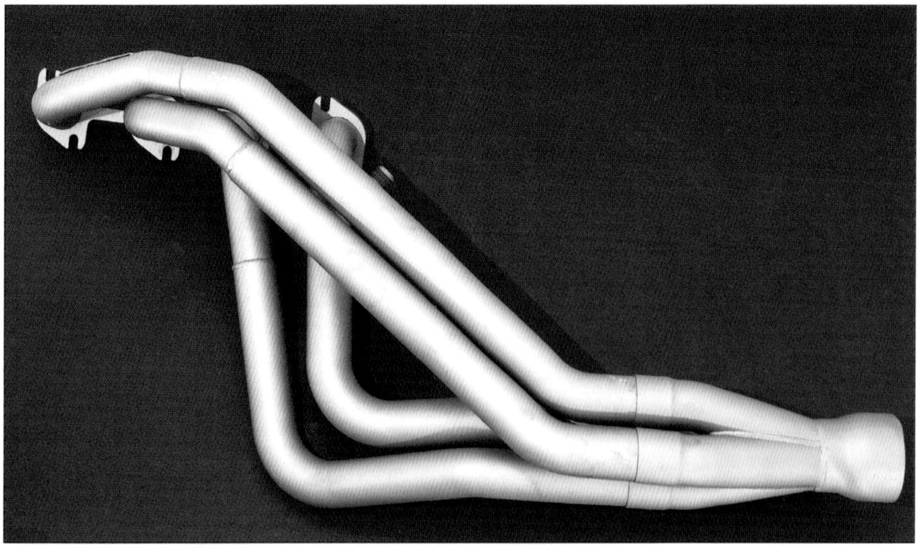

This head looked so promising that I was eager to go through a couple of builds to test it. At the time, I was no big expert on Ford's Modular engine, so I teamed up with Chris Harrington of Harrington Racing Engines (a well-known engine machine shop having top NASCAR stature) and Andy Wood, who has built many a fast Mod motor.

The first time around it was an out-of-the-box deal, in terms of intake, etc., on a conventionally modified 4.6L. With what is truly a street cam, this engine was treated to a set of TFS Street Heat heads after chassis dyno testing, with a set of nicely prepped but otherwise stock heads. Figure 5.23 shows the dramatic improvement these heads delivered.

Mod Motor: Round-2

After the preceding dyno tests, a comparison was made of the 2004 two-valve engine in its final TFS-equipped form with a stock three-valve 2005 GT. The good news is that the TFS two-valver won out everywhere over a stock three-valve-equipped engine. Basically, it was

Fig. 5.25. Although not back-to-back tested here, the test car was very competitive. This is a good indication that these Edelbrock merge collector headers are working just fine on our TFS-equipped 4.6 Mustang.

The test engine for this series of tests was a Dart 302 block bore to 4.165 with a 3.4-inch-stroke Scat crank for 370 ci. The Edelbrock Victor Jr heads were ported for all the tests.

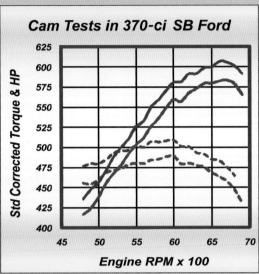

The blue curves are for a cam that was spec'd by one of the top techs at a very well-known cam company. The red curves are for a cam spec'd per my How to Build Horsepower book. Over the RPM tested there is an average gain of 19.5 lbs-ft and 21.5 hp. Need I say more?

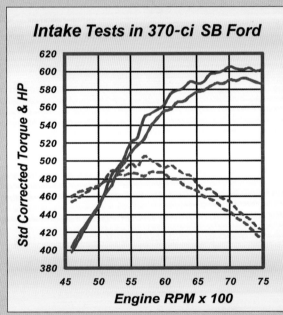

If the heads are good and the cam spec is right, the flow that the carb and intake provide becomes more critical. Here is what happened when we substituted an Edelbrock Victor intake for the larger Super Victor.

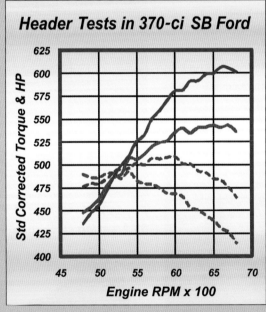

In this particular test, we used a set of off-the-shelf long-tube (average of 41 inches) 1-inch headers with a 2½-inch regular-shape collector 23 inches long (blue curves). This set was tested against a set of custom headers with 1½- to 1¾-inch stepped primaries with an average length of 32 inches. The primaries were grouped with a merge collector and with an overall collector (secondary) length of 15 inches by 3¼-inch diameter (red curves).

up 20 hp and 20 ft-lbs more than its newer three-valve sibling. However, my thoughts led me to look further into these TFS heads. The problem as seen at this point was that a stock or stock-like intake was not the best for flow and could be seriously holding these heads back. So I started a brand-new engine build with the intent of using the Edelbrock 4-barrel-carb intake because this had already shown better than 50 hp more than the stock fuel-injected intake.

With Chris Harrington doing all the machine work and balancing, etc., the new engine shaped up over a couple of months. Good results were expected so a very real effort was made to upgrade critical parts. Stock rods break, so they were replaced with Scat rods. D.S.S. Racing responded to the piston issues with a set of the race pistons. Finally, I decided to put some compression into this engine and use E85 pump gas-station fuel.

As for a cam, well, this was to be one of my computer-spec'd items. This cam only had 236 degrees at 0.050 lift at the follower, so it was more of a moderately stout street cam than a race cam (a race cam for this application is more in the range of 260 to 265 degrees). The exhaust was dumped through an Edelbrock-built set of headers, which from the dyno testing seen so far work just fine.

As you can see from the chassis dyno results in Figure 5.29, our 4.6 Mod Motor made some really healthy numbers. At the time of this writing, all I can say about porting these heads is that they are about as easy as it gets. On my bench, the 1.84 intake version flowed about 258 cfm at 0.600 lift. After a basic porting job, this rose to a little more than 270. Given a 12.5:1 CR and a suitable cam, that's enough air to make about 550 normally aspirated horsepower from a 4.6-ci motor.

At the time of this writing, I am experimenting with a 1.9-inch intake version of this head. So far, with a very special seat design, I have seen some really encouraging results but reporting on that has to wait until a later date. To sum up these TFS heads, I have to say that they are about the best thing that ever happened for the two-valve-per-cylinder Mod Motor community.

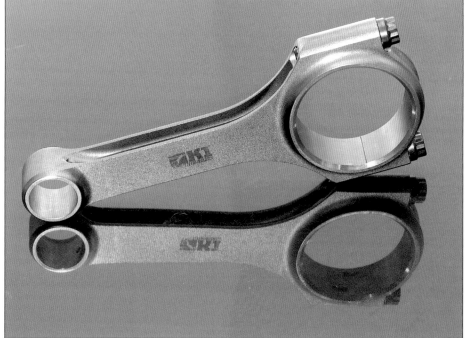

Fig. 5.27. If your Mod Motor has more than 425 hp, a set of Scat rods is the fix for breaking stock rods. These are good to about 9,000 rpm.

Fig. 5.26. These D.S.S. pistons worked well in the Mod Motor builds done to test the TFS heads.

Fig. 5.28. Be aware that when power figures get much above about 425 hp, the Mod Motor can break stock rods.

Chevy 18-Degree Head

In the late 1980s, the stock design 23-degree-angle head made it difficult to develop an efficient burn in a high-compression chamber, and this difficulty was inhibiting the output of NASCAR's Cup series engines. The factory's answer to this and better porting was the 18-degree head.

This particular head is a Dart 18-degree casting CNC machined by UPM. In essence, the 18-degree head was the grandaddy of all the later lower angle heads.

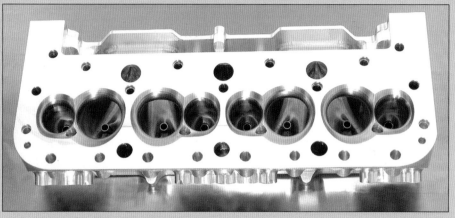

This 9-degree UPM water-jacketed billet head is patterned after the original Chevy 18-degree head. The valve angles and spacing were fine tuned. In addition, this head is able to sport 2.230-inch intake valves along with the usual 1.6 exhaust. The shallow chamber allows for high compression without the necessity of a high dome on the piston. Flow figures are outstanding with 425 cfm on the intake and 252 on the exhaust.

From this angle, the compact form of the UPM 9-degree Chevy head can be seen. Chamber volumes typically range from 52 to 30 cc.

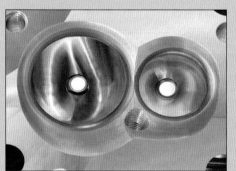

Because of the RPM, it is likely to see the 9-degree UPM heads with 50- or 55-degree seats. This steeper angle reduces low-lift flow somewhat but increases high-lift flow. Also the steeper angle tends to dampen unwanted seat bounce.

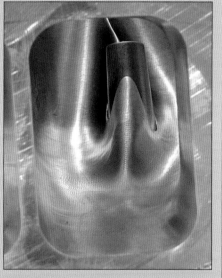

Intake port volumes are available to suit any typical high-end race application. The ideal port volumes generate an appropriate cross-sectional area for the engine size and RPM. This is one of the bigger ports, which flows some 425 cfm.

Chevy 18-Degree Head *CONTINUED*

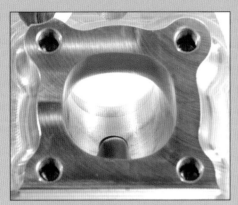

The UPM 9-degree head's exhaust port shows very-high-flow efficiency numbers. My flow tests indicated 252 cfm at 0.800 inch lift.

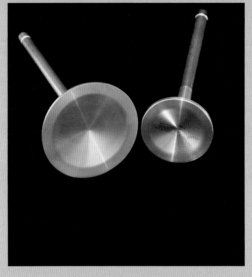

These high-end heads typically have titanium intake and exhaust valves. However, since the exhaust is much smaller, a more durable and less costly steel exhaust valve can be used rather than a titanium valve, with no downside in performance.

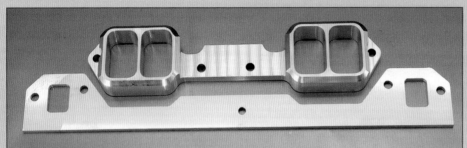

Unlike the all-in-one 23-degree intake manifold the 18-degree family of heads has two-piece intakes, which comprises the valley cover and the intake itself. The position of these two pieces is shown as installed. From this, you can see just how much the port runners have been raised. The runner entrance piece is precisely machined to the intake ports of the cylinder head. To achieve a spot-on port alignment, the bolt face of the intake is machined off, and the remaining part of the manifold is welded to the machined runner entrance.

For those wanting the ultimate in CFD design and CNC production UPM offers this billet intake for its 9-degree heads. Single-carb 410-inch circle-track engines using the 9-degree UPM parts produce close to 1,000 hp.

To achieve the high-valve-lift figures needed to access the high-flow cams with high lobe lift, high-ratio rockers (typically 1.75 to 1.9) are needed. Shown here are rockers from Jesel made just for this application.

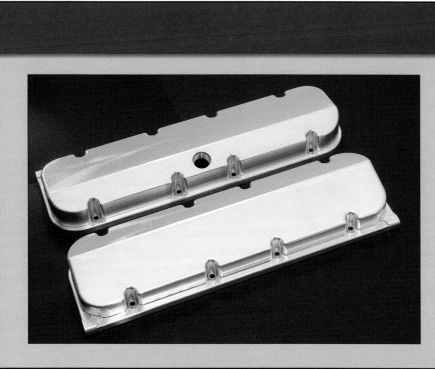

These UPM billet valve covers feature spring oilers to cool the valvesprings. This increases spring life by a substantial margin.

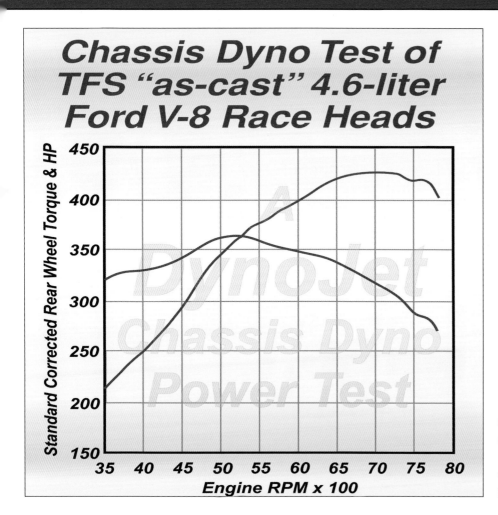

Fig. 5.29. These power curves were as measured at the wheels. Almost 100 hp per liter at the wheels is an outstanding figure for an engine with what is essentially a hot street cam.

Hand Ported vs CNC Ported

So, when ported by relative novices as per the instructions within these pages, how do the heads described in this chapter stand up to the CNC heads put out by the pros? Well, there's nothing like putting it to the test. The test engine was a 351 Ford Windsor bored 0.030 over and stroked via a Scat 1/2-inch stroker crank for 408 ci (6.69 liters).

This long block assembly went through a lot of iterations testing heads, intakes, carbs, and exhausts. All the testing was done with a 10:1 to 10.5:1 CR and a fully streetable hydraulic cam. The heads I choose to make the comparison had to be top notch in CNC form otherwise we would prove nothing. In addition to this the as-cast versions of the CNC head had to fit the easy-to-port format that is the primary feature of the heads. The heads I chose were the Victor Jrs from Edelbrock. (I have run a number of these heads and, without excep-tion, they produced stellar results when used with my cams specs.)

The heads were hand ported by a relative novice, being the third set he had ever done. All the work was done before the heads hit the flow bench. the They flowed less in the low and mid range than the CNC heads. I suspected this would be the case as the work in and around the valve seats was better on the CNC Edelbrock heads. Still, the assumption here is that the novice porter is unlikely to have seat-cutting equipment so the seats on the hand-ported heads received no special treatment other than a safe hand blend. (By safe I mean not venturing too near with the die grinder so as to avoid damage if a slip of the hand occurs.)

From the result charts you can see that there was a price to be paid for the reduced low- and mid-range flow but overall the hand-ported Victor Jr. heads still produced some really good results.

This stroker 351 (for 408 inches) was the dyno mule for these tests. The spec was nothing out of the ordinary and affordable. The reason it worked well was that the overall spec was well orchestrated. Anytime a regular-pump-gas build hits or exceeds 1.35 ft-lbs per cube (82 ft-lbs per liter), you can safely assume the overall spec is close to optimal.

The hand-ported Victor Jr. head has an overall 80-grit finish. The work involved to get to this stage took up about 20 hours of porting time.

Our novice-ported Victor Jr. head is ready to install. No glamorous high-shine finishes here, just a focus on shape using 80-grit finishing media.

This closeup shows the overall finish of the CNC-ported Victor Jr. It is smooth but not by any means shiny.

This is the Victor Jr. CNC intake port. While appearances can be deceiving, it does not look anything out of the ordinary for a CNC small-block Ford Windsor port, but the flow bench and dyno demonstrate excellent results.

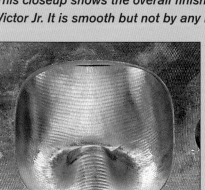

The Victor Jr. exhaust delivered a strong flow curve with good numbers at low, mid, and high lift.

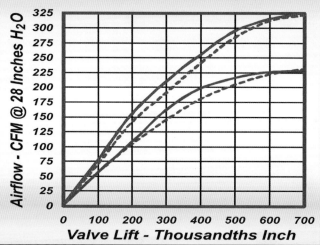

Edelbrock Victor Jr. Flow Tests
Hand Ported vs CNC Ported

The difference between a novice-ported (dotted curves) and CNC-ported (solid curves) Edelbrock Victor Jr. can be seen here. The lower mid-range figures of the hand-ported head can almost certainly be attributed to less effective valve seat forms.

The Edelbrock CNC-ported Victor Jr. heads are capable of excellent results as this street 408-ci engine with a hydraulic roller cam and 10.5:1 compression demonstrates. Also we can see the penalty for the loss of just a moderate amount of low- and mid-range flow. In terms of output the loss of this low- and mid-range flow shows up as an increasing loss as RPM increases.

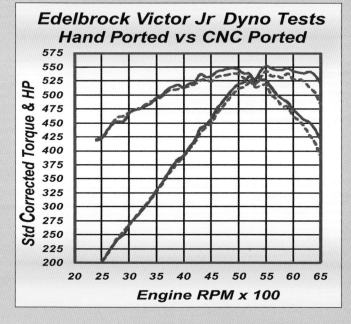

Edelbrock Victor Jr Dyno Tests
Hand Ported vs CNC Ported

Hemi Chamber Design and High Compression

The stock Harley head shown here is a classic example of copying the hemi head, which delivered exceptional results, but the copy was used entirely out of context. The classic hemi head, as per the stock Harley head shown here, is a relatively faithful copy of the chamber and valve layout of some of the best World War II aircraft engines. This works well for a big-inch, supercharged, low-compression engine but not for a small, higher compression, naturally aspirated engine. The principal problem with a full hemi-style chamber is that a suitably high-compression ratio requires a substantial piston dome, and this inhibits the flame travel as well as producing a poor surface area to volume ratio. As can be seen from this series of heads, the compression/quench problems with the stock head are progressively eliminated.

This stock pattern Harley-Davidson head is as basic as it gets for a hemi-style valve and chamber layout. The large quenchless chamber means a big piston dome is needed to achieve higher compression ratios. Also zero quench can mean reduced low-speed torque. This classic design layout looks good on paper, but this example is poorly thought out and as a consequence the flow advantage of a hemi head is far from fully realized.

This Harley head was machined from a dedicated casting by Ultra Pro Machining. Note the quench pads on each side of the chamber making this a semi-hemi layout. Improved combustion characteristics here lead to more low-speed torque while a far greater airflow considerably boosts top-end horsepower.

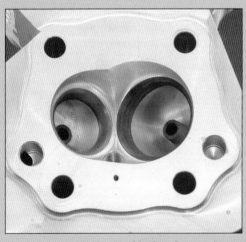

By making the head from billet, Ultra Pro has removed all the limitations of a casting. Here you see a design that utilizes just about every positive design aspect short of being four valves per cylinder. The power potential of these heads can put any Harley into the performance realms of a superbike.

Ultra Pro Machining's ultimate expression of power is in the form of this Harley Top Fuel head. Points to note are the twin spark plugs (super rich nitro methane fuel air mixes are not the easiest to effectively light off) and twin injector nozzle tapping (one can be seen just above the intake guide). All this comes with well over 500 cfm of intake flow and some 350 cfm on the exhaust. Usually these heads are used atop a 190-ci (3.2 liters) engine.

PORTING TOOLS, CONSUMABLES AND SAFETY

Granted, this chapter is titled "Porting Tools, Consumables and Safety," but I address the safety issues first because it is vitally important you understand just how critical they are.

Eye and Lung Safety

Make no mistake about it—an 18,000-rpm die grinder with a carbide cutting metal is a nasty little predatory critter spitting out fine, razor-sharp shrapnel. It's not just the very sharp shards of metal, but that they also

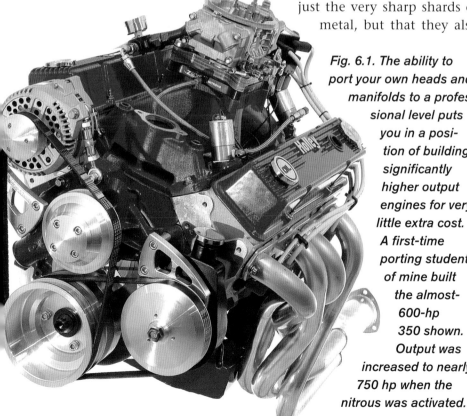

Fig. 6.1. The ability to port your own heads and manifolds to a professional level puts you in a position of building significantly higher output engines for very little extra cost. A first-time porting student of mine built the almost-600-hp 350 shown. Output was increased to nearly 750 hp when the nitrous was activated.

come off the work piece at speeds up to 60 ft/sec. If they hit you, the end on these razor-sharp shards will, with ease, penetrate your eye up to 1/16 inch deep. That means a "right now" trip to the hospital for some painful eye care. So get a good set of safety glasses, the type that wraps around, so that ricocheting shards don't get into your eyes from the side.

With your eyes taken care of, it's time to consider your lungs. Do not, for any reason, use abrasives without first putting on a mask. You don't need to do that many times before lung damage (usually silicosis) goes from a possibility to a certainty. I can be very categorical here because I found out the hard way!

Using a shop vac to keep the work area clean is also a very good idea. Sticking the end of a shop vac into the open end of the port you are working on not only helps keep your shop a whole lot cleaner but it also allows you to see what you are doing in the port while it keeps it clear of 99 percent of the cutter/emery-roll debris.

Fig. 6.2. Do not shortchange yourself when it comes to safety glasses. Eyeglasses with sideshields (shown) or wrap-around-style eyeglasses are a must. Also a cap with a bill as is being worn here is a good idea; it stops cutter debris from dropping over the top of the glasses onto your eyelids and later being rubbed into your eyes. Also note the mask. You want something a little better than those very cheap paint masks, and any good auto-parts retailer has suitable versions.

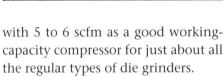

Fig. 6.3. If you use this air tool oil from BND, your cheap die grinder will last at least three years. Use any other oil and it may not last three months.

Fig. 6.4. This 3.6-scfm-at-90-psi grinder just barely made the grade for air-powered die grinders. I recommend a 4-scfm-at-90-psi minimum.

Grinders–Air or Electric

Other than the components we are going to port for more airflow, there are many aspects of an engine that can be improved with the aid of a die grinder, some carbide cutters, and a box of emery rolls. If you are just starting out, you need to consider the pros and cons of the two most popular types of die grinders: air and electric. Air grinders are cheaper, if you already have a compressed-air source. Consider 4 scfm at 90 psi a minimum

with 5 to 6 scfm as a good working-capacity compressor for just about all the regular types of die grinders.

The compressor takes your main cash outlay for an air-powered porting system. After that, there are some low-cost options open to you in terms of air die grinders. There are many discount tool outlets that sell cheap die grinders costing as little as $18. They are of lower quality than grinders costing $50 or more, but there is a fix. If you use the BND Automotive air tool oil as I do, the cheapo

grinder's life is extended about ten-fold. That gives them about the same life porting heads as a grinder costing three to five times as much.

Electric grinders are a little more costly and there are a few underpowered models you should avoid. For instance, don't buy a model-maker's grinder; it's grossly underpowered for the intended task. If you intend to get an electric grinder, it needs to have at least 1/4 hp but preferably 1/2. For speed, you require about 20,000 rpm max.

Fig. 6.5. In 2009 I bought this air die grinder for $22. It has been lubed with BND oil and is still in fine shape as of 2012.

Fig. 6.6. A right-angle die grinder as you see here is a great asset for doing combustion chambers, so put it on your list of "must haves." This particular grinder came in at less than $25 in 2010.

Again, electric grinders cost a lot more but tend to be of better quality. Also consider that they are more bulky, which can make using one more tiring over a day's grinding. The preference of many cylinder head specialists I come into contact with seems about split down the middle. My position is: For home-based porting you need air. After what my friends jokingly called my retirement, I built a shop in the basement of my house. I had to have a compressor for a multitude of other jobs, so air die grinders made a lot of sense.

Speed Control

If you bought the right die grinder, it should be capable of 15,000-plus rpm. But some jobs call for a lot less, so a speed controller of some sort is needed. For an air grinder the solution is a simple pressure regulator. Many compressors have one as a matter of course. Regulating this to 30 or so psi slows a typical air grinder to about 2,000 to 3,000 rpm, a speed ideal for finishing intake ports with a relatively coarse emery roll. Many hand-held electric die grinders are in the 500- to 600-watt range, so you can use an SCR dimmer light switch as a cheap and effective speed controller. This type of switch can be rated at 600 watts or more and is up to this job.

Carbide Cutters

The only type of cutter that removes metal and lasts is of tungsten carbide. Do not consider any other type. For cast-iron heads, a fine-tooth cutter removes metal faster and produces a finer finish. For aluminum, the tooth form needs to be coarser to minimize clogging during use. For what it's worth, you can

Fig. 6.8. These three cutter shapes and sizes cover almost all your porting needs. For cast iron, the tooth form needs to be fine like the cutter on the right. For aluminum, the tooth form needs to be coarser like the other two cutters.

spray WD-40 onto whatever aluminum part you are reworking, and it almost eliminates clogging. The best anti-clog/finish-enhancing lube is supplied in the porting kit sold by Dr. J's Performance.

For most porting jobs you need only have the cutter forms and shank lengths shown in Figure 6.8.

Support Porting Tools

At this point, you should be up to speed with whatever metal-removal tools are needed to get you started. Next, we look at tools that physically aid the production of shapes that best meet the goals of airflow and port efficiency and for achieving the best sizing to maintain good port velocity.

Dr. Air's E-Bar

Although this book covers porting in general, for two-, three-, four,- or

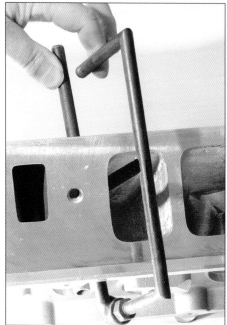

Fig. 6.10. The E-bar tool in use. The gap between the two bar components (arrow) indicates twice the thickness of material remaining.

five-valve heads, it's a fair bet that most of you are porting something with a pushrod hole running right up past the side of a port. Here, I am referring to such heads as small- and big-block Chevy, Ford, Chrysler V-8s, and the like. If that's the case, you have to widen the port at the pushrod pinch point. The problem here is quickly gauging just how much metal there is left before breaking into the area where the pushrod passes through. If you do break through unintentionally, it can be welded closed but that's an inconvenience to avoid. To get the

Fig. 6.9. This simple E-Bar tool makes accurate, failsafe porting of the pushrod pinch point a breeze. It pretty much stays in place as the porting is done, allowing for fast and frequent checks of the remaining metal thickness.

port width to a maximum without breaking through, and in a fast, efficient manner, I strongly recommend using Roger Helgesen's E-Bar tool.

Tagging the Flow

To successfully port any head or manifold, you need to know about two aspects of the flow: where flow is most restricted and the direction it is flowing at any particular point. The

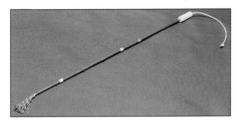

6.11. If you want a more universal tagger, this item from Thorpe Development has adjustable-length threads and does a nice job of highlighting the local flow patterns.

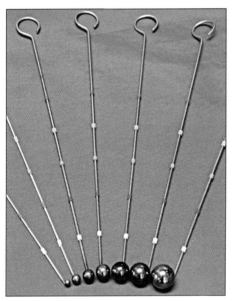

6.12. These "flow balls," also from Thorpe Developments, are a useful aid toward finding where the dead areas and the busy ones are in the port. Thorpe has a nice video on its website demonstrating the use of the flowballs and is well worth the time to check it out.

easiest way to establish the general direction of the flow is to use strands of cotton epoxied onto a piece of welding rod. While you are making one of these, you may as well go ahead and make three: one with 1/2-inch-long strands of cotton, one with 1-inchers, and one with 1½ inches.

Inserting these into the port indicates the general direction of the flow at any particular point. Now, it may seem like I am being a little vague here about this technique for ascertaining the flow direction. That is indeed the case and for good reason. The flow is turbulent at any port velocity that exists in a running engine (I address port turbulence in Chapter 10). Depending on the size

Fig. 6.13. Although strongly influenced by turbulence, this handy little device allows tagging of the airflow's direction of motion.

Fig. 6.14. As simple as it looks, a screwdriver like this can be a handy tool for checking the potential for flowing extra air around the short-side turn.

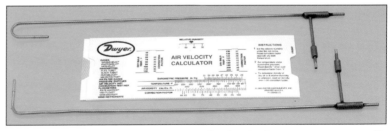

of the vortices, the cotton strands vibrate, leaving you to make an estimation of the general flow direction that is taking place at the point of interest.

Big Screwdriver

As simple as it sounds, a suitable long screwdriver with a tip about 3/8-inch wide can be a handy tool for investigating the short-side turn of any port that has a downdraft angle of less than about 30 degrees and/or a tight short-side turn radius. Get one and place it somewhere handy.

Velocity Probe

Knowing how fast the air is going at any point is probably going to tell

Fig. 6.15. The two types of Pitot tubes typically used. It is the accepted tool for making accurate fluid velocity measurements. Its characteristics are known for aircraft use and its output can be corrected for altitude. Unfortunately, for port work, the "U" tube is somewhat unwieldy and does not lend itself well to probing around corners.

you in which direction it is going. Probing a port to determine speed at any given point can be very informative. Like most things, there is a good and bad way of doing it and a cheap or expensive way of making the measurements. The more costly way of making the measurements is probably the most common and not necessarily the best. The usual tool for port probing is the Pitot (pronounced Pete-Oh) tube named after Henri Pitot, who resided mostly in France during the 1700s. Pitot tubes are commonly used for airspeed indicators in aircraft. They do this by referencing the stagnation pressure, due to head-on motion into one orifice, and referencing it against the ambient or static pressure as measured from a second orifice.

With a little calibration and some math, we end up with the air speed in the port. You can source Pitot tubes suitable for this use from Performance Trends but the reality is that they are far from essential. In the past, I used regular Pitot tubes, but they can be cumbersome in the confines of a curved port and are sensitive to yaw. A few degrees of misalignment with the flow, and the measurements are wrong. About 1985, I adopted the far simpler and significantly cheaper method Roger Helgesen showed me. This simple method employs a length of hose with a piece of welding rod inserted into it.

One end of the hose is connected to a manometer, and the other end is located in the port at the point where you wish to establish the velocity. The purpose of the welding rod in the business end of the hose is to give it some rigidity to allow you to probe around corners. Do this by bending the welding rod and hose to a suitable shape to explore areas not accessible by a regular Pitot tube. By suitably bending and making hand-held adjustments within the port, you can position the end of the test tube so it is aligned along the direction of flow, giving a more meaningful reading. To make this test probe easier to use, put a loop in the hose (and the welding rod inside it) so that everything stays in place.

Although this probe is far easier to use and costs almost nothing, the reasonably consistent results do not fully agree with those of a regular Pitot tube. To get a good idea of the port velocity, Figure 6.17 is the graph I generated to calibrate a device such as this.

At the other end of the scale, we have Laser Doppler Anemometers. I was first introduced to these in the 1990s when a salesperson came into my shop in California and tried to convince me I needed one. He told me that he had just sold one to Cosworth. The salesman said that he could sell me the same model as Cosworth's at a whopping $440,000! I said I felt it best to pass on that offer.

What is a Laser Doppler Anemometer? Basically, it is a device for

Fig. 6.16. This simple velocity probe made from hose, with a length of welding rod inserted for stability, is cheap, easy to use, and, though less accurate, gets better results than a costly commercial Pitot tube.

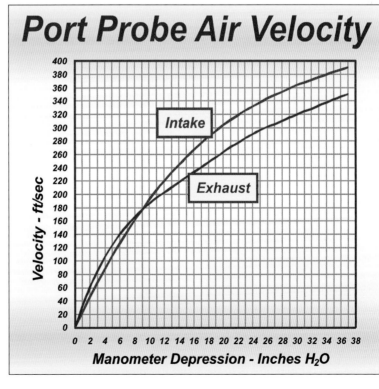

Fig. 6.17. This graph can be used to convert the manometer pressures of our probe into feet/second with reasonable accuracy.

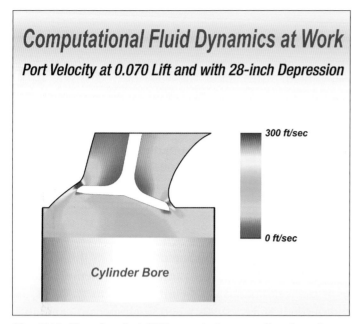

Fig. 6.18. Here is what CFD can do for you—the day of affordable fast-run programs is, as of 2012, almost upon us.

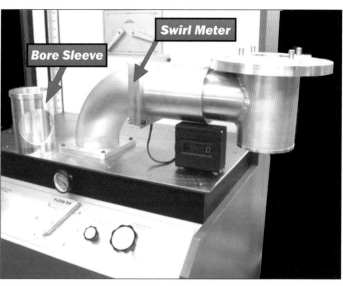

Fig. 6.19. This setup from Performance Trends measures the tumble typically generated by a four-valve or Hemi head. The swirl meter used to measure the tumble action is sandwiched between the two plates.

unobtrusively measuring the velocity of a transparent medium. A laser beam is first split into two beams, which are then both focused on the point of interest. Where these beams intersect, a moiré effect (light and dark bands) is created. As particles pass through this area, their reflectivity fluctuates. By measuring the rate of particle fluctuation, velocity can be determined. As good as this sounds, it still takes a fair amount of time to do a complete 3-D velocity plot of a port. Worse, you could only plot where there was a straight line of site to the area of interest. A better bet for investigating velocities within a port is by computational fluid dynamics (CFD).

This exciting subject is coming of age for the serious head porter and is something I delve into in Chapter 10.

Swirl and Tumble

There are many standards used throughout the industry for swirl; so unless you are using the same system as someone else, comparisons are not that readily done. There are several ways that I am aware of and have used to determine charge motion, whether it's swirl or tumble. Torque is where a strain gauge is located at the center of the bore and has torque applied to it by means of a honeycomb. The greater the swirl, the higher the torque exerted. This type of swirl meter is rare and I do not know of any company currently offering it.

The RPM swirl meter is probably the most common. Performance Trends and Audie Technology make these meters. The Performance Trends unit is a paddle-wheel-style instrument and requires a simple paddle wheel be made for each bore size that is to be used for the test.

Seat Flow Distribution

It is very useful to know where the air is exiting the port (intake) or the chamber (exhaust). Like many others, I made up valves that had a small hole in the seat that then communicated to a hole up the stem. From here a manometer was connected and by observing the pressure drop at a given lift around the whole circumference of the seat, a good idea of the flow pattern could be established. A fancy tool to do

Fig. 6.20. This paddle-wheel swirl meter from Performance Trends is about as reliable as it gets, but the paddle needs to be sized for the bore.

Fig. 6.22. For multi-valve engines, the RTS Tooling fixture needs an indexing plate, such as shown here for a BMW head.

Fig. 6.23. Rick Touchette of RTS Tooling runs the tests on a big-block Chevy in about three minutes per lift station. This is much faster than probing up the bore while blowing into the intake.

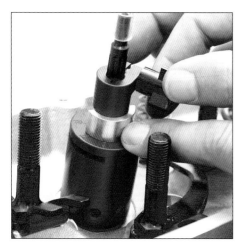

Fig. 6.24. Lift on the pressure differential valve (PDV) is set with the spacer shown here.

Fig. 6.25. With the valve lift set, the spacer is removed and the flow tests run with the valve indexed at eight stations covering 360 degrees.

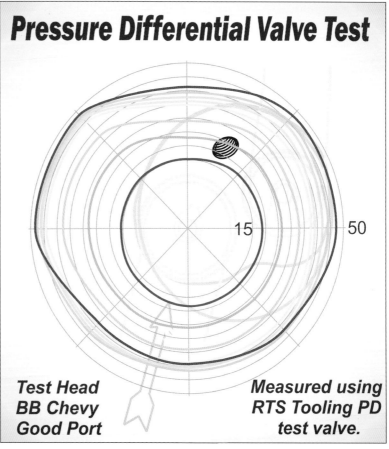

Pressure Differential Valve Test

15 50

Test Head
BB Chevy
Good Port

Measured using
RTS Tooling PD
test valve.

Fig. 6.26. This PDV test shows the results on an Edelbrock Super Victor big-block Chevy head that I am just about to start porting. Ghosted in the back-ground in gray is the outline of the intake port and the combustion chamber. The scale here is 15 cfm per 45-degree quadrant on the inner circle and 50 on the outer in 5-cfm increments. The red line is flow at 0.100-inch lift, the dark orange at 0.200, the lighter orange at 0.300, and so on. Typically, you expect the highest flow exiting the intake valve would be toward the center of the cylinder in the 1 to 3 o'clock position. While this is a high-flow area, there is a section in the 9:00 to 10:30 position where flow is unexpectedly very high. As I have said elsewhere in this book, the only thing you can expect for sure when flow testing is the unexpected.

just this is made by RTS Tooling. This method (though a little more costly if you buy one or more time intensive if you make one yourself) is very effective and delivers a wealth of data very rapidly. The RTS setup comes complete with a computer program that does 99 percent of the number crunching for you. It also produces a situational chart for each lift value investigated, to show where the air is flowing. My system for showing the flow is a little different from the RTS system and is shown in the nearby test done with an RTS setup on a big-block Chevy head (Figure 6.27).

Another way to do this kind of test is to set up your shop vac to blow air into the intake port and test from the cylinder side. For a test like this, it is the flow patterns that are being investigated, so it is not necessary to measure the CFM during the same test. If you are clever about it, you can create a system that allows chamber de-shrouding to be optimized without actually taking the head off the porting bench. All you need is to have a couple of valves that can be preset to a given lift. If the system is coupled to a manometer, you have a floating test pressure bench that actually resides on the grinding bench.

To establish where the flow is going, use the velocity probe around the valve. This works very well for the specific job of optimal valve de-shrouding. If you can't afford CFD, this is the next best thing for chambers.

Sourcing Consumable Supplies

You can get carbide cutters, emery rolls, and the like from almost any tool and machine outlet that supplies regular engineering machine shops. If you live in or near any sizable community, there is likely to be at least one such outlet. The problem with buying at such places is they tend to charge much more than some other sources. Auto swap meets are a much less costly source for die grinder supplies.

If you can wait for one of these swap meets to be held nearby, you are likely to get your porting supplies at 30 to 50 percent less than from a typical machine shop supplier. This is all well and good, but you have to know what you are looking for and have the time to go get it. I know exactly what I am looking for, but an extremely busy schedule often prohibits driving 50 miles to get such supplies. For that and other pertinent reasons, I deal exclusively with Dr. J's

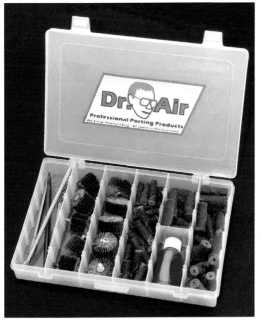

Fig. 6.27. If you are about to tackle your first serious porting job, this starter kit from Dr. J's Performance makes for a convenient starter package. At about $140, it comes with an appropriate selection of carbide cutters and mandrels on which to mount the abrasive. Along with that, there are sufficient 60- and 80-grit emery rolls to do the finish work on a typical pair of V-8 heads. Also the kit contains a bottle of the very effective cutting lube to use on aluminum. The small bottle you see here is good for at least three sets of V-8 heads.

Fig. 6.28. Most abrasive supply companies sell their product in boxes of 100. While this may be fine for someone porting heads on a daily basis, it is usually more than is needed for the home porter who typically does fewer than half a dozen heads a year. Dr. J's Performance sells boxes of 50, which is much more cost-effective for the smaller-time porter. These Bonus Boxes are so called because Dr. J's does not have time to count out 50 rolls per box, so they weigh them and then throw in some extras to make sure the quantity is there. This means a better deal on as many as 55 rolls per box.

Performance. This is where Dr. J's Performance and my good friend Roger "Dr. Air" Helgesen teamed up. Over the years, Roger has worked with several carbide cutter manufacturers to develop tooth forms that provide specific advantages for the head porter. The carbides remove metal faster and leave a better finish due to, among other things, a reduced tendency to bounce. These cutters can be had at prices that equal or beat swap-meet prices.

For the most part, only two forms of porting abrasives are needed for effective porting. These are emery rolls, or cartridges as they are some-

times called, and emery disks. The rolls cover the work that needs to be done on the ports and the walls of the chamber, while the discs (usually on a right-angle grinder) are best used for the floor of combustion chambers. If you want to refine what you are doing, emery flap wheels of various sizes can speed up smoothing the short-side turns and the like.

For the best all-around results, go for coarser grits than you might at first suspect you need.

Since shape is far more important than finish, it is best to use a coarse-enough grit to actually reshape the metal in a reasonably rapid fashion.

The 80- or even 60-grit rolls and the 80- to 100-grit discs are about the best. Initially, these coarser grades remove metal fairly fast, making them ideal to carry on where the cutter work left off. After some use, they wear and cut as if they are a finer grade; so they are able to produce a finish appropriate to the job at hand. If the work is on the intake port, I usually use an 80-grit roll in new condition and finish the port at a slow tool speed. Here, about 2,000 rpm gets the job done. This method delivers a constant finish for good appearance, while still being a coarse enough surface to counter the forming of fuel rivulets.

Jon Kasse Ford Small-Block Heads

The aftermarket head industry is constrained to some degree or other to produce heads that will install on an otherwise production engine with a minimum of hassle. But at the same time each company is looking for the edge over its competition. Here we see how Jon Kaase (four-time Engine Masters Challenge winner) tackled the problem. The easiest move was to angle the valves; the photos show some of the other power moves Jon applied to these heads.

Although out of production at the time of this writing this Jon Kaase–designed head has some novel features that made it a real power producer. The most obvious was the inclined valves but other less obvious features greatly contributed to its success.

This is the as-cast chamber of the Kaase small-block Ford head. Note the plug position. It is located near the hotter, faster burning charge that resides in the exhaust valve area. Although swirl plays a part here this tends to leave the cooler, less-detonation-prone charge by the intake valve to be burned last.

Jon Kasse Ford Small-Block Heads *CONTINUED*

A generous bowl volume plus an appropriate port bias contributes toward the high-flow capability of this head.

The as-cast ports on the Kaase heads have a cross-sectional area that works on almost anything from a hot 302 to a moderately cammed stroker 351. Here, we would be looking at outputs from about 375 to 500 hp.

The ported intake was only about 8 cc larger than the as-cast port. Here, the intake valve inclination can clearly be seen. Also note the lack of a high polish. This port was finished with an 80-grit emery roll. The final flow was a fat curve with almost 340 cfm at 0.600 lift.

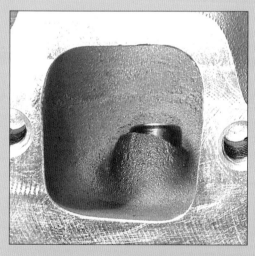

Although it does not look like much from this shot, the as-cast exhaust port flowed well delivering almost 190 cfm at 0.700-inch lift.

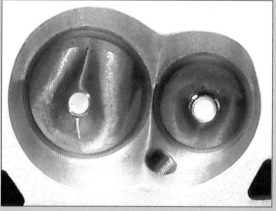

This is a ported Kaase head. With a keen eye, some of the other changes Jon Kaase did become apparent. At the 2 o'clock position for the exhaust, the chamber wall is as per the cylinder wall. Exhaust valves can stand to be cylinder-wall shrouded far better than intakes.

By moving the exhaust valve over, the intake valve could be moved to a less shrouded position nearer the center of the cylinder. Also note that I ported the upstream part of the guide boss to slightly push the roof flow toward the cylinder wall side of the port. This has the effect of making better use of port bias at high lift and improving swirl.

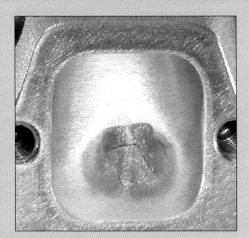

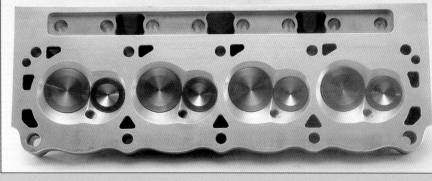

Here is the finished head ready to go on a big-inch small-block Windsor Ford.

As can be seen from a comparison with the stock exhaust port there is not much done to the original Kaase port. All that was done was to apply the basics outlined within these pages and the result was a very respectable 237 cfm at 0.700-inch lift.

The as-cast flow figures were very good (dotted lines) and, as was expected, this head responded well to porting by delivering almost 340 cfm on the intake and almost 240 on the exhaust. Power delivered when installed on a stroker 351 (418 ci) was a stout 632 hp and 580 ft-lbs from a 10.5:1 hydraulic roller-cam-equipped engine (240 degrees at 0.050 lift).

Kaase Windsor Ford Head Flow

Ported

Intake

Exhaust

Airflow - CFM @ 28 inches H$_2$O

Valve Lift - Thousandths Inch

The Value of Velocity Probing

A basic high school introduction to the Otto cycle of the four-stroke engine tends to leave the incorrect impression. Some believe air simply travels through an engine strictly from the entry into the intake side through to the exit at the end of the exhaust pipe. But this is far from the truth because the reality is that with any cam there is overlap and delayed intake closing. There is almost always reverse flow unless port velocities are up to a certain speed. This is called "reversion." Usually reversion of exhaust flow is the biggest culprit toward killing low-speed torque.

In the 1970s I worked on a Chrysler Competition UK project: a turbo motor for a production-line sports sedan to take on Ford's Lotus Cortina. It was a stroke of luck for Ford that an oil crisis struck and Chrysler canceled the project because we had been able to extract a 0-60 time of 5.2 seconds and a 0-100 time of 13 seconds from our engine. This performance would have not merely beaten the Lotus Cortina, but it would have crucified it.

On that project, I spent a lot of time with velocity probe sizing and shaping both the intake port and the exhaust port using velocity gradients. I attempted, by changing the port shape, to modify them so they would enhance the port's capability to flow predominantly in one direct. The intake port was, for a pushrod two-valve head, in really good shape. In this instance, I had to deal mostly with port cross-sectional area to get both a flow and a port velocity distribution that favored one-way flow.

Unfortunately, the exhaust was significantly off the pace. A check of the velocity gradient across the port showed certain areas were very slow while others were relatively fast. The velocity distribution across the port showed the slowest flow was only 20 percent of the fastest. This almost certainly meant that at low-speed and wide-open throttle exhaust reversion was occurring. A look at the way the torque curve dropped off indicated that this could be so. With these heads' exhaust ports, the only way to get a decent low-speed torque output was to shorten the cam about 15 to 20 degrees. That led to an unacceptable reduction in top-end output.

With a cam that met the stringent top-end requirement for this 1,500-cc engine (minimum of 110 bhp), the way to a good low end did not allow a shorter cam to be an option. Certainly at wide-open throttle the engine signed off at about 1,500 rpm in about the same fashion as turning off the ignition.

Well, I worked diligently on that exhaust port putting my velocity probe into overtime usage. I was mentally prepared to do some welding on the exhaust if it proved to be necessary, but in this situation, as with many heads, this was not required. Fortunately for me, the exhaust port was a little on the small side so when I installed a larger exhaust valve I managed to get a much better short side seat and turn form.

This with some judicious port biasing helped produce a port that had both strong flow characteristics and a slow speed close to 90 percent of that on the fast side. The port itself, in terms of total area, was only marginally bigger than stock.

So how did all this work out on the dyno? It produced a well-sorted high-flow, small-diameter intake port and an exhaust port that not only flowed well, but also utilized the available area well. The results, with an appropriate cam, intake, and exhaust system, were "truly outstanding," according to one of the test drivers from UK's *Motor* magazine after an extensive performance test.

But "truly outstanding" is hardly a quantitative assessment of the engine's performance, so let me put some numbers to the final result that was subsequently demonstrated for Des O'Dell, Chrysler's competition manger at that time.

First, the engine pulled strong and smoothly from just 400 rpm. As for the top end this motor pulled hard to right around 8,000 rpm, which was the valvetrain limit imposed by the valvesprings I had to use. Now there is a power curve that even today's variable valve timing engines are hard pushed to replicate.

Driving the test car with this motor was about like driving an electric car; it had torque everywhere. When tested against the then-new Cosworth twin cam 16-valve 1,600-cc Ford Escort, the 1,500-cc two-valve motor ate it alive in every respect—from outright acceleration to in-one-gear acceleration, flexibility, drivability, and fuel economy.

Sure a lot of this was airflow but that super-wide powerband was mostly due to diligent use of a velocity probe and getting the ports to fully utilize the areas involved. The moral here? Don't dismiss the value of velocity probing.

FIVE GOLDEN PORTING RULES

Follow the five rules discussed here, and you are sure to avoid making a power-breaking move.

The title of this chapter is self explanatory—but why now? Why wasn't the explanation in an earlier chapter or even Chapter 1? I gave this considerable thought when I started this book and decided that it was best to first get, to an extent, immersed into the subject of cylinder heads. By introducing examples early on, I felt that any general rules that may be made from there on would have more significance. For instance, I won't need to explain the impor-tance of getting the port size right—you now have a better appreciation of how port velocity affects things because you now appreciate how heavy air is. Really, what I am going to do here is take a breather and sum up the implications of what has been covered so far—so here goes.

Fig. 7.1. The success of any engine as a high-output unit entirely depends upon successful combinations of flow, velocity, and mixture motion (swirl or tumble).

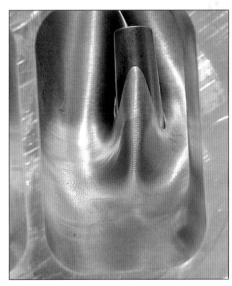

Fig. 7.2. A port for a naturally aspi-rated, 410-ci small-block-Chevy race engine that cranked out more than 1,000 hp on a single 4-barrel carb. Results like this don't happen by accident, so heed the rules shown in this chapter.

Rule Number 1:
Locate the point of greatest restriction
and work on that first.

As obvious as Rule Number-1 seems, the big problem for the novice is almost always a question of recognizing exactly where the greatest restriction is in the induction/exhaust tract. Primary restriction points are dealt with in Chapters 1, 8, 9, and 10. If you did not absorb what was in Chapter 1, here is a good reason to re-read it. One pleasing note for the novice porter is that tackling the most restrictive part of the system and freeing up some flow potential delivers the best power return for the time invested. For the record, pocket porting heads (reworking and blending the seats into the first 2 or so inches of the port) is all about focusing on Rule Number-1, to the exclusion of almost all else. At the end of the day, pocket porting may not produce the fastest-looking set of heads or the most photogenic, but the results can be very satisfying.

Rule Number 2:
Let the air move the way it wants to,
not the way you think it should.

Any time you force air to flow along a particular path, the total flow almost certainly drops. If you investigate where the air in a port is flowing, you find that there are two distinct situations that determine its path. In the first situation, a substantial amount of air is flowing in a certain part of the port because the route along which it is flowing has minimal flow resistance. In the second situation, a lot of air is flowing at a certain point/area because of the shapes upstream, downstream, or both of that high-flow or "busy" area.

It is important to be able to recognize the difference between these two types of busy areas. In the first situation, there is a strong indication that the area needs to be enlarged to make room for more air to flow along what can be seen to be a flow-efficient path. The roof of a typical port is a good example here.

In the second situation, the fix for more airflow is to add material at and around the point of fastest flow. A prime example here is the very-high-speed flow that can occur on, or just in front of, the short-side turn of a relatively low-angle intake port (small-block Chevys and Fords are prime examples).

The trick here is to distinguish one source of high-speed flow from the other because they require totally opposite responses.

Rule Number 3:
Air is heavier than you think.
Keep up port velocities and
avoid redundant cross-sectional areas.

When we get to the stage of flow testing ports, we find that not only is there a need to know how much air is flowing, but there is an equal need to know where it is flowing and how fast it is flowing. After a head porter or head designer appreciates just how heavy air is, he tends to have a whole different perspective on the importance of port velocities and cross-sectional areas. The port-area dyno tests covered in Chapter 10 serve as a good demonstration of the need to have the ports appropriately sized for the job.

All this, in one form or another, comes under the heading of velocity probing, and the cost of the equipment necessary to do that falls into the "peanuts" category. We have looked at how to build a flow bench, and down the road we look at what it takes to make and calibrate a velocity probe for just a few bucks.

One last thing before moving on: an explanation of what redundant port area is. As the term "redundant" suggests, it is an area of the port where little flow is taking place. If this is the case, it is redundant to requirements. The best action to take here is to fill it in. Redundancy in a port makes for a lazy port, and that results in a less-than-optimal torque output everywhere in the RPM range.

Rule Number 4:
Mixture motion is important.
Do not ignore the need for it.

A charge that has little motion not only burns slower but also burns less effectively. This is most noticeable at low engine speeds. Lack of adequate mixture motion can cut torque output at, say, 1,000 to 2,000 rpm by as much as 25 percent. When engine speeds are 5,000 to 6,000 rpm, the need for port/chamber-induced mixture motion is far less. Mixture motion from quench action between the piston crown and the cylinder head face can be instrumental toward increased torque at all engine speeds. At part throttle, lack of mixture motion can also have a direct negative impact on mileage. Another desirable engine characteristic to suffer when you have low mixture motion is throttle response.

Rule Number 5:
Shape is all-important,
a shiny finish is not!

The flow capability of a head absolutely cannot be judged by its reflectivity! This is a big one. Heads with a rough-finished right shape always out-power heads with a shiny-finished wrong shape! So don't be in too much of a hurry to start work with those 180-grit or finer emery rolls.

DEVELOPING FUNCTIONAL PORTS

In Chapter 1, I brought attention to the fact that the number-one impediment to flow on both the intake and exhaust side of things is the valve seat. You can know how influential it is, with reasonable accuracy, by determining the mean velocity at the gap between the seats of the valve and head and then comparing it with the mean port velocity. If these two velocities are put in graph form, we can see the relative importance of both the seat geometry and the port configuration.

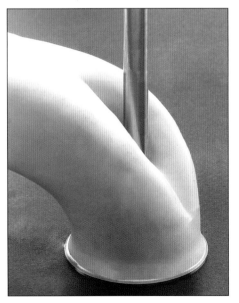

Fig. 8.1. In this chapter, I look at the importance of valve seats and how best to get high efficiency from them.

Figure 8.4 shows how this works out for a stock production head in as-new condition. Where the two lines cross is the point at which valve seat priority gives way to port priority.

On this particular head, a 2.02-inch intake valve was used and the cross-over point was at 0.390 lift. This is probably a lot higher than you may have previously thought. As a rule, the intake seat is the number-one influence until valve lift has reached about 0.18 of the valve diameter. On the exhaust side, the seat has influence until higher lift values. In fact, for an exhaust valve, the seat and its immediate throat form can have a significant influence right up to 0.35 of the valve's diameter.

Valve Seat Forms

The more rounded and streamlined a seat and the approach and departure areas are, the more efficiently it's likely to flow. Figure 8.5 shows about how much the average flow efficiency of the first 0.250-inch lift of an approximately 2-inch-diameter valve varies with seat design. Although a hypothetical knife-edge valve seat as on cylinder number-1 gives the largest throat area, note that its efficiency is pathetically low at 45 percent. Number-2 is really the first seat that can actually be used, and at best this is 56 percent efficient.

By streamlining the underside of the 45-degree seat, the situation is further improved when a 30-degree top cut is applied as on number-4. For number-5, a surface is present to constrain at least one side of the jet of air/fuel as it enters the cylinder (or exits for the exhaust). With suitable attention to detail, the flow efficiency of an intake valve in the first 0.100 to 0.150 inch can closely approach 100 percent while the exhaust, at higher lift values, can actually exceed 100 percent by virtue of nozzling. That is, the seat and port is starting to emulate a nozzle similar to a venturi of a rocket nozzle. All this only comes about by virtue of a well-developed form before and after the seat.

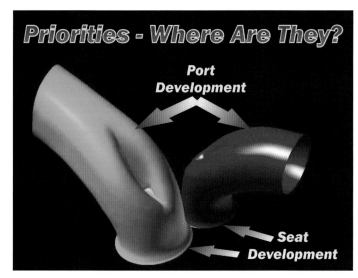

Fig. 8.2. How much effort should be put into seats compared to the ports? Answer: A great deal more than you may at first suppose.

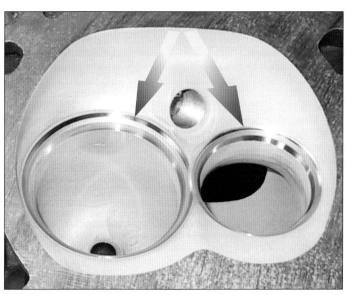

Fig. 8.3. For any high-performance development program, here is where the work starts.

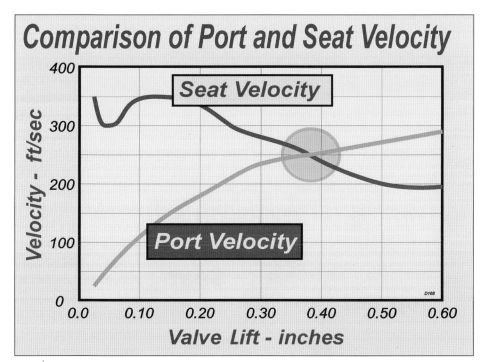

Fig. 8.4. Where the two lines cross on this graph is the point where the port becomes a greater influence on flow than the seat design.

Working Valve Seat Shapes

All the forgoing begs the question: What shape should you use for best results? Ultimately, each application may need something a little different to suit the particular head.

That said, the seat form in Figure 8.6 can be made to work very well. SAE efficiency figures at as much as 0.250 lift can be as high as 84 percent. With a three-, four-, or even five-angle valve job, efficiency figures mostly top out at about 76 percent

by the time the valve has reached 0.250 lift.

For an exhaust valve to flow well, it is quite imperative that a reasonably generous radius follows the seat. If the seat progresses into a generous radius, having the throat of the exhaust port at as much as 12.5 percent smaller than the exhaust valve itself can be beneficial to flow. Flow efficiency right off the seat is not so critical with an exhaust valve. At low lift, the flow is supersonic, and flow is dictated by area rather than flow efficiency seen on a flow bench. Where the flow of the exhaust valve is more critical is from about 0.100 inch of valve lift on up. That said, be aware that the seat form and the following 0.250 inch can measurably effect flow over the entire lift range for an exhaust port, so getting the seat form right is a key factor toward success.

The Top Cut

Making a top cut, as seen in Figure 8.6, on the intake seat helps low-lift flow in almost every case. However, there is a downside to such

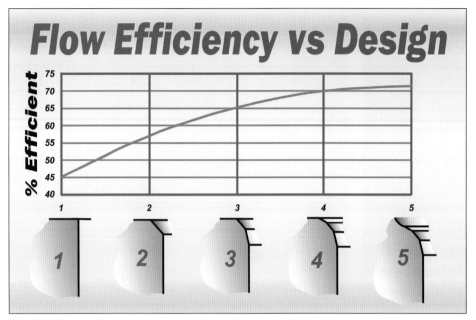

Fig. 8.5. The point to note here is how the flow efficiency rises as the seat is given even basic modifications to streamline the approach and departure shapes.

a top cut. In practice most intake ports flow better in reverse than in the forward direction. A top cut increases this tendency. What we really want is a port that flows well in the right direction but poorly in the wrong direction. If low-speed output is important to you, foregoing a top cut is a move in the right direction.

If high-speed power in the top half of the RPM range is a greater priority, the form following the actual seat needs to allow a slower expansion into the chamber. As of 2012, there has been a growing tendency to make the top cut at 38 degrees on both the intake and the exhaust. Note the dimensions in Figure 8.6, especially the seat width. It is often tempting to reduce the seat width to as narrow as possible to achieve the largest throat diameter possible. The reality is that a 45-degree seat of anything significantly less than 0.055-inch width flows less than a wider seat, as does anything significantly more than 0.065. Targeting 0.060 for most applications is about as surefire as it gets.

Alternative Seat Angles

Although a 45-degree seat is the most common, there are good rea-sons for adopting other angles. For instance, the heads for the 358-ci V-8 engines used in NASCAR's premier series typically use 50- and 55-degree seats. Where an engine is extremely air starved, such as for a typical stroker big-block Chevy or Ford, I sometimes use a 30-degree seat. To understand why, let us first look at the flow capability of a 30- versus a 45-degree seat, so we can see what happens as far as area presented to the cylinder during the initial phase of opening.

If you are working with simple plain-angle seat cutters, this design of seat works well. If you have the option, the lower angles can be sub-stituted with a radius that emulates the form shown in Figure 8.8.

Back to Figure 8.7 for a moment. Here is a comparison of the opening area delivered by a 45-degree seat versus a 30-degree seat. The flatter the angle, the quicker through-flow area is presented to the cylinder.

On the face of things, it looks like an open-and-shut case for using

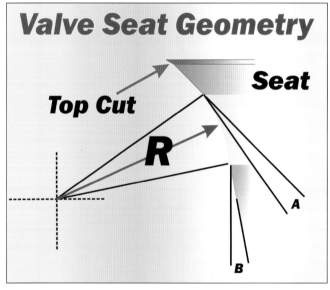

Fig. 8.6. For intake valves in the 1¼- to 2¾-inch-diameter range, a seat such as shown here makes a good starting point because this form achieves most of the efficiency likely to be seen. The seat should be between about 0.055 to 0.065 wide. A top cut of 30 to 38 degrees of about 0.015 to 0.025 should be on top of that. The radius should be between 0.200 (for smaller valves) to 0.300 for those big valves for mountain motors and the like. The last part of the cut (B) is at 75 to 80 degrees and should be blended with the rest of the port.

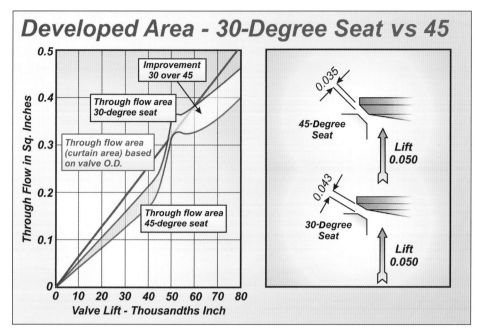

Fig. 8.7. Clearly shown, a flatter valve seat (in this case of 2.02-inch diameter) angle initially presents breathing area to the cylinder faster than a steeper angle. The opening areas shown here are based on the minimum gap between the head and valve seats. As the valve is lifted, the geometry changes in a complex manner and produces the curves shown. The red line is the area based solely on lift multiplied by valve circumference.

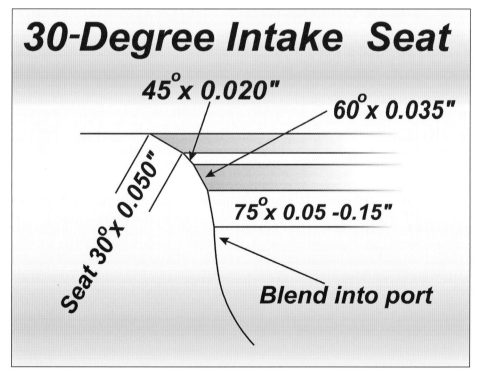

Fig. 8.8. If you are working with just plain-angle seat cutters, this seat design works well. If you have the option, the lower angles can be substituted with a radius that emulates the form shown here.

30-degree seats, but things are not that simple. As the angle becomes shallower, the "wedging" action that helps seal the valve to the head is reduced. And the flatter the seat, the greater the tendency for the valve to bounce on closing. Flatter seats are better at low lift, but without some serious geometry studies, they tend to flow worse at higher lifts.

On the other hand, the 50- and 55-degree seats used on Cup Car motors tend to deliver better high-lift flow (in conjunction with the steeper downdraft angle these heads have), and the increased wedging action at seating tends to act as a bounce dampener to create a more stable valvetrain. At the end of the day, you can see it's very much a "horses for courses" deal.

No doubt, a 30-degree seat delivers high flow at low lift, and for many, it's a compelling argument to use it. Factory engineers have used 30-degree seats in many engines. A prime example is the flathead Ford V-8 introduced in 1932 and produced until 1953. Also Pontiac used 30-degree seats extensively in the 326- to 455-inch engines built from the late 1950s to the late 1970s.

Granted, 30-degree seats offer considerably more low-lift flow. That extra opening area translates, for a typical intake in the 2.000- to 2.400-inch range, to an increase of about 20 percent at lifts just off the seat (declining to zero at about 0.300 lift). Unless suitable care is taken, a 30-degree seat can be down on flow at the higher-lift figures commonly used by a big two-valve engine, such as a typical V-8. Above about 0.600 lift, making the 30-degree seated intake port work can consume quite a lot of flow bench time. However, it can be made to rival a 45- or even

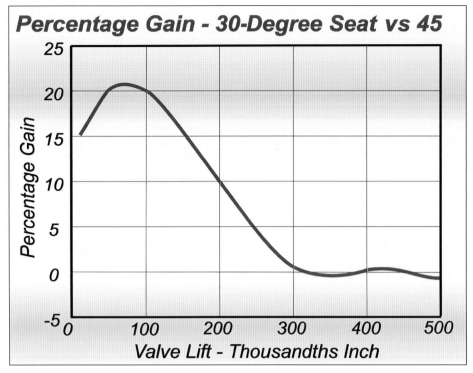

Fig. 8.9. The gains possible from a typical small-block V-8 port using a 30-degree seat instead of a 45.

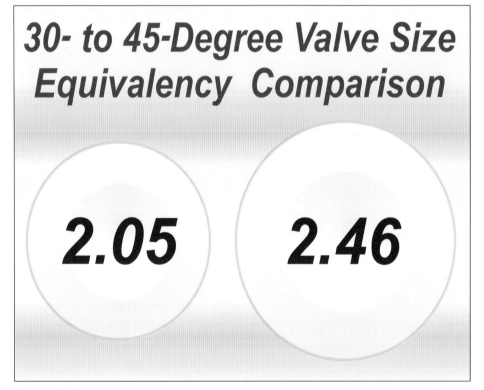

Fig. 8.10. To put things into graphic perspective, a 30-degree seat in the first 0.100 lift makes a 2.05 valve flow as if it were a regular 45-degree seat but of 2.46 diameter. In the first 0.100 lift, at least, this is more than halfway to having two intake valves instead of one!

a 50-degree seat on most occasions if you spend the time perfecting it in detail. The dimensions of a 30-degree seat are as shown in Figure 8.8.

Even though a functional seat (as shown in Figure 8.8) produces excellent flow bench results, an improved performance deal is still far from sealed. There are other issues with a 30-degree seat (or any seat significantly flatter than 45) that you must address to see positive results. First, there can be a sealing problem, especially at RPM much above 5,000. Because of the reduced wedging action as the valve sits down on the seat, leakage can (and most often does) occur at higher RPM. This is especially relevant to heads that have any instability in seat form at the temperatures seen in a high-performance engine at sustained wide-open-throttle (WOT) conditions.

To combat this, I have used what I call a conformation groove in the top face of the valve. For what it's worth, I have seen this also improve the high-RPM sealing capability of regular seats where big temperature differences across the chamber have been suspected. Figure 8.12 shows a conformation groove for a 30-degree seat.

Per the blueprint in Figure 8.15, a conformation groove is almost a given. Also be sure that a 30-degree seat seals; it does not hurt to increase the valve-spring preload by 10 percent or so more than what was needed for a 45-degree seat. Another move is to coat the seats with a high-adherence dry-lube film. Tech Line Coatings provides a suitable coating (CermaLube or C-Lube) for this job. By reducing the friction between the seats, the valve can more easily centralize itself and thereby develop a 100-percent seal.

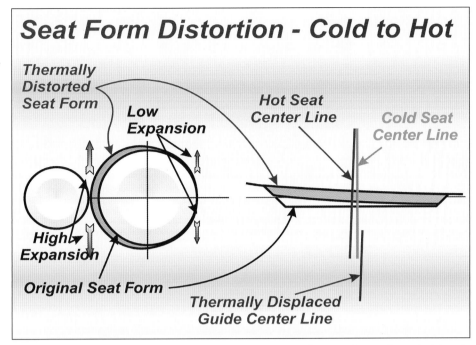

Fig. 8.11. The big temperature difference between the very hot exhaust side of a chamber and the relatively cool side of the intake causes thermal distortion, which we must allow for if a valve is to seat and seal properly. This is especially the case with a 30-degree seat.

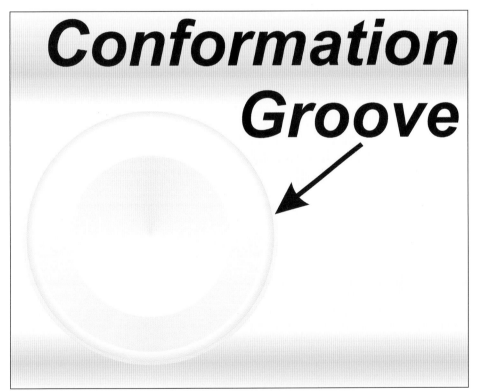

Fig. 8.12. Without a groove in the front face of the valve, a 30-degree seat used for a high-RPM engine almost certainly leaks. Cutting this groove gives enough compliance to the valve head for it to seat on a thermally distorted head seat.

Seats on Valves

The valve seats in the head are only half the equation. Though it is not practical to streamline the exit from the intake valve itself, it is not only practical but very simple to streamline the approach to the intake seat. On the exhaust side of things, the outward-bound gases are usually aided by having a radius between the front face of the valve and the valve margin, plus a 30-degree back cut— same as the intake.

If you use a 30-degree intake (it is not really any advantage on an exhaust in terms of potential power increases), you need to ensure the valve seals at high RPM. This involves the conformation groove mentioned earlier. This, for intake valves in the 1.6- to 2.8-inch range, can be cut per the blueprint in Figure 8.15.

For what it's worth, the conformation groove also acts as a means of anti-reversion. Using even a moderate-performance cam, I have on numerous occasions seen an increase in torque output in the lower-RPM ranges of engines.

One last point on 30-degree seats: It is not that important in most instances to back cut the valve at a shallower angle, such as 20 degrees.

Valve Shapes

Just as the ports affect the flow, so do the shapes of the valves, but to a much lesser extent. In the 1920s, when building racing engines was in its infancy, it was assumed that a tulip valve was the best because it looks so much more streamlined in form than the lighter and what was to be the more commonly used "penny-on-a-stick" valve. Here, again, we find that nothing can be taken for granted.

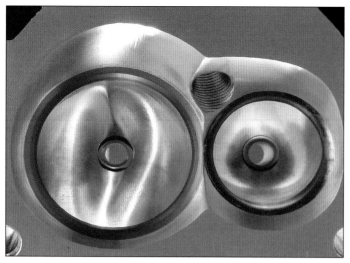 

Fig. 8.13. Producers of all-out race-car two-valve heads (left) go through a lot of pain to optimize the flow delivered by the valve seat form. As it happens this is an easy route to better airflow from cost-conscious CNC street heads such as this small-block Chevy head from AFR (right).

Fig. 8.14. When a standard 45-degree seat is used, back cutting the intake valve with a 30-degree angle helps form a venturi-like shape between the head and valve seat at low lift. Though usually only a minor aid to high-lift flow, it usually aids low-lift flow measurably.

For a cylinder head in which the approach is relatively flat (not much down-draft angle) a flat valve not only allows more flow, but it is also considerably lighter.

I have experimented with valve forms, from a spherical back, through the tulip shapes, and on to the nearly flat back. The flow bench can come up with some surprises, but for the most part tulip- or spherical-shaped backs on intake valves need to be

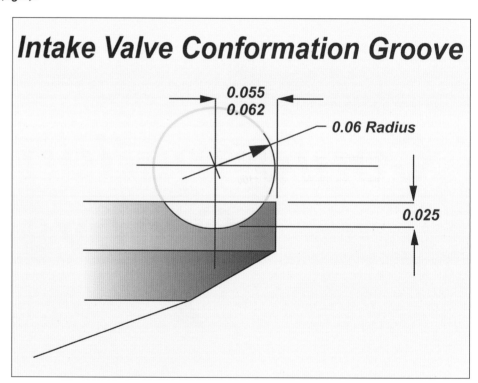

Fig. 8.15. If you wish to explore the potential of a 30-degree seat, this is the way to cut the front face of the intake valve so it can more effectively seal against the high cylinder pressures seen during the combustion phase.

restricted to use in ports with steep (45 degrees or more) down-draft angles. For all other cases, a relatively flat back of 15 degrees to as nearly flat as 10 degrees gets the job done best.

For exhaust, something more closely resembling a tulip shape often provides not only a flow advantage but also a better heat path to the valvestem, and as a result heat is removed more effectively. It's worth emphasizing that keeping the

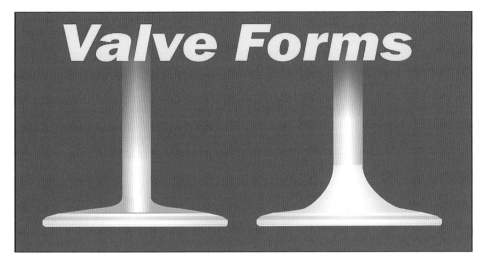

Fig. 8.16. These two intake valve shapes encompass the approximate range needed for most heads. For shallow ports the form on the left is usually the way to go. As the ports become more steeply inclined, the optimal valve shape tends to move toward that on the right.

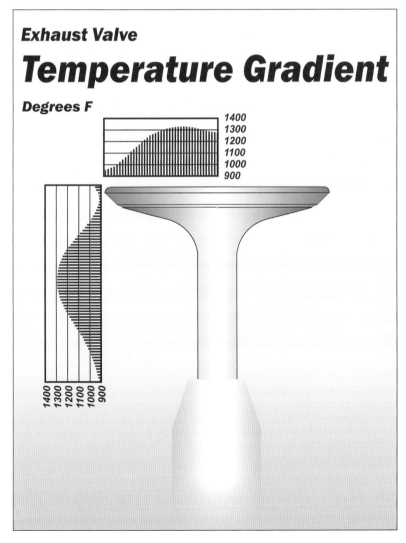

Fig. 8.17. Typical exhaust valve temperatures. Heat from the valve is dissipated through the seat and guide.

exhaust as cool as possible staves off detonation and, ultimately, detonation fixes the limit on the power a cylinder can make.

Clearances and Temperatures

It is important to keep the valves as cool as possible. The exhaust valve is likely to be the most problematic, so I'll start with that. First, a great deal of heat from the valve is passed to the head and on to the cooling system via the valve seat when the valve is closed. For this reason, apart from flow, the exhaust valve width needs to be not less than 0.060 inch wide.

Also, as you can see from Figure 8.17, a substantial amount of heat is dissipated through the valvestem to the guide. Just how well it does that depends on the clearance and the oil film thickness at the guide/stem interface. Too much clearance and the valve overheats and fails to seal properly. Too little and the valve seizes in the guide. A good working clearance for the exhaust is 0.0018 to 0.0021 inch. For the intake valve, this can be reduced to 0.0014 to 0.0016 inch. Although cast-iron guides are fully functional, I prefer to use a good-quality bronze guide.

The effect of guide clearance on power output is an issue that is well worth bringing up here. Many years ago, while developing the Ford 2-liter SOHC Pinto engine for a book, I had run some tests of stem clearance versus output. The results were surprising. Switching from 0.002 to 0.004 clearance on just the intake dropped the output of a nominal 165-hp mule engine by about 3 hp. Increasing that clearance to 0.006 inch reduced power by no less than 9 hp! This should make the point that valvestem clearance is an important factor, but what if we can find a way to tighten it up more?

Guess what? I brought this up because I have something to say on the matter. As it happens, the K-Line guide liners (very functional to fix worn guides and highly recommended if done properly) have ultra-high anti-seize properties. It is possible to run an intake valve with a 0.0001 clearance and not have it seize.

On that same Pinto mule engine, I ran a test with the intakes as close to zero clearance as I could make them. The result was a loss of about 4 hp! That begs the question: Why?

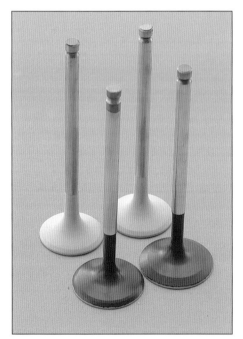

Fig. 8.18. Some intake (foreground) and exhaust valves that I very successfully used in a 1,170 observed (uncorrected), rear-wheel-horsepower 2-liter turbo Mitsubishi engine. The red coating is a non-stick high-temp polymer. The gray coatings are thermal-barrier-type coatings. Calico Coatings did these high-tech coatings. If you want to coat your own valves, Tech Line could be the company you need to deal with.

My thoughts here are that it was almost certainly due to the valve's reduced ability to center itself on the seat because of the reduced clearance. The real clincher to this theory is that when a conformation groove was machined into the front face of the valve, that lost power returned.

Thermal Coatings

Thermal coatings can be used to manage and mitigate valve heat issues. Coating the front face of an exhaust valve is very effective for the minimal effort involved and coating the entire surface (other than the seat itself) is better yet. I do not have definitive figures of the valve's bulk temperature reduction, but from prolonged tests I estimate it to be in the region of 150 to 200 degrees F for the exhaust.

On the intake valve, there is little chance of overheating, but we do have a power-influencing factor at work here. First, the intake valve temperatures in a high-output engine under WOT conditions is far higher than you might think. While looking down the stacks of a Cosworth BDP Midget engine with the dyno cell lights out, I noticed that the intakes were glowing dull red.

That indicates something around the 900-degree-F mark. The only reason they did not get even hotter is that the incoming charge was cooling the valves. Putting combustion heat into the incoming charge is not what we want for power. When the front face of the valve receives a good thermal barrier coating, the intake valve heat is reduced by at least 100 degrees. Doing the whole exposed valve surface is even better. On that same Cosworth BDP, treating the entire valve surface resulted in an increase of 2 to 4 hp.

Fig. 8.19. Phil at Advanced Induction cuts the seats on a set of Dart small-block Ford Windsor heads. The results of the advanced seat form were excellent.

Cutting Valve Seats

I have focused on the need to optimize valve seat form, so it's worth saying a few words about seat cutting equipment. At one time or another, I have used almost all the seat-cutting machine/equipment out there. At the time of this writing, my number-one choice for getting a really superb job done is Newen's CNC single-point cutter machine.

The beauty of this machine is that it allows you to design a seat right on the machine, and the accuracy is phenomenal. For the record, most of my work on seats was done using a Serdi 100 seat and guide machine. I was very happy with the results of this machine, but it was necessary to get whatever seat form was required ground on a cutter. These were not that expensive, considering they were precision carbide pieces, but when you are testing seat forms, the bill for multiple cutters can become a sizable amount very quickly.

As it happens, Serdi-style cutters are about standard for the industry. Here, I can recommend high-flow form cutters at a good price from

Fig. 8.20. I have used a Serdi seat and guide machine, such as seen here, for about 20 years. Most of the test seat forms for the results discussed in this book were done on this type of machine.

Goodson. If you want to cut your own seats, entry-level seat cutting equipment can be had from Soiux, Neway, and a few others. If you want to step up a little in cost, but still be far from the $40,000 budget for high-end equipment, check out the head-mounted Hall-Toledo orbital grinder. Once the seat you require has been formed, it does an outstandingly good job of replicating it on the head.

High-Performance Valvetrain Components

Our "porting" deals largely with gas dynamics, but for our efforts to produce improved output, we also have to be cognizant of the valvetrain's mechanical dynamics. In essence, this is all about valvetrain control, and the following are some important recommendations to make the best upgrades in this department.

Bigger valves weigh more and usually need higher lifting. Neither of these factors help with the production of a stable high-RPM valvetrain. Short of a super-light and expensive titanium valve, a hollow-stem steel valve, or a valve with a reduced stem diameter is a big help.

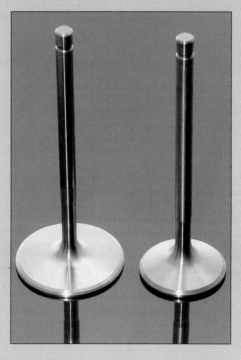

Although seemingly minor, weight reduction at the valve has a significant effect on valvetrain stability and RPM potential.

If you can afford titanium valves, they are the best option. However, a titanium intake and a steel exhaust will do just as well and runs up a valve bill about 25 percent less.

Solid Steel (119 Gr.)	*7,600 rpm*
Hollow Steel (101 Gr.)	*8,000 rpm*
Titanium (89 Gr.)	*8,300 rpm*

This SpinTron test uses a good but conventional valvespring. As you can see going with a hollow valvestem (or the skinnier valvestem) pays off in terms of more RPM for a given spring or a lighter spring for a given RPM. As expected, the titanium valve was a quantum step better but even this could have been improved on if a beehive spring had been used.

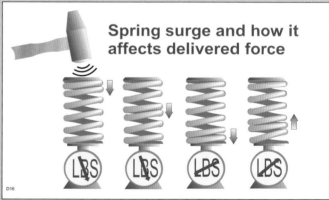

Spring surge and how it affects delivered force

A heavy blow to the top of the spring momentarily compresses the top coils. This coil compression then travels back and forth along the spring's length until it dies out. Note how the force exerted by the spring momentarily drops when the coil reflection occurs.

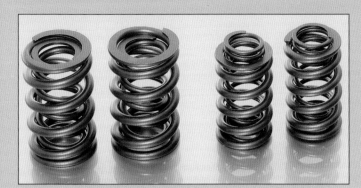

A valvetrain is only as good as the valvespring. When buying, you are looking for reliability, delivered forces, and as high a resonant frequency as possible. The PAC Racing Springs catalog is a really good place to start your search for such a spring.

The beehive spring on the left ran to over 1,000 rpm more before loss of valvetrain control occurred. The beehive spring's principal asset is that it has no clear-cut natural resonant frequency. This changes as the lift progresses, so if a certain frequency might be a problem, the spring goes through that frequency so quickly it has no measurable negative effect on the valvetrain. Another factor, though much lesser important, is the fact that a steel retainer for a beehive spring is usually marginally lighter than a titanium one for a regular spring.

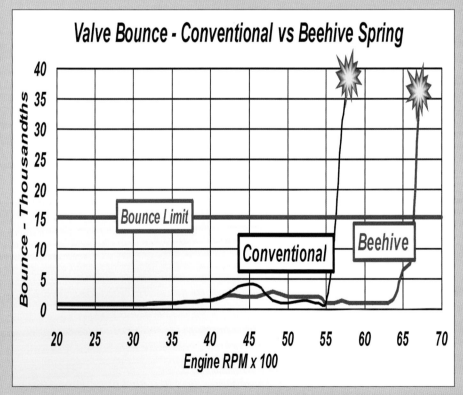

This test pits a conventional spring against a beehive version. Even with 12 pounds or so less seat preload and about 20 pounds less over the nose the beehive spring ran an additional 1,000 rpm before valvetrain crash occurred.

One of PAC's beehive springs originally intended for a hot street cam in GM LS6 engines is shown. Even though it was significantly less stiff than the conventional spring recommended, it ran this big-block Chevy's heavy valvetrain with a valve lift of more than 0.600 inch, to over 6,500 rpm.

High-Performance Valvetrain Components *CONTINUED*

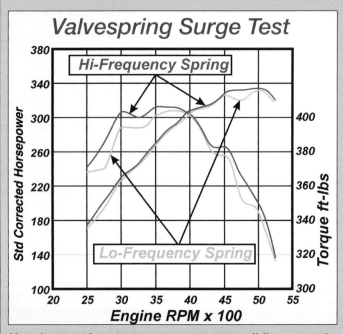

Valvespring Surge Test

Here is a test I ran many years ago on a mildly cammed 305 small-block Chevy. In this instance, the low-frequency springs were a no-name brand from a not-so-reputable discount warehouse. Although they met the cam company's requirement in terms of seat and nose spring forces, they were overly heavy in terms of weight (or more correctly, mass). The result is they had a much greater propensity to surge and lost control of the valvetrain at several points in the RPM range other than at peak valvetrain speed. When surge occurs, it usually means a drop in power. A good set of springs (sourced this time from Iskey Cams) change the power curve considerably for the better as is shown here.

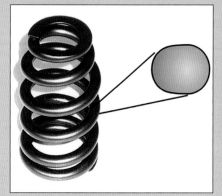

There is more to the top-of-the-line bee-hive springs than just variable pitch and diameter. This example has ovate section wire to more evenly distribute stresses. This gives greater reliability and capability.

If you are building heads, you almost cannot do without a spring tester. A pro-quality one such as this is available from many tool supply outlets (Goodson has a good price on these) but be aware that Moroso has a low-cost unit that can be used in a drill press at a price most home porters find more than acceptable.

Beehive springs became common in production vehicles, but aftermarket use lagged significantly. At first, the aftermarket only offered OEM replacements, such as the Ford Modular motor and GM LS range of engines. Since about 2000, the range of springs has increased and many applications can be catered to. One of the assets of a beehive is that just one spring part number can often replace as many as half a dozen conventional springs. The three PAC springs shown here cover almost every street V-8 application, for small- and big-blocks.

Valvestem Lubrication Tips

You need to use top-quality oil stem seals when you assemble a cylinder head. If oil gets by the intake valve, it effectively "dilutes" the octane rating of the fuel. On the flip side: if you use good oil seals, very little lube is present on the stem.

Most guide/valvestem material combinations have been developed to supply a minimal amount of stem lube. But you need to take care of the valvetrain during initial start-up. Here, I recommend using a good high-temperature, high-pressure grease. I usually use moly or lithium grease.

To ensure the stem and guide are completely lubricated, liberally grease the stem, and push it through the guide, first from one side and then from the other side until you are sure the entire contacting stem/guide bore surfaces are lubed. Next, put some of the grease under the oil stem seal and install the seal using the proper seal install tool.

If the head is for a turbo motor, the exhaust valvestem is under constant pressure from the manifold. As such, the exhaust tries to flow from the manifold up around the stem and into the engine. This tends to push oil up the stem into the engine, and as a result, it leaves a very dry exhaust valvestem.

The first thing to do here is to make sure you use a specific grade of valveguide bronze that requires a mini-mal amount of oil to survive.

Second, use a lube that has really good high pressure and minimal film thickness capability. My three-part break-in lube is ideal for this.

A Good (Bad) Example

I did a test of my three-part break-in lube on an already broken-in engine. This was at one of my seminars in front of a big audience of pro engine builders.

In essence, I could not have picked a worse way to demo the effectiveness of this break-in lube, but that was a deliberate move on my part so as to distance myself from all the "snake oil" additives that are peddled these days (and it is a whole lot more than you think). The results were great and I made believers of that group of very skeptical guys.

This beak-in lube, which has already been taken up by several of the top NASCAR teams and a few of the Indy-Car teams, not only effectively services the break in, but if about half a bottle of the #3 stuff is used at every 3,000-mile oil change, or proportionally less at shorter interval oil changes, then an effective high-pressure, low-friction lubrication film will be maintained. All this adds up to more power and significantly longer life.

VALVE SHROUDING

Valve shrouding may be something you have heard of (or maybe not), but it and its effects are closely tied with both the seat and port design that works best.

So what is valve shrouding? It is easier to see from a drawing than to explain, so take a look at Figure 9.2. When you have absorbed this concept, move on to Figure 9.3. This is the intake valve in the intake side of the infamous Weslake A-Series engine combustion chamber that I talked about in the Introduction. The point to note here is that the walls of the chamber are, for much of the valve's circumference, close to the edge of the valve. So this setup shrouds that part of the valve, and flow is limited around that particular section. The green line represents the radius of the stock chamber wall, and the airflow produced by this is shown by the green line on the graph. Obviously, we cannot cut the chamber away where it is adjacent to the bore diameter (gray line), but elsewhere we can cut it to alleviate the shrouding.

We can look at the chamber wall as a continuation of the valve seat. At an angle of 36 degrees from the valvestem, from the valve seat on up, the area around the valve is always as much as the curtain area. This represents a geometrical de-shrouded valve.

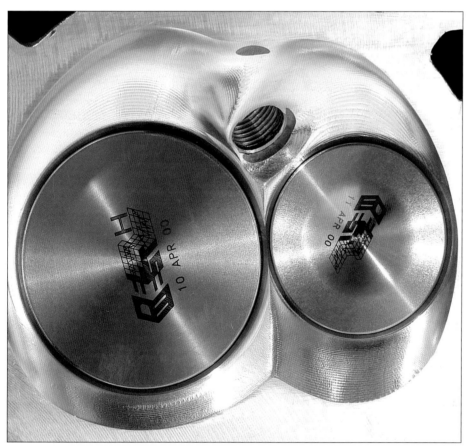

Fig. 9.1. As exotic as this head for a 7-liter Corvette may look, it is not without a basic problem: valve shrouding.

Practical De-shrouding

All this talk of shrouding raises a question: Is it possible to have zero shrouding within a head that still utilizes the largest valves possible?

A hemi-style combustion chamber can provide just that. And it does so because the valves are always moving away from the cylinder wall as they open.

Many World War II aircraft engines had a hemi-style combustion chamber. These typically employed valve angles of as much as 90 degrees inclusive. This accommodated the biggest valves, but it also produced a very deep chamber (a

Fig. 9.2. On the left is a totally shrouded valve. This doesn't happen in practice, but it demonstrates what shrouding is. No air passes by the head of the valve because it is completely enclosed by the chamber walls. By pulling the chamber walls away from the valve's circumference, as on the right, air (green arrows) can pass freely around the valve head.

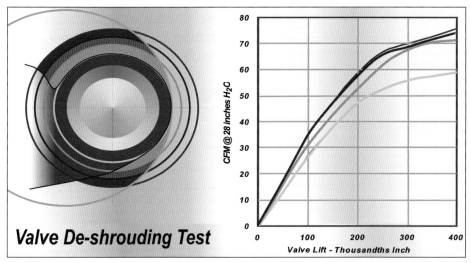

Fig. 9.3. On the left is a drawing of the infamous A-Series 850 Mini head. This so-called magic combustion chamber from Weslake suffered acute valve shrouding. Progressively cutting back the chamber as shown here produced an initially marked increase in flow but, as the graph on the right shows, subsequently diminishing returns. This is exactly as you would expect.

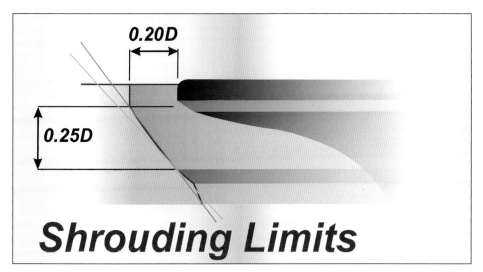

Fig. 9.4. We can say a valve is geometrically and fully de-shrouded when there is a clearance around the valve head equal to 0.20D at 0.25D lift. This equates to an angle, for the combustion chamber wall, of 36 degrees from vertical.

hemisphere). Deep chambers were okay for the low-compression ratios used for heavily supercharged engines but were bad for high-compression use because of the high piston dome needed. In practice, it turns out that about the optimum angle for the intake valve from the bore centerline is about 18 degrees. For the exhaust, where shrouding is less important, the optimum angle is approximately 10 degrees.

Chrysler has been synonymous with Hemi engines from the 1950s and with good effect. It introduced the 5.7 in 2003 and a 6.1 version

came later. The engine is a very-well-conceived design, with heads that flow every bit as well as you expect a good design to do.

So far I have referred to "geometric" shrouding. It's a good start to understand what shrouding is, but simply applying it without further thought about what might be going on may not be the way to go. If air entered all around the valve in a uniform fashion, geometrically de-shrouding the valve works every time. However, air is heavy stuff and tends to flow in a straight line. There is no point in de-shrouding a por-

tion of the valve's circumference if there is minimal flow there. So we must first understand where the de-shrouding needs to be done to make the most use of material removed from the combustion chamber. This can be important; for every cc carved out less compression-ratio potential is available.

Fig. 9.7. A lot of effort went into minimizing shrouding on this D3 Ford Cup Car head from Ultra Pro Machining. The result of this and other intensive airflow work is an 850 hp, 5.8-liter, 358-ci pushrod engine equipped with a single 4-barrel carb.

Fig. 9.5. We can do little to remove shrouding caused by the bore diameter (red), but chamber shrouding (green) can be effectively minimized.

Fig. 9.6. The latest Chrysler Hemi engine is the latest high-tech design. In stock form the heads flow as well as many good aftermarket heads for the small-blocks from GM and Ford. In ported form, they rival a set of $10,000 Cup-Car heads.

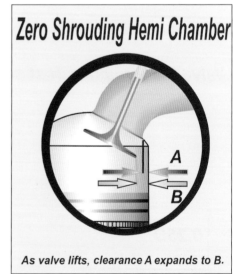

Fig. 9.8. A hemi-style cylinder head has zero valve shrouding. This comes about because as the valve opens, the distance from the edge of the valve to the cylinder wall increases from A to B.

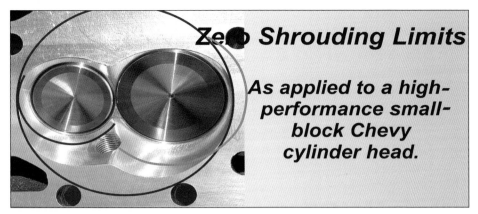

Zero Shrouding Limits

As applied to a high-performance small-block Chevy cylinder head.

Fig. 9.9. This small-block Chevy Dart CNC-ported head is a good example of shrouding reduced to a minimum. The red and the blue lines represent zero shrouding. Only the cylinder walls cause any shrouding.

Fig. 9.10. Air does not enter the cylinder evenly all around the intake valve. Here, better than 60 percent enters via the valve's "A" half. This means the "B" half is in less need of de-shrouding. Note: the flow exiting the valve is turning, thus generating swirl.

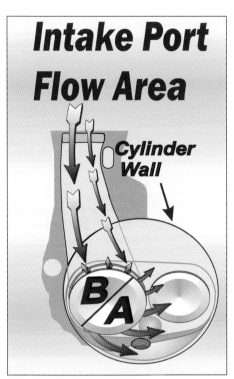

Intake Port Flow Area

Cylinder Wall

B A

Shrouding in Multi-Valve Heads

Multi-valve heads are not free from valve shrouding, as you can see here. At the lift value 0.25D, the area around the valve in a zero shrouding situation would equal the actual valve area. Therefore, the gray area outlined in red shows the flow area actually available. For a four- or five-valve head, we can run into the situation in which a valve-diameter increase is totally offset by an increase in shrouding.

Many factory heads are close to this situation already. This means there is little point in increasing the valve size more than 1 mm or so on many heads. A good way to estimate the valve size increase possible is to draw it out as seen here, but on graph paper so that the relative areas can be determined.

It's important to understand that multi-valve heads generate their own kind of valve shrouding. Shown here is a shrouding pattern for a four-valve-per-cylinder head. With a five-valve head, the possibility for shrouding increases if the valves are too big.

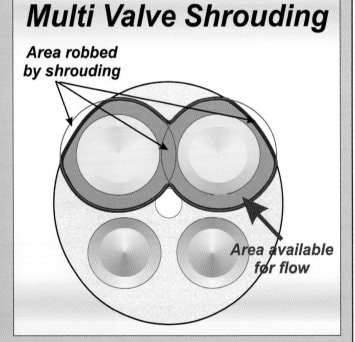

Multi Valve Shrouding

Area robbed by shrouding

Area available for flow

DEVELOPING FUNCTIONAL HEADS

So far I have covered a lot of technical details that could be described as peripheral. It's important, but is not actually the hands-on stuff. I am now about to set that right.

Optimizing Cylinder Head Airflow

With the classic poppet-valve-style engine, air cannot make a straight shot into the cylinder. There has to be a bend in the port to accommodate the valvestem and, worst of all, the air must make its way around the head of a valve. So we can confidently assume that the number-one skill a head porter must develop is the ability to get air to "corner" well. If you have any doubts about this, refer to Figure 10.1. What are we looking at here? It is a port for an all-out-race, two-valve engine.

The color gradients indicate velocity. Red is 450 ft/sec, transitioning through yellow at 350 ft/sec, to aquamarine at 250 ft/sec, and then to blue at 150 (or less) ft/sec. Despite this port's very substantial short-side turn, you can see that the air has a propensity to move in a straight line

as indicated by the ghosted arrow in the port. We learned earlier that air was a lot heavier than is commonly believed and this is a manifestation of that property. Because of its mass and the speeds involved, the air really wants to travel in a straight line. Check the high speed exhibited on the long-side valve seat. This demon-

strates that valve seat form is a factor even at this head's 0.900-inch lift.

The left-hand arrow indicates the combustion chamber wall. Examine this closely because the flow is not following the curve of the chamber wall but is in a free stream. This tells us we could use a chamber wall that was flatter (not concave) here (as I

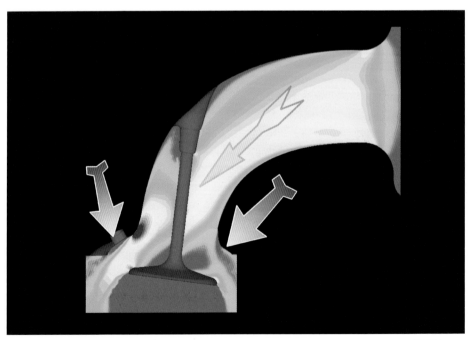

Fig. 10.1. Here is just one of a series of computational fluid dynamics (CFD) illustrations from Dr. Rick Roberts of Edelbrock. The port is a prototype for one of Edelbrocks's high-performance heads.

describe in Chapter 9). Also, because this is a very active area we need to make sure that there is as near minimal valve shrouding as possible on this side of the port.

Let's now move to the right-hand arrow. Here, we see that because there is much less activity, de-shrouding this side of the chamber to the same extent as the long side is unnecessary and possibly detrimental to the overall performance of the head. Keeping in mind all we have so far learned on valve seats and valve shrouding, let's move on to the ports, chambers, and CR, which has all-important effects on initial head design.

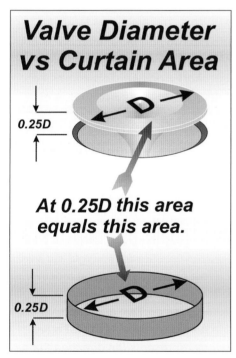

Fig. 10.2. To better understand how flow efficiency can vary as valve lift progresses, it is helpful to look at lift values in relation to the valve diameter. Here, we see one of the most important lift points that occurs at 0.25D. Depending on the style of head, a number of important things happen around this lift point that are pertinent to making big power numbers, especially on two-valve heads.

Valve and Flow

Within either port, the valve is the only component that, as it opens and closes, delivers a variable geometry. At low lift, the flow is entirely dependent on the size of the gap between the valve seat, the seat in the head, and the efficiency with which they flow. At high lift, the port size and shape primarily (but not wholly) dictate the amount of flow delivered.

A key proportion in the valve's opening cycle is a lift value equal to 1/4 of the valve's diameter. This is commonly known as 0.25D, and Figure 10.2 shows its significance. At 0.25D the "curtain area" is exactly equal to the valve head area. By applying the same criteria, we can say that the valve seat influence, though continually diminishing, is the major influence on flow up to a valve lift equal to about 0.18 to 0.20D. In other words, the seat is the number-one priority until the valve has reached a lift figure between 18 and 20 percent of the valve's diameter.

At this point, you may ask how much difference a valve seat shape can make to the efficiency delivered during the lower lift regime. The answer is: a lot. Up to the 0.20D lift point, a typical production three-angle valve seat usually delivers efficiency figures starting at about 65 percent and quickly dropping to around 55 percent. Spend a lot of time on a flow bench, and those

Air is almost ccertainly heavier than you might expect. Guess how much a 100 x 100 x 100-foot cube of air is.

Answer: 38 tons!

figures can be as high as 85 percent or more.

A point worth raising here is that there is a commonly held belief, among many successful engine builders who specialize in high-output two-valve V-8 engines, that too much low-lift flow hurts power. I won't go into a lot of detail here, other than to put forward a simple explanation. First, the cylinder does not know how far an intake valve is open. All it knows is how much flow is being presented. Therefore, if too much flow is being presented at any given moment, it is because the valve events are not what the head wants. That means the wrong cam is being used. Claiming a cylinder head has too much low-lift flow is a little like claiming your race team has too much cash on hand!

Ports

Remembering that everything in terms of flow starts at the valve seat, let's move on to the subject of the ports themselves. Although a flow bench is a prime requirement for optimal results, there are many ground rules that can be applied to improve a typical stock cylinder head of two- or four-valve design.

Port Requirements

If we assume the port is paired with a good valve seat design, priority number-one is maximizing airflow. Second, high airflow must be achieved by high-flow efficiencies, not by an overly large cross section. If the cross section is too large, the port velocity is low; this reduces cylinder ramming and increases flow reversion. The result: poor low-speed output with possibly no benefits at the top end.

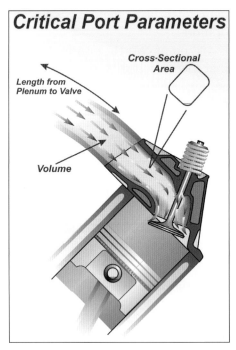

Fig. 10.3. Apart from total airflow, a successful port design must also address issues relating to cross-sectional area, total length, and wet flow.

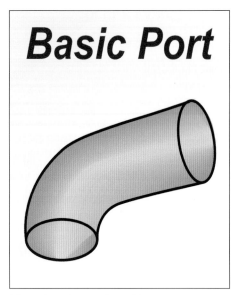

Fig. 10.4. Assuming this as our starting point, we intend to progressively change the port's form into a much more efficient shape.

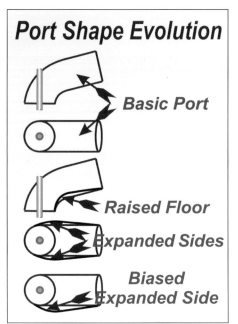

Fig. 10.5. The first move toward making a basic port more effective is to raise the floor, starting just before the short-side turn. This allows the radius of the short-side turn to be increased. Doing this, though, leaves the port with a small cross-sectional area around the turn. To compensate, the port needs to be made wider as viewed from above. This works fine for a Hemi or with four inclined valves as in most four-valve designs. For a parallel (or nearly so) valve head with two valves, the expansion of the port almost always needs to be mostly on one side, the cylinder wall side. By biasing the port we allow, at high lift, the port to follow a form that more nearly represents the direction the air wants to travel in.

Another factor that can greatly affect low-speed and, to a lesser extent, high-speed output is swirl or otherwise-induced mixture motion within the closed cylinder.

Next it helps to make sure no big problems exist with fuel management within the port. This comes under the heading of "wet flow."

Finally, we have to look at the combustion chamber form as defined by both the combustion chamber and the piston crown. That simply means getting the required CR without producing a poor-burning chamber in the process.

Port Evolution

The most basic port we could have is a round port (see Figure 10.4), which has a bend in it to accommodate the valve. Using this as a starting point, we can develop a port using some simple logic.

With any port, the radius of the short-side turn is usually the number-one obstacle to achieving good mid- to high-lift flow figures. F1 engines have a very large short-side turn radius, and the port's downdraft angle is only about 30 degrees off vertical. This makes for a very simple port that requires very little in the way of Band-Aid fixes to make it work extremely well. Unfortunately, the dictates of less-than-ultimate power on a less-than-ultimate budget and low hood lines mean ports that are severely compromised. Figure 10.5 shows the basic steps that need to be taken for improved efficiency.

If you are modifying a typical parallel-valve head with two valves, the last step in the illustration is a very important one. Understanding that the port more than likely needs a bias is the key to getting those big high-lift flow numbers. This leads ultimately to high-lift flow efficiency figures that exceed those delivered by many four-valve heads.

The recovering flow efficiency of a parallel two-valve head is one of the reasons why this type of head responds to high valve lift, so bear that in mind when it comes time to spec out the cam and valvetrain. The target lift to shoot for is 0.30D for a hot street machine and as much as 0.35D for an all-out racer.

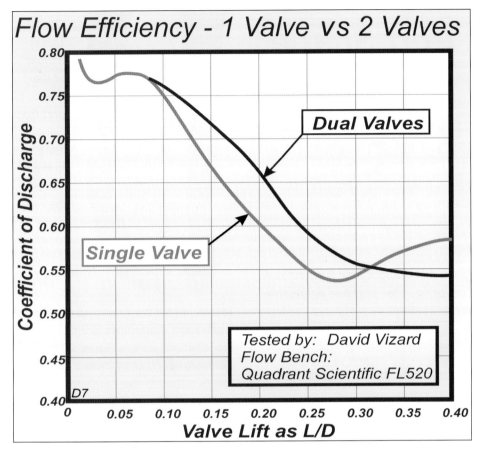

Flow Efficiency - 1 Valve vs 2 Valves

Tested by: David Vizard
Flow Bench:
Quadrant Scientific FL520

Fig. 10.6. Past 0.10D two-valves show better efficiency but at about 0.27D the single valve recovers and ultimately wins out.

Cross-Sectional Area

The optimal cross-sectional area for a given size of cylinder can vary somewhat, depending on the size of the intake valve, how tortuous the port is, and the bore/stroke ratio of the cylinder. A good starting point for the intake is to have a nearly parallel section of the port, about 1½ to 2 intake valve diameters up from the intake valve itself, sized to a cross section equal to 77 to 80 percent of the area of the intake valve.

The optimal area of this parallel section gets bigger as the port gets steeper and vice-versa (see Figure 10.10). This parallel section needs to extend, if necessary, into the intake manifold for about two to three times the diameter of the intake valve for a two-valve head and about four to five times the diameter if we are dealing with a four-valve head. For the record, it is better for the widest powerband and best torque if you err on the smaller side because this produces a "punchier" driving experience. Making the port too big can hurt output everywhere, as the test results from a small-block Chevy in Figure 10.13 show.

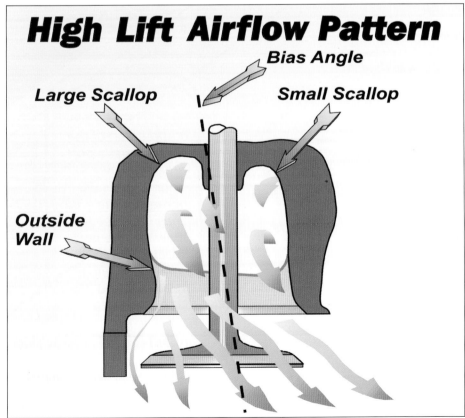

High Lift Airflow Pattern

Bias Angle

Large Scallop

Small Scallop

Outside Wall

Fig. 10.7. Above about 0.27D, the flow of a typical two-valve head starts to move predominantly across the back of the valve, as shown here. The efficiency increases because of change in this flow characteristic. This is why engines with two-parallel-valves like a lot of valve lift.

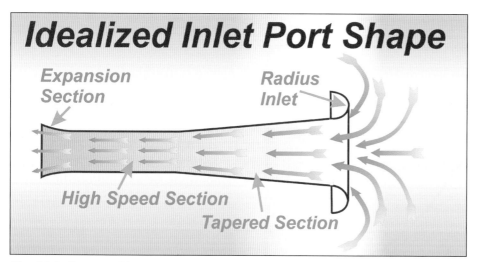

Idealized Inlet Port Shape

Expansion Section

Radius Inlet

High Speed Section

Tapered Section

Fig. 10.8. If we could straighten an intake port, this is about how it would look for optimum performance. The severity of the bend in the port has an overriding influence on the final form for best results.

Fig. 10.9. This is a mold of the intake port from valve head to the end of the ram stack for an Australian V-8 Super Tourer. Within the rules and casting limitations, it attempts to emulate the idealized port in Figure 10.8. This particular port, at 14 inches long, favors output in the 7,000- to 7,500-rpm range.

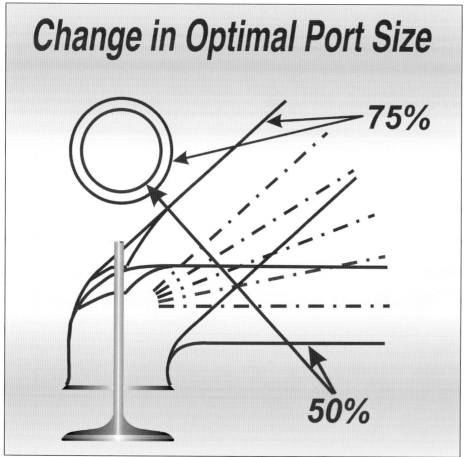

Change in Optimal Port Size

75%

50%

Fig. 10.10. The more poorly the turn into the valve throat area is, the smaller the valve appears to the port, and therefore the port needs to be smaller in cross section to keep a lesser amount of air up to speed for inertial ramming of the cylinder. As the port inclination becomes steeper, it is able to utilize the valve better and the valve appears to the port to be bigger; hence, a bigger port is optimal.

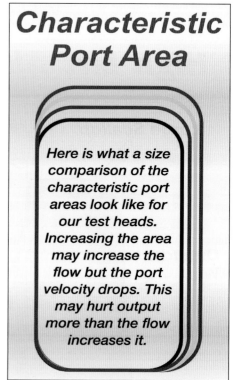

Characteristic Port Area

Here is what a size comparison of the characteristic port areas look like for our test heads. Increasing the area may increase the flow but the port velocity drops. This may hurt output more than the flow increases it.

Fig.10.11. To gain in one area, you typically sacrifice in another area. If you enlarge the ports, typically port velocity decreases.

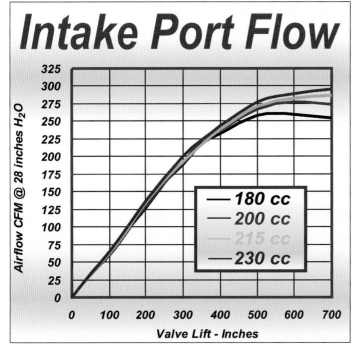

Intake Port Flow

Fig. 10.12. The flow curves produced by progressively enlarging the port (as measured in cubic centimeters of port volume). Note the bigger ports only showed an improvement in the higher lift ranges, showing again that the valve and seat control flow at lower lifts.

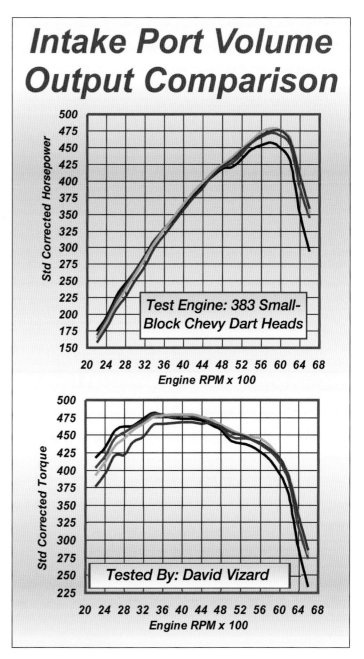

Intake Port Volume Output Comparison

Test Engine: 383 Small-Block Chevy Dart Heads

Tested By: David Vizard

Fig. 10.13. The outcomes from increasing port size are easy to see from these tests. The smallest port at 180 cc produced the best torque up to about 3,300 rpm. The 200-cc port lost a little at the low end but gained a worthwhile amount at the top end. At this point, the port size for optimal results over a wide rev range was close to being achieved. The 215-cc port delivered a slightly better top end than the 200 but lost out everywhere else. The 230-cc port produced no more top end than the 215 but lost everywhere else.

Port Velocity

Although the sidebar on page 106 gives a theoretical picture of port area requirements, it does assume that the stream of air in the port can reasonably make it around the turn. Remember, the air has mass and is inclined to stay in a stream a little like water from a hose. What this means is the throat or bowl area before the valve becomes really critical. That is

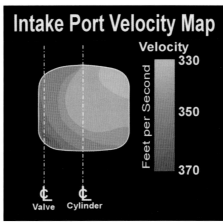

Fig. 10.14. One of my port velocity maps for a high-performance head for a small-block Ford Windsor engine. Note how well the port area is utilized. The slowest velocity is 330 ft/sec while the highest is 370; a difference of some 11 percent. Many production heads have a velocity gradient of as much as 50 percent. Since the port area is underutilized, it has the effect of reducing the mean port velocity at which peak power occurs.

where the flow bench is needed to make the best job possible of getting the air around the bend and on past the valve.

One last point: The reason the different head configurations in the Sidebar "Calculating Peak Power RPM" below have differing maximum port velocities is tied to the fact they have differing port utilization characteristics. The more uniform the velocity is at the area considered, the higher the peak-power port speed is.

Limiting Port Velocity

Air drawn into the engine is done so in a stop-start fashion. There is a price to be paid in terms of the energy taken to accelerate the air up to speed for each induction stroke. As you may suspect, there comes a time when the energy required to accelerate the air to higher speeds costs more in power than any extra power the additional air may have produced. During the World War II era, Charles Fayette Taylor, a highly respected tech pioneer of the day, deduced that the peak port speed, at peak power RPM, reached a limiting value at about Mach 0.5 to 0.55 (at standard temperature and pressure, that's 580 to 640 ft/sec). Although this limiting number has been pushed up on really high-tech engines, such as F1 units (I have heard of numbers as high as Mach 0.62), those numbers hold really well when we are considering a high-performance two-valve-per-cylinder engine and four-valve engines with ports of less than about 30 degrees of downdraft to the valve axis.

By the time the port's Mach number has reached about 0.6, the power curve is very much on the way down for most engines.

So how do you determine the Mach number of your engine's ports, short of measuring it? Well there are some formulas that were developed by Taylor and others but they almost all relate to slow-revving aero engines. The fact that we have so much of a better handle on tuned

Calculating Peak Power RPM

Although the following figures and formulas look like they wrap things up neatly, nothing could be further from the truth. While these numbers apply quite well when we are dealing with heads other than F1-style stuff, the results given are about okay for short-cammed, moderate-compression engines. When compression ratios go much above about 10:1, the peak power RPM indicated tends to be on the low side.

For instance, a 12:1 small-block Chevy with a hot street/strip cam in it can produce peak power as much as 10-percent higher than indicated here.

I have included this info because so many other books do, but they usually fail to qualify it. Use it as a guide but don't for one moment assume it to be exact.

$$\text{Peak Power RPM} = \frac{\text{Port Velocity (ft/sec) x Port Area (sq. in.) x 360}}{\text{Cubic Inches Displacement}}$$

The number you need to know to make this work is the port velocity. Use the appropriate figure from the peak power port velocities shown here.

Two Valves per Cylinder

Pre 1985 stock production low-performance	280 ft/sec
As above pocket ported	300 ft/sec
Newer precision cast high-performance stock	300 ft/sec
As above, pocket ported	310 ft/sec
As above, fully ported	320 ft/sec
Race-spec stock-port location	330 ft/sec
CNC-ported race non-production	340 to 360 ft/sec

Three, Four, or Five Valves per Cylinder

Production, unported	300 to 310 ft/sec
Production, fully ported	300 to 360 ft/sec
F1-style	380 to 420 ft/sec

If you know the engine's peak-power RPM, you can calculate the mean port velocity with the following formula:

$$\text{Mean Port Velocity} = \frac{\text{CI x RPM}}{\text{Port Area Square Inches x 360}}$$

Port Velocity Spread

In the sidebar "Calculating Peak Power RPM" on page 106, the chart gives peak power port velocities of various head configurations. I also mention a few factors that affect the accuracy of these port velocities. There, I mostly focus on port-area utilization. Here, I want to help you understand how those numbers can change.

This is a lesson on "combinations," which are also a factor a good head porter needs to know to enhance his own engine building skills or those of a customer. So let us look at port velocities and what affects the peak power velocity.

As an example, assume a test engine with, say, a 9:1 compression ratio, a stock head, and a good but not necessarily optimum intake and exhaust. A 2-liter SOHC two-valve Ford Pinto engine as used in U.S. and European cars from about 1970 to 1980 fits the bill because it is a basically sound engine with a poor cylinder head.

This example looks at various changes and how they affect the peak power port velocity.

Move #1

Increase compression ratio. Raising it from 9:1 to, say, 11.5:1 increases output throughout the RPM range and puts the peak power at a little higher RPM. The result is that this engine now produces its peak power at a higher port speed.

Move #2

Install a larger valve with a far more efficient valve seat than the stock design. The bigger valve is blended into the existing port, but the main body of the port gets nothing more than a cleanup, and so it remains virtually stock size.

This change on a stock-cammed 2-liter Pinto results in about a 12-hp increase and moves peak power up the RPM range by about 200.

So what you now have is a motor that peaks at even higher port speed.

Move #3

Because the Pinto intake port is poorly conceived, the bottom 1/4 inch of it is largely redundant. Filling in that lower 1/4 inch and blending it out at the valve bowl

(throat) produces a port with a much more even flow across its area. It also flows the odd CFM or so more from a port about 15 percent smaller.

On the dyno, the torque increases throughout the RPM range, and because of better cylinder ramming at higher RPM the power goes up as well as the RPM, at which peak occurs.

What you now have is a substantially different (higher) port velocity at peak power RPM.

Move #4

Although far from obvious on a high-performance or race engine, the strongest pull on the intake port during the induction process is not from the piston. I have demonstrated this on a 525-ci big-block Chevy street motor. This engine had a well-designed intake and exhaust for the job at hand. With port and in-cylinder pressure measuring gear installed, this engine had a vacuum of 11 psi (4 inches absolute pressure) at the exhaust valve and 3 psi positive at the intake valve during the overlap period when the piston was parked at TDC.

This means that while the piston is stationary at TDC, there is a pressure differential across the chamber of 14 psi because of the wave tuning of the intake and exhaust. (FYI, suction, due to the piston going down the bore, was just a shade under 1 psi.) By starting the charge motion into the cylinder early (this reached about 135 ft/sec, or, about 90 mph), the depression later in the cycle as the piston is near or at peak velocity is lower.

This intake/exhaust action causes peak power to go up as well as the RPM at which it occurs. So the better the exhaust, the higher the intake velocity where peak power occurs.

Move #5

Next is a very obvious change in engine spec, which can move peak power RPM up the scale considerably. That means a change to a cam of longer duration.

Again you see that an increase of as much as 20 hp from our Pinto can be had while the RPM at which it occurs can be as much as 1,500 rpm or so higher.

lengths today, especially the exhaust, means that determining the Mach number with any useful accuracy involves way more than just a single, simple formula. My recommendation here is that you get an engine simulation program, such as those from Motion Software (Dynomation) or Performance Trends (Engine Analyzer). With these programs, you can experiment with different port cross-sectional areas to determine what works the best for your application, to within some pretty close limits.

Applied Basic Porting

Having plowed through the basics in theory, it's worth asking: What's it worth in terms of power? This obviously varies from head to head and engine to engine. The better the head is to start with, the more

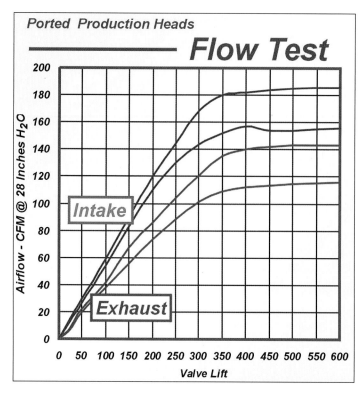

Fig. 10.15. Just how poor a typical pushrod, two-valve as-cast factory exhaust port is can be seen here. The top port mold is a factory-stock 5.0 exhaust port, and its shortcomings are obvious. The middle port is an as-cast aftermarket head and is much better in all respects. The bottom port mold is the center one after porting. Note the seat-to-port blend.

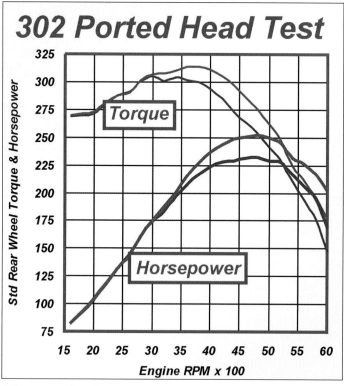

Fig. 10.16. These graphs show what even a basic porting job can do on a pre-1990s production head casting (1989 5.0 Mustang). Just basic porting moves resulted in the flow increases (top) and on the dyno showed the power gains (bottom): peak torque up by 10 ft-lbs and peak horsepower up by 21. A compression ratio increase improved torque throughout the RPM range.

your efforts are likely to resemble a basic porting job. The following tests should give you a good idea of the worth of any porting or compression raising you are likely to do. Figure 10.16 shows what can be achieved with just an easy weekend's porting exercise on a set of production 1989 Ford 5.0 heads.

But let's go one step further. We start with a pair of airflow-tested heads on a Ford 5.0 Mustang mule engine and develop a set of baseline power and torque curves. From there, we look at what a set of as-cast Dart Pro 1 170-cc port heads can do. And then, the 170s are swapped out for a set of 195s and a set of basic ported 170s, milled for 1.2 points of extra CR.

The cam used for all the test heads was a 280-degree Comp Cams High Energy, single-pattern street roller (profile number 1474). The 1.6 rockers, after lash, delivered 0.560-inch lift at the valves. Other than Comp Cams rockers and Icon pistons, all the other parts, including the timing chain, oil pump, water pump, etc., were stock. We also used a Moroso pan, as its greater volume and surface area help dissipate the heat of repeated dyno runs.

For induction, we used an Edelbrock Performer RPM Air Gap intake along with a 650-Holley-style carb and a billet Petronix distributor with a mechanical advance curve to suit the cam spec, provided ignition. You can see our dyno mule was far from exotic, and actually had considerable test time on the card already. At this point, making power might look simple—just make the heads as big as possible to flow as much air as possible. Unfortunately, there is far more to it than just plain old flow as measured on a flow bench.

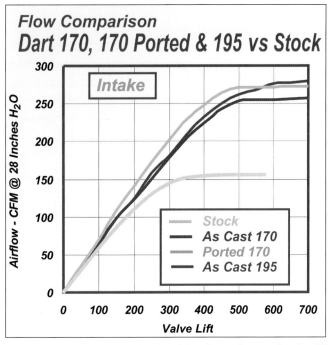

Fig. 10.17. The flow of the 170 or 195 Dart head was a huge increase from stock. The ported 170 head (green curve) took advantage of the Dart's inherently good as-cast form by allowing effective porting by simply refining the as-cast form. Note how the ported head delivers more flow right off the seat. Also note how it tops out at about 0.550 lift. This is a good indication that the port is optimally sized for the valve and valve lift (0.560) involved. If a port flows significantly more at valve lifts much above those to be used, it is a fair bet the port is too big for the job!

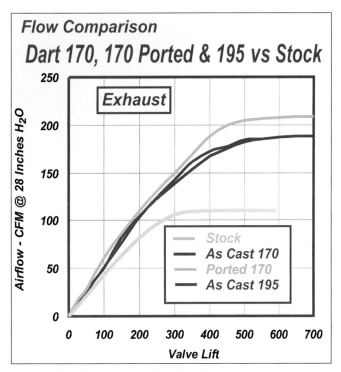

Fig. 10.18. Dart's exhaust seat is a very effective form and largely follows what is successfully used for the ultra-high-tech heads used on NASCAR Cup Cars and Pro Stock. With this in mind, the form just downstream of the seat itself was blended into the cast part of the port without altering the machined form on the seat insert. This, along with some streamlining of the guide boss and a short-side clean up, resulted in the green curve seen here. With only 2 cc of material out of the port, our detailing of the exhaust gave an increase in flow from about 0.075 lift on up. Again, note how the curve flattens out by the time our intended 0.560 valve lift point is reached, indicating the port is no bigger than it need be for the job at hand.

As I have tried to stress, air has considerable mass and is heavier than you might think. If that air is moving fast, we can utilize the kinetic energy it contains to not only ram the cylinders at high speed but also reduce flow reversion at low speed. Getting that port area just right for a particular engine combination means more power at the top end, where a previously air-starved engine can now breath, and also at the low end. And we use the low end 95 percent of the time on the street, so it should at least be a realistic priority.

Another item on the agenda is swirl. The stock 5.0 head is very poor in this respect. Here, the test Dart heads show excellent swirl for a Ford-style casting, though it is still less than a typical small-block Chevy casting. Without good mixture motion, the combustion process is compromised. If a head has good swirl, it helps improve combustion quality, especially at low speed. In a nutshell, good swirl most often equates to good low-speed torque.

The last factor to consider is the compression ratio, which I cover later in this chapter. At this juncture, you are getting an idea of the impor-tance of understanding just what the CR, especially when suitably high, can do for an engine's output. This is as important for a street-driven machine as it is for an all-out race car. The compression ratio has a considerable influence on the size of cam that can be used before low-speed output becomes unacceptable. The higher the compression ratio, the greater the cam duration that can be used. Also more compression equates directly to improved fuel efficiency, and that is something that cannot be overlooked these days.

Physical Comparisons

Now let's look at a few physical dimensions of the heads under review here. First, the as-cast 170-cc Dart Pro 1 has a 165-cc measured intake port volume and a 62-cc exhaust volume. The flow figures of the heads tested are shown in Figures 10.17 and 10.18.

As a reference point, the stock heads are typically in the low to mid 120 cc on the intake and low to mid 50 cc on the exhaust. The 170 Pro 1 heads are intended to be used as a direct replacement on an engine that has an otherwise-stock bottom end. That means they must have valves that are not too big to be accommodated by the stock piston's valve cutouts. To do this, the intake valve is 1.94 inches in diameter. That's up appreciably from the stock 1.84 inches but significantly less than the typical 2.02 inches that can be used when aftermarket pistons are in the engine.

To make flow comparisons fast and easy, we'll look at two reference lift points that, for all practical purposes, define the head's ability to get the job done. These two points are the flow at 0.250 lift, and the flow at peak valve lift as delivered by the cam and valvetrain. In this particular case that is 0.56, but to make life easier here we use the 0.550 lift point because it is close enough.

At these two key lift points, the intake on a stock head delivers 121 and 155 cfm, respectively. On the flow bench, the 170-cc Dart Pro 1 in as-cast form delivered 151 and 255 cfm. Let's put that into perspective here. First, even at as low a lift figure as 0.250, the Dart head delivered flow numbers almost as good as a stock head at maximum lift. At the peak valve lift point, the Dart Pro 1 head produced a full 100 cfm more than stock!

Fig. 10.19. Unless the two are side by side, it is hard to see the difference in port size between the 170-cc port (left) and the 195 (right).

Fig. 10.20. It can be seen that even in out-of-the-box form the bowls or throats of both ports are relatively well streamlined. To get from here to a nearly optimal bowl form takes very little metal removal.

Fig. 10.21. Here you can get an appreciation of the valve sizes and chamber form used on both the small- and big-port Dart Pro 1 heads. This chamber is well conceived in that it minimizes shrouding and tends to maintain any port-developed swirl.

Swirl was also measured during the flow tests. The Dart heads all showed excellent swirl characteristics. In spite of having bigger ports (which, all other things being equal, typically reduces swirl) all the Dart heads tested had significantly better-than-stock swirl performance.

As far as port velocity is concerned, we have somewhat more challenging concepts and principles to get a handle on. The Dart head has a significantly bigger port than stock; so for a given flow, the velocity is less. However, the valve is bigger and so, for a given lift and flow bench depression, more air is pulled in and this boosts the velocity.

Okay, that all looks simple enough, but the engine does not inhale air in the same way that a flow bench does. Let's consider the situation at low RPM. If the valve is open to the extent that it can more than satisfy the instantaneous need of the cylinder, the depression drawing air in could be lower than we see on the bench. The net result is that the port velocity could actually be lower even though it was (as in our case here) higher on the flow bench. If we throw all the variables of port velocity, swirl, and flow into the melting pot, and do not have many years of experience, it is difficult to confidently predict the outcome of this type of proposed head change.

Although swirl, because we are considering the exhaust, is out of the picture, the exhaust ports flow and flow velocity are also factors affecting the low-speed output as well as the top end. One of the worst enemies to low-speed torque, when a big cam is used, is exhaust flow reversion. Higher uniform port velocities on the exhaust side can have a considerable positive influence on low-speed output. For the exhaust side, our 170-cc Dart Pro 1 had, with its measured 63-cc exhaust port at the two key lift points, flowed 123 and 185 cfm, respectively. The stock 52-cc port, at those same key lift points, delivered only 92 and 121 cfm. This means that even though the port was bigger, the Dart exhaust had more velocity because of the greater quantities it could flow.

The 170s on the Dyno

With the flow, swirl, and velocity characteristics so far discussed in mind, let's see how the as-cast 170 Dart Pro 1s fair on the dyno. Check out the curves in Figure 10.27. The green lines are the ones to look at, compared to the stock head results shown in black. Even though it had a much-bigger-than-stock intake runner, the combination of swirl, flow, and runner velocity was such that output was improved right down to 2,200 rpm. At this point, the Dart 170 put out a creditable 14 ft-lbs more than the stock heads. This combination also led to the peak torque going up by 16 to 17 ft-lbs and peak power by a very satisfying 68 hp. The usable top-end RPM figure also rose by about 700 to 800 rpm. That is pretty good for just a cylinder head change by any standards, especially ones that are still as-cast.

The Bigger Sibling

The 195-cc Dart Pro 1 differs from the 170; the intake measured 25 cc more and the exhaust 2 cc more. Also the 195 had 2.02-inch intake valves instead of the smaller 1.94s of the 170 heads. At the two key points of 0.250 and 0.550, the 195s flowed 159 and 268 cfm. That's up by 8 and 13 more than the 170-cc head. For swirl, the bigger port was a little lower until about 0.400 lift, then it picked up to numbers very similar to the 170-cc head variant.

Here is how it plays out for port velocity. By enlarging the port by 25 cc, the mean cross-sectional area of the bigger port is 13 percent greater. However, the flow increases we see are about 5 percent at the 0.250 and 0.550 check points. The net result is a decrease in port velocity by a nominal 8.5 percent. In simple terms, this means that this head would be better on an engine that was either 8.5 percent bigger or turned 8.5 percent more RPM. The exhaust port, 3-cc bigger, was marginally better on flow between 0.300 and 0.500 lift. This makes them close to the same as the ports in the 170-cc heads.

The 195s on the Dyno

On the dyno, the 195s produced the output curves shown in dark blue in Figure 10.27. Notice the torque at low RPM is down compared to the 170-cc heads. This is how it remains until about 5,000 rpm. From there to 5,500 rpm, the bigger port heads matched the smaller ones. It was not until the RPM exceeded 5,500 that the bigger, higher-flowing ports produced any additional output. Even then, the power increase only

Fig. 10.22. The finished seat job. The form used on both the intake and exhaust was a radius joining a 45-degree seat at 15 degrees (see Chapter 9).

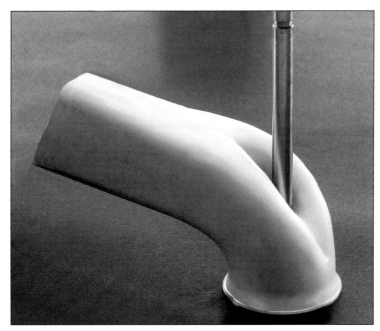

Fig. 10.23. Points to note here on the modified intake are: 1) the blend of the port into the seat, 2) the significantly broader and higher port shape at the turn, and 3) the relatively small main body of the port. With

only 5 cc removed to bring it to 170 cc, this port flowed 275 cfm at 0.600 lift. I have reworked these to flow 301 cfm at that lift with still only 177 cc of port volume and essentially the same size for the main body of the port.

amounted to 4 or so HP. Increased output at 2,200 rpm amounted to just 1 ft-lb more than stock. Peak torque was up by 12 ft-lbs and peak power by 72 hp. This means that although the 195-cc head is still a very effective piece on a relatively big-cammed 302, it appears much more suited to a 331- or 347-ci engine where its port size is more appropriate.

If Some Is Good—More Is Better

From the tests so far, it looks like port velocity is instrumental in delivering more area under the curve. If keeping port velocity up to some key value, such as we are doing here, can produce a fatter curve without sacrifice at the top end, then we effectively make a smaller engine run like it has more inches. Let's take the 170-cc heads and pose a question. How would they perform if they were given a basic porting job, plus the bigger 2.02-inch valve as on the 195-cc heads?

A basic porting job, as defined earlier, means limiting the metal removal to skinnying the guide bosses, blending in obvious irregularities (there were only a few of those), making the most of a progressive radius on the short-side turn, and, in this case, replacing the 1.94 intake valves with 2.02-inch ones. Installing the bigger valves also allowed for a more sophisticated-radius valve seat to be used.

All things being equal, this should improve the low-lift flow, which has the effect of improving the top-end output and helping power hang on longer after the peak point has been passed.

Unfortunately, flow graphs do little to show the extent of improvement at low lifts on the finished 170-cc Darts, so let's look at some numbers to bring the point home. First the intake: The new valve at 2.02 inches diameter is 4 percent larger, so it has 4 percent more circumference.

This means, if it is utilized at exactly the same efficiency as the valve it replaces, it should be 4 percent better. If the seat form is also more efficient, that also increases the flow. Countering this is the fact that as the valve size increases, so does the shrouding caused by the cylinder wall.

Let's see how the numbers shape up here. First, at 0.025 inches lift the flow with the new, bigger valve was up from 16 to 19 cfm, for a 14-percent improvement. Not bad for a starter. At 0.050-inch lift the gain was from 34 to 36 cfm for almost 6-percent improvement. We see this trend all the way up to the peak valve lift that we are going to use. On average, the flow increase is about 8 percent, and this has been achieved with a port volume that is only up from the measured 165 to 170 cc. That's just 3 percent. What this means is that for any given flow rate, the port velocity has also increased.

Now we have heads that deliver both more flow and more velocity. If we have not altered the basic port

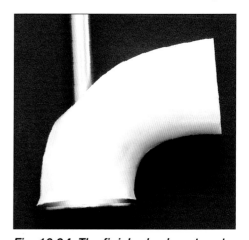

Fig. 10.24. The finished exhaust port, as seen here, on the 170 Dart Pro 1 produced some impressive numbers for what was essentially a simple and fast porting job. Note the transition of seat into port.

Fig. 10.25. The finished chamber on the Dart 170 Pro 1 looked like this. Other than a cleanup, this shape is much as it came from Dart. These shiny valves are hollow-stem items from Ferrea; I highly recommend them. They don't bounce off seats as easy and they typically rev about 300 rpm higher on a hot street application.

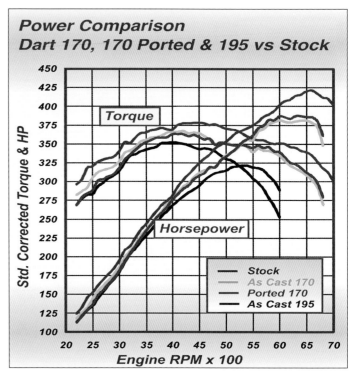

Fig. 10.26. There is a lot going on here with all the curves on this graph. The most obvious is that the ported Dart 170 Pro 1 paid off handsomely.

form, we should also see a little more swirl activity. Our swirl meter confirmed this was in fact the case. So far, so good—now on to the CR.

Compression Increase

The stock heads and the as-cast Dart heads delivered a measured compression ratio of between 8.87 and 8.94:1; so, for the sake of simplification, we average this out to 8.9:1. The ported Dart heads were machined 0.0050 to reduce the chamber size to a final 52 cc. This, on the mule's short-block combination, gave a CR of 10.1:1. Using a basic equation for thermal efficiency, this increase in CR should deliver 2.9 percent more torque everywhere in the RPM range.

However, the formula assumes that the intake valve opens at top dead center (TDC) and closes at bottom dead center (BDC). We actually have a pretty big cam in this engine and the valves open and close way before TDC and way after BDC. This means the effective compression ratio, the one that applies using the intake valve closing point, is much lower than the theoretical, or static, CR. As a result, an increase of 1.2 actually gives the engine a bigger percentage increase of the CR than it initially seems.

The result is, with a big cam, the low-speed torque can increase considerably more than you might otherwise expect. Also increasing the CR causes the exhaust gas speed to increase at just the time when it's most important to do so—right around TDC in the overlap period. This reduces the tendency for the exhaust flow to go into reversion and delay the onset of intake flow into the cylinder.

Modified 170s on the Dyno

Maintaining (or even slightly improving) the swirl and port velocity at low speed should mean we don't lose anything at those lower speeds. While the increase in flow won't really pay off until higher RPM, the increase in compression should return dividends everywhere, but most especially at low RPM. A check of the red output curves in Figure 10.26 confirms just that. If this had been a very short cam, we would have seen only about 8 ft-lbs increase at the 2,200 rpm point; but because the cam was quite big (for a street cam), an extra 16 ft-lbs was realized. This little exercise should bring home the importance of matching cam and compression; the bigger the cam, the more compression is needed to make it work.

Moving up the RPM scale, we see that the ported 170 Darts pushed up the peak torque to 20 ft-lbs better than the best of the unported heads. And peak power went up by some 30 hp more than the bigger-port 195 Darts and hung on longer, allowing shift points to be raised to near the 7,000-rpm mark. About 10 of those extra horses are from the compression increase and the other 20 from a combination of airflow and port velocity improvements.

From these results, you can see that having good airflow, port velocity, swirl, and compression results in a vastly superior power curve. The numbers speak clearly here. Not only was the low-speed torque better for street use, but the ported heads added a staggering total of 101 hp at the top end. That's like having a 100-hp nitrous system installed that you never have to fill! Mission accomplished.

An increase in the CR was part of the equation that made the example head porting successful. It is a key ingredient toward making power, and understanding the implications involved helps make porting and cam selection decisions that put you at least one step ahead of your competition.

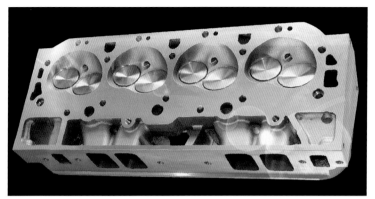

Fig. 10.28. We have arrived at a point where we need to look at combustion dynamics and the CR. Combustion dynamics have to be good no matter what, but just how much compression an engine needs or can tolerate for a given application and fuel octane needs to be well understood. It depends greatly on the engine's basic design parameters. On a multi-valve engine with a lot of valve area for the displacement involved, the CR is important but far less so than, say, on a big-block Chevy, which has a lot of displacement for too little valve area. As good as this Dart big-block Chevy head flows for a 2.3-inch valve, it is way short of outright CFM to feed what can easily be a 630-inch (10.4 liter) engine. If you are building a big-block Chevy, be sure to make the most of any means necessary to get the CR as high as the fuel octane allows.

Fig. 10.29. If you follow the guidelines I have detailed, you should be able to achieve what is shown here. Power in a 383-ci small-block Chevy went from 505 to 536 hp.

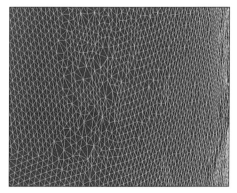

Fig. 10.27. This is the mesh developed from a drawing or a digitized port for CFD testing.

The Virtual Flow Bench

With anything that involves the passage of air through or over solid objects, it really helps to see where the air is going. As we all know, the problem is that air is invisible. All those tests we do to map out the velocity using the probes as described in Chapter 6 are to establish where the air is moving. Computational fluid dynamics (CFD) does just that, but until recently, it has been a valuable tool that only F1 and Cup Car teams could afford. But that is changing. Beginning in early 2011, I have been working with Design Dreams, a small company that has been developing ways and means to bring a virtual flow bench or wind tunnel to the market at a price that is little more than the most expensive commercial

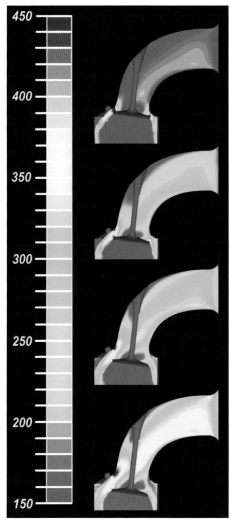

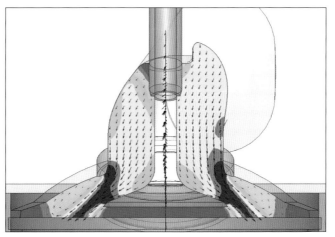

Fig. 10.31. Even at moderately high lift, you can see from this Design Dreams CFD illustration that the busiest (red is high speed, blue is low speed) area is still at the gap between the valve seats. This should remove any doubt about how important the valve seat form on the valve and, especially, the head is. Also note the angle of the main stream in red and the angle of the chamber walls. The difference between the two demonstrates that the chamber wall could beneficially be a lot steeper.

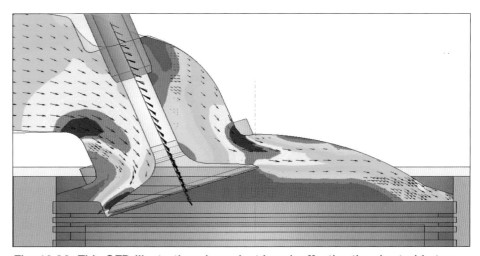

Fig. 10.30. This CFD illustration from Dr. Rick Roberts of Edelbrock shows how port/valve seat activity changes as the lift progresses from 0.300 through to 0.900 in 0.200-inch increments. Note at 0.300 lift the high-speed activity is concentrated at the valve seat. However, even at low valve lift, a flow pattern is developing in the port. Even though the speeds in the port are little more than 150 ft/sec, the tendency for the air to want to travel in a straight line is just beginning to be apparent. At 0.500 lift, this characteristic is plainly obvious and at 0.900 lift it is the dominant feature of the port. I claim that a head porter's number-one job is to find ways and means to get air around corners.

Fig. 10.32. This CFD illustration shows just how ineffective the short-side turn can be without careful attention to its counterpart. Also check out the hot spot on the back of the valve at the location of the piston valve cutout.

flow benches. The work here is being done by David Woodruff and his aim is to bring CFD capability to any serious head shop.

The downside to CFD is that you need to be able to develop a mesh that describes the form of the head. I am going to use some CFD results contributed both by David Woodruff and the ever-resourceful Dr. Rick Roberts, who could best be described as Edelbrock's chief research engineer.

First, take a look at Figure 10.31. You can see that the area between the seats is the busiest but also how, on this shallow hemi-style head, the flow is virtually even out of both sides of the valve. This is a virtue of a head with nearly zero shrouding.

A CFD result from the same head as viewed from the side is also revealing (Figure 10.32). First, note the high velocity occurring on the beginning of the short-side turn. Immediately after the high-velocity plume, the flow separates from the port wall. This demonstrates the need to spend whatever time is required to get the

Turbulence and the Reynolds Number

Some years ago, Johnny Hunkins, who was then editor of *Muscle Mustangs & Fast Fords*, wrote a very complimentary review of one of my university lectures that he attended. In that article he reiterated a comment he had overheard during the first break of the day on this two-day seminar. One of the attendees commented that "Vizard could explain quantum physics to a 10th-grader and they would understand." While that comment might be stretching things a little, because what I know about quantum physics would barely fill two sides of a postage stamp, I do get a great many people telling me they have managed to grasp highly technical subjects when I have explained them. I say this because I am going to try here to explain something that is proving to be somewhat of a challenge to simplify.

So what am I about to tackle here? I am trying to deliver a more simply understood explanation than typical text books give of what the Reynolds Number is and, more importantly, its significance to airflow in the induction system, cylinder heads, and exhaust system.

My Initial Exposure

I was first introduced to the Reynolds Number while studying for my degree. The class was given a test question that involved calculating some aerodynamic properties of an airship (like I was ever going to design one). After that little exercise, the Reynolds Number did not crop up again until I was deep in a porting discussion with Dr. Tom Boyce of, as I remember it, Queen's University in London. Dr. Boyce was a hotshot engine guy in the truest sense and was getting power figures from his 1-liter SOHC race engines that I was not even in sight of. During our conversation, he brought up the subject of the Reynolds Number of a typical intake port and its relevance to airflow in a running engine.

His words of wisdom have stuck in my mind since that day in 1969. What he said relates to a comment I so often hear. That comment goes something like this: "We cut the port [guide boss, short-side turn, or whatever] like that to eliminate turbulence." Although that seems like a comment with all the earmarks of a reasonably factual statement, it is actually the result of a total misconception of the type of flow taking place in a working port. And what makes that comment so erroneous is all related to the Reynolds Number of the system we are dealing with.

Help from DB

Currently addressing the subject, I reflect that I have had opportunity to think up a lucid explanation of the Reynolds Number for about 42 years. But when I started to write on this subject, I found myself sinking in a sea of mud. The difference between being able to use the Reynolds Number and to explain it without resorting to any real math looked really daunting. The Reynolds Number has an almost abstract quality about it. So to cover my bases here, I bounced my explanation off my good friend and whiz-kid mathematician/theorist (as well as one of the sharpest head porters I know) David Baker, of Puma Race Engines.

I am very glad I did. Although I had a working knowledge of the Reynolds Number and could apply it to whatever I might be doing with airflow through an engine, the difference between what I knew about the Reynolds Number and what David knew was about the same as opposite ends of a 12-inch ruler. So, after many failed attempts at simplifying things, here is what I put together after a considerable amount of aid and guidance from David Baker.

Mr. Reynolds?

The Reynolds Number is a dimensionless number (has no units) used to quantify the ratio of inertial forces to viscous forces. In the context of fluid dynamics, this gives us a measure of the relative importance of these two types of forces within or around the conduit/object with which we are working. In our case that is the port or the gap between the valve and seat.

You could, with good reason, believe that the Reynolds Number was named for the person who conceived it, but that is not actually the case. It was originally developed by one of the great minds of the nineteenth century–Sir George Stokes (the Stokes of the Navier-Stokes equations that play such an important part in computational fluid dynamics). Originally conceived and developed by Stokes around 1851, the value of the equation was put to extensive practical use by Osborne Reynolds in about the mid 1880s.

The Formula

But back to our definition of the Reynolds Number. It can be viewed as a number for determining the type of flow regimen within the system being considered. These flow regimens include laminar, transitional, and turbulent flow under conditions where the flow pattern has fully developed, which means it has stabilized after the last change of direction. As such, it can be applied directly to describe the type of flow that occurs within the ports of cylinder heads. Conceptually, the Reynolds Number uses the density and viscosity of the fluid concerned (air, in our case) along with the velocity and what is called a characteristic dimension. Again, in our case, that characteristic dimension is either the port diameter (or its equivalent, if it is not round) or the gap between the valve and the valve seat.

$$\text{The Reynolds Number} = \frac{\text{Velocity x Characteristic Dimension}}{\text{Kinematic Viscosity}}$$

I imagine most people are used to the concept of absolute viscosity, which tells us how "sticky," or viscous, a fluid is. For example, it's used to grade motor oils. Kinematic viscosity is absolute viscosity divided by the fluid density, so it tells us how viscous a fluid is relative to its density. Air is obviously much less viscous than water, but after taking density into account it actually has a much higher kinematic viscosity.

The units (in Metric) of kinematic viscosity are m^2/s, so when we multiply velocity (m/s) x dimension (m) and divide by kinematic viscosity, we get m^2/s divided by m^2/s, which leaves the number dimensionless.

So what does the Reynolds Number tell us? Well it doesn't directly tell us whether the flow is laminar or turbulent. That has to be determined empirically for each individual situation and the shape of the test piece. However, when we know what the flow regimen is at a given Reynolds Number for a given situation, we know whether the flow will be laminar or turbulent for differently sized but similarly shaped test pieces at different fluid velocities.

Testing Realities

The general rule is: When testing flow on a scale model of the real item, then, for the rule of similitude to apply, the Reynolds Number must be kept the same for the model being tested as it was in the full-scale situation (if the flow regimen is to remain the same). This leads us to a finding that is not very intuitive. We could easily suppose that if we were testing a half-scale model of a real car doing 100 mph in a wind tunnel, we would need to use a wind speed of 50 mph in the wind tunnel so everything stays in proportion. The reality is that we need to use a wind speed of 200 mph in the wind tunnel for the half-scale model. When the characteristic dimension halves, the velocity must double for the Reynolds Number to stay the same (as the equation shows).

For systems that we are concerned with in engine development (ports), when the Reynolds Number is less than about 2,300, the flow within the port is laminar because the viscous forces of the air are dominant. At about 2,300 things begin to change. Between 2,300 and about 4,000 the flow is in a transitional phase between being fully laminar and fully turbulent (at these levels, flow is influenced by surface finishes and abrupt changes in flow direction). More than about 4,000, the flow is almost certain to be fully turbulent, and there is nothing that can be done to make it otherwise. During turbulent flow, the inertial forces dominate.

Higher Reynolds Numbers produce eddies and vortices, which can be summed up as turbulence. This leads to the point that I want to make: Assume for the moment a typical port-area/valve-area ratio along with typical exhaust extraction pressures (below atmospheric) during the overlap event of a high-performance engine. Under these conditions, the intake port flow is such that the Reynolds Number exceeds 4,000 (fully turbulent) when the valve lift is only at 0.003-inch lift. By the time the valve is at full lift in a running engine, the Reynolds Number for a typical port is easily more than 200,000. Result? There is absolutely no sign, nor can there be, of laminar flow within the port in

Turbulence and the Reynolds Number *CONTINUED*

most situations. It is always highly turbulent except for the first few thousandths of valve lift.

At the test pressures typically seen on a fixed-pressure-drop flow bench, the flow is fully turbulent from lift figures as low as 0.006 inch at 28 inches H_2O test pressure and 0.010 inch at 10 inches H_2O test pressure. As David Baker pointed out, the port flow in a typical port of about $1^5/_8$-inch diameter is fully turbulent at velocities as low as 5 ft/sec, and I'm betting that is a lot less than most people guess.

A Deeper Understanding

Here, among a number of interesting issues, is another David Baker tech point that I am sure appeals to all you hardcore techies. For a given ratio of port diameter to valve diameter, the port Reynolds Number is totally dependent on the valve lift and completely independent of valve size for valve lifts up to about 15 percent of the valve diameter. I was a little skeptical when David first pointed that out—it

seemed just too convenient. But a little time spent going through the math showed that it was actually so. It means that regardless of engine size or valve size, the port flow becomes fully turbulent at very small valve lifts.

Conclusions

So what does all this tell us? In the very simplest terms, it tells us that the Reynolds Number is essentially about describing the relative viscosity of the fluid in relation to the size of the object. For a given velocity, a smaller characteristic dimension produces a smaller Reynolds Number. What that means is the smaller object sees the medium (air, in our case) as being more viscous and, therefore, more likely to have laminar flow at any given speed. A classic example is the airflow through the tiny holes of a paper air filter. This flow is laminar and flow through a laminar orifice(s) is proportional to the pressure drop, not the square of the pressure drop. In other words, double the suction produces double the flow.

Four-Valve Porting Tips and PolyQuad Conversion

It might appear that I have said way too little that pertains to porting four-valve heads. The reality here is that, for the most part, a four-valve head follows the same lines of approach toward good flow as a two-valve cylinder head. I do have one almost universal beef, though, when it comes to four (or more) valve heads: OE manufacturers, for some reason beyond my understanding, seem hell-bent on over-sizing the ports (especially the intake).

On most of the heads I deal with, the number-one issue is how best to make the main body of the port smaller. For a multi-valve engine, a good starting figure for port area versus valve area is about 85 percent.

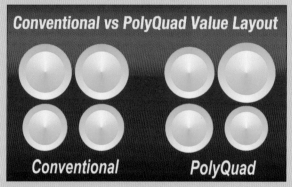

Figure 1. The most visible feature of the Poly-Quad design, and the one for which it is named, is the valve layout. A conventional four-valve layout is shown on the left.

Without sacrificing valve area, the PolyQuad design, at right, employs four distinctly different-sized valves. The benefits are reduced fuel consumption and emissions, more low-speed output, and better top-end horsepower. That's everything variable valve timing (VVT) does but with no additional parts.

Four-Valve Porting Tips *CONTINUED*

I have seen good results from 85 percent to a little less than 80 percent but it's never good when that figure goes much above about 88 percent. When the ports are needlessly big, it is important to get as much additional flow from valve and seat work as possible.

If you find that installing bigger valves, without the need for bigger ports, helps flow from the seat up (usually the case), the bigger valve helps the situation with no downside. If you want to really get results from a four-valve head modification program, you really need to PolyQuad the head. PolyQuad is the patented name for my porting development for three- and four-valve heads. It delivers the results of variable valve timing (VVT) without actually having any VVT involved. In fact, it involves no additional moving parts whatsoever. It can also be used with VVT to amplify the effect of the VVT. In essence, a fully developed PolyQuad head delivers the low-speed torque of the best two-valve heads along with the high-speed output of the best four-valve heads.

The results can be quite dramatic. I did one head for a competition-annihilating (and here "annihilating" is not just a figure of speech) turbo 2-liter Mitsubishi engine that, on 5 psi less boost, outperformed the original race head by no less than 98 hp and 110 ft-lbs. For most heads, this PolyQuad conversion is not difficult to do even by the home porter. There is not space here, but you can find the full details of the procedure and results on my Web site: www.motortecmagazine.net. If you are doing a head like this for your own use, that's fine. But if you intend to sell it, remember, the process is patented, and you then owe me 7.5 percent of what you get for it.

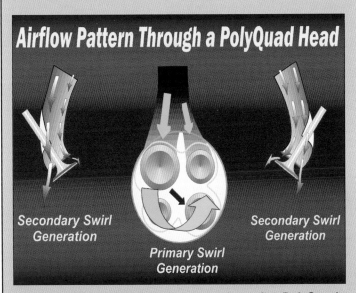

Figure 2. Here is the airflow pattern through a PolyQuad head. Note the flow that the bigger intake valve dominates, thus turning the charge in the direction of the green arrow. Since the charge is spiraling downward and the big exhaust valve is as far from the intake as possible, cross flow is minimized. The shape of the intake port is a secondary contributor toward swirl generation.

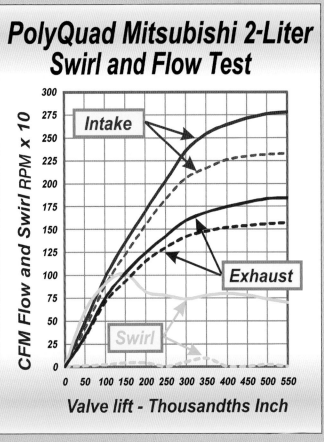

Figure 3. Here are the test results for the Mitsubishi race head I ported for a winning turbo drag-race car. Attention to port size, an increase in flow, and the generation of swirl produced an increase of 98 hp and 110 ft-lbs on 5 pounds less boost.

Piston Porting

Combustion chambers and cylinder walls are not the only part of the combustion space that can cause valve shrouding. First acquaint yourself with the CFD illustration in Figure 1. See how air that wants to flow around the short side turn is being somewhat blocked by the wall of the piston's valve pocket. Air is trying to flow out of the short-side turn and the wall of the valve pocket is restricting flow. A total fix can be difficult, but if the piston is cut as shown in Figure 2, any shrouding effect is minimized.

Once it is pointed out that the piston causes valve shrouding, it all looks pretty obvious. Unfortunately, a high piston dome causes flow restrictions but usually this is far less obvious. Although proportionally great compared to the overall flow, a typical domed, 24-degree big-block Chevy piston can cut the flow both into and out of the cylinder and the precise points of the restrictions are far from obvious until pointed out. Take a look at Figure 3.

Here you see the areas that tend to hinder the flow into and out of the cylinder during the overlap period. The one way to determine, with any degree of precision, just what needs to come off the piston crown to maximize flow is to install a piston into the bore of the engine/flow bench and suck air through the exhaust port with the valves in the overlap position.

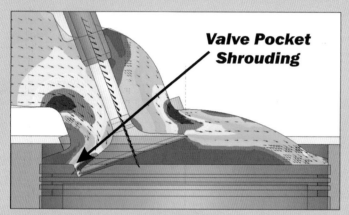

Figure 1. It may be less than obvious but valve pockets can also restrict flow due to shrouding during the close approach at overlap.

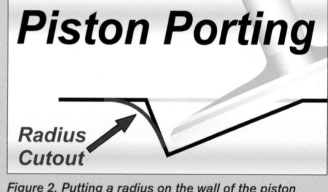

Figure 2. Putting a radius on the wall of the piston valve pockets (as shown here) helps with both the inflow of fresh charge and the outflow of exhaust during the overlap period.

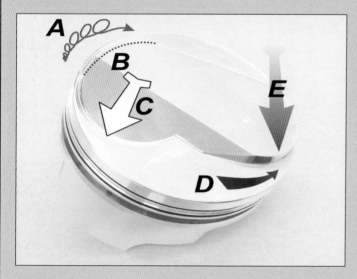

Figure 3. Most big-block Chevy pistons also need to be "ported" if they have any kind of dome more than about 0.100 inch. During the overlap period, the intake air rolls past the edge of the valve as shown by arrow A. Unless the piston crown is cut back to about the position of the blue dotted line B, the bore and the edge of the piston shroud the flow. As in Figure 2, the edge of the valve pocket needs to be radiused-off (arrow C) to reduce shrouding at this point. At TDC, considerable exhaust flow is along the direction of arrow D. To allow an easier exit path, the edge of the dome at E needs to be angled about 45 degrees, right down to the piston's deck face. This needs to be done right around the dome wherever it is close to the cylinder wall.

How Much Air Makes How Much Power

The question of how much airflow is needed to deliver a target power output is one of the most often asked questions I get. I have a down-and-dirty, but super-quick answer to that, plus one that is a little more time consuming to work out but is also more meaningful. If you want to really get with the program, I suggest you invest in a good high-end engine simulation program for the enthusiast. That way you can project airflow and horsepower targets. I can recommend programs from Performance Trends and Motion Software. Both give a good indication of the power increase you are likely to see as well as what changes may be beneficial in other areas such as the valve event timing and the exhaust.

But back to some simple stuff to calculate the power potential of your heads. First, let's look at the down-and-dirty calculation for the cylinder's horsepower output.

You will, of course, need to multiply your answer by the number of cylinders. You take the CFM flow (at 28 inches H_2O) at the peak valve lift that you intend to use for the engine. Multiply this figure by 0.2625 for a roller cam and by 0.248 for a flat-tappet cam. For a 12.5:1, two-valve pushrod, wet-sump, carbureted engine with a good intake and exhaust system, and having four, six, or eight cylinders, this works well considering its simplicity. It does, of course, assume you built a reasonably good short block, and by that I mean one without undue friction.

This next formula works very well if you are targeting 100 hp per liter from a 10.5:1 pump-gas motor.

To make 100 hp per liter or 1.56 hp per cubic inch a viable proposition, we have to be a little more specific when correlating flow numbers with our expected output results. To achieve this goal, the head, at the full intake valve lift, needs to flow 6.4 cfm (as measured at 28 inches H_2O) for every cubic inch it has to feed (39 cfm for every 100 cc). Along with this, you need to have 4 cfm for every

One of my UNCC students built this 350 small-block Chevy to see if he had learned enough to build a 100-hp-per-liter street drivable two-valve V-8 with 10.5:1 compression. The result was 584 hp from 5.82 liters with a useable powerband from 2,500 to 8,000 rpm. And just in case you think otherwise, the budget on this was also pretty tight.

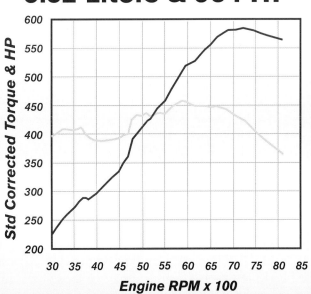

355 Small-Block Chevy 5.82 Liters & 584 HP

Other than some carb and manifold testing this build utilized building and spec practices right out of one or other of my books on small-block Chevy's and building power in general.

How Much Air Makes How Much Power CONTINUED

cubic inch to be fed (24 cfm for every 100 cc) while the intake valve is in the overlap sequence at TDC.

This means you need to draw a lift-versus-flow curve and establish the amount of lift needed at TDC to get the job done. You now have two points on the lift curve to meet the output requirement. From this you can figure out what cam profile and rocker ratio gets the job done. If you want to figure out the right LCA for the head and displacement combination you have, things get a little more involved, but my book, *How to Build Horsepower*, has all you need to know, plus the charts to get this important and so often wrongly selected factor right the first time and in a speedy manner.

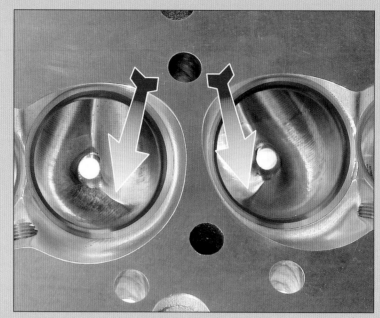

The example 100-hp-per-liter engine featured here used the highly effective AFR Competition Eliminator heads. These feature a fuel dam as indicated by the arrows.

short-side turn to be as effective as possible. In a real-world situation, that only happens if you flow the port at a working pressure drop, not a fixed 28 inches or so!

With CFD, you can flow the head not only with real-world pressure differentials, but you can also do so with the piston in the appropriate place. This means you have the ability to flow the head from the intake right through the exhaust port during the overlap period. When I am teaching students at a university or in seminars, I go to great lengths to emphasize the importance of optimizing the effectiveness of the overlap period. My time with flow benches, dynos, and in cylinder pressure measuring gear has shown that what happens during the overlap period, and the first 30 degrees of the intake stroke,

is the making or breaking of a high-output engine.

Using the traces of intake port, cylinder, and exhaust port pressures allows us not only to see, but to refine the intake and exhaust systems of test engines. So, we can feed a CFD program with real-world data, in order to realistically flow the head during the overlap period as well as the entire induction stroke. Tests, such as this, are very cumbersome, and in some respects impossible with a conventional flow bench. For instance, take a look at the interaction of the valve pocket with the valve during the valve's and piston's closest approach in Figure 10.31. Note that air wants to flow off the back face of the valve and into the cylinder.

Unfortunately, the process is short-changed by the fact that the

valve cutout is shrouding the valve at this point. By modifying the valve cutout, as shown in sidebar "Piston Porting" on page 121, additional airflow into the cylinder can be had. I have tried pistons with and without the mods described here. On a nominal 520-hp mule engine, the so-called piston porting looks to be worth about 5 hp. Not much, but that's 5 more that was not there before doing the mod.

Though in a different form, the same applies evxen more so to the tall piston crown on a big-block Chevy. On high-compression pistons, the dome that is near the wall, and is directly in line with the flow out of the intake valve during overlap, shrouds and reduces the flow. The same applies to the approach on the exhaust valve. I won't go into more detail here except to say that if you want to modify big-block Chevys like a pro or better, my big-block Chevy book, *How to Build Max-Performance Chevy Big-Blocks on a Budget*, is what you are looking for.

It takes little imagination to appreciate the huge potential that an affordable virtual flow bench has for serious head development. By the time this book is published, David Woodruff of Design Dreams will be well on the way to having working copies of the virtual flow bench. If you are already into CNC head porting, applying the virtual flow bench is a straightforward job. If not, you need to do some drafting work to draw out what you want to test, or some digitizing on an existing port to create the mesh outline of what you want to test.

Porting for Restricted Motors

Here is a subject that is worth almost a book in its own right. Although I don't claim to be the authority on the subject of restricted intake race engines, those that I have done have always run up front and often as not in the number-one position.

Success in this arena can be summed up as: Whoever, to the greatest extent, defeats the effect of the restriction, wins.

To defeat the effect of the restrictor (carb, plate, or a venturi) as much as possible means communicating cylinder demand to the manifold plenum as efficiently as possible. That is the same requirement of any max-output engine. However, it is worth emphasizing the areas of importance. These are:

- Optimize the exhaust system's effectiveness in terms of chamber scavenging during the overlap.
- Develop the intake port to give the most flow possible (especially at low lift) from an efficient port shape, not from a big area. Velocity probing the intake ports (including the manifold) to find and fill the low-activity areas can help immensely. The intent is to keep port velocity high in the early and late part of the valve opening and closing events.
- Check the intake port's reverse flow. Usually an intake flows better backward than forward. Reduce reverse flow as much as possible by means of a reversion ditch in the intake valve face, similar to the conformation ditch shown in Chapter 8. A similar technique can be used around much of the valve seat in the head.
- Keep the intake temperature as low as possible. Use thermal barriers everywhere the transmission of heat into the intake charge can take place.
- Use a fuel with fewer of the volatile front-end hydrocarbons than normally used for an unrestricted engine. You do not want excessive fuel vaporization to occur in the intake tract because it cuts the engine's volumetric efficiency potential.
- Use as high a CR as possible.

THE COMBUSTION PROCESS

I really wanted to title this chapter "In-Cylinder Turbulence and Combustion Dynamics," but it wouldn't quite fit. Nonetheless, it is where we are going here, because cramming a cylinder full of air is just one aspect of making power. Exactly how it is filled, and what we do with it once filled, still has a great deal to do with the production of power.

Fig. 11.1. Here is one of my mules on the dyno at the University of Northwestern Ohio. This 525-ci stroker build is being put through its paces with the TFX in-cylinder and port-pressure measuring gear. For this three-day test session, I had top-grade help from Randy Lucius and his eager students.

Defining Combustion

Before even getting into our discussion of "in-cylinder mixture dynamics," I want to make sure we are on the same page when it comes to the term combustion, as it relates to the internal combustion engine. I want everybody to understand this, so I offer no apologies for oversimplification. First let's look at the overall, grand scheme of things. Refer back to Figure 1.1 in Chapter 1. It is the summation of everything you need to know about the production of power from an engine.

In the "Long-Block Assembly" area of that illustration, there are more factors to take care of in the "Optimize Cylinder Head Airflow" box than in any other box. To do this we have to take care of the six issues quoted within that box. That is our goal here. And to start with, let's take a very basic look at what goes on in the cylinder.

Burn: Yes, Explode: No

First, the charge in the cylinder does not explode when the plug fires. It burns and the rate at which it burns in no way resembles an explosion. In a NASCAR Cup Car engine at peak RPM, the charge burns at approximately 150 mph across a 4-inch bore. That's slower than the car is usually racing! An explosion is something that ignites at more than 2,000 mph—and dynamite burns a whole lot faster than that. At a 700-rpm idle, the flame speed barely makes 10 mph! This is why we have distributors with ignition advance and advance curves.

"It's an explosion that pushes the piston down the bore." "It's the burning fuel that pushes the piston down the bore, not the air. The air is there just to support combustion." "It's the flame that pushes the piston down the bore." All of these statements are erroneous and demonstrate the fact that a working understanding of what is involved is not common. Before we can go on to look at, and hopefully optimize, the combustion process, we need to understand some basic principles. The easiest way to do that is to start with an external combustion engine, i.e., a steam engine. With this engine, combustion takes place outside, or external to, the working cylinder.

Two factors make a steam engine work: 1.) combustion of a fuel to generate heat and 2.) a working medium. The fuel for heat can be oil, coal, or wood, but in every case, the working medium for a steam engine is steam generated from water. Heating water creates steam at high pressure. This high pressure is then applied to a piston/crank mechanism and turned into motive power. The key factors to note here are: the generation of heat and a working medium.

Let's now consider the internal combustion engine. For "internal combustion," we could substitute "internally generated heat source." Let's do just that. Imagine a cylinder full of air that has been compressed by the piston going to the top of the bore. Instead of burning gasoline to provide the heat, we substitute a piece of thick wire and put a high voltage and several thousand amps through it. Assuming it is suitably sized, the wire acts like a fuse and instantly vaporizes. The heat it produces expands the air (such as what a typical-size V-8 cylinder could do) on this power stroke, and generates about 50 hp.

The interesting thing is that most of what is released from this cylinder is not exhaust but hot air and atomized particles of metal. From this example, we can see that heating the air places the pressure on the piston, and it's the expansion of this hot air that pushes the piston down the bore.

Unlike with a steam engine, which uses air only to provide the oxygen for combustion, the air taken into an internal combustion engine has to serve two purposes: It has to supply the oxygen for combustion and it also has to be the working medium. My point here is that it is the heat of combustion expanding the air that supplies the power. If we could, at the moment after combustion, somehow suck all the heat out of the air in the cylinder, the pressure would immediately drop back to whatever the compression pressure was at that point in the stroke.

So, what we can say for sure at this point is: We need to generate the most heat possible by fully utilizing the heating value of the fuel, and also make sure that, after producing heat, we don't aimlessly squander it. All this falls under two headings: combustion efficiency and thermal efficiency. Let's define these two parameters so we all remain on the same page.

Let's tackle combustion efficiency first. In practice, it's a complex process that involves not only how much of the fuel is burned compared with what should have burned, but also how fast it was burned. Thermal efficiency is the amount of power developed at the flywheel divided

Fig. 11.2. The orange arrow shows the intake port pressure sensor. The green arrow is the equivalent for the exhaust. The blue arrow is the cylinder-pressure measuring sensor that is in the form of a spark plug.

by the amount of power that could have been developed had all the heat energy of the fuel been turned into mechanical work. In this second context it needs to be stated that the compression ratio, as discussed in Chapter 10, is the principal influencing factor toward high thermal efficiency.

Combustion Efficiency

I rarely have access to the sophisticated and diabolically expensive equipment that the big auto makers use to do combustion research. The test gear I have been able to beg, borrow, or steal falls more into the super-equipped hot rodder's category. That being the case, the plan here is to bring to bear what is now my 50-plus years of race engine building and development experience. This means looking at the things we can, as hot rodders, practically apply to make our engines better. There won't be too much SAE-type hardcore (hard to understand and nearly always impossible to apply) stuff, unless we can physically apply the info gleaned from such sources.

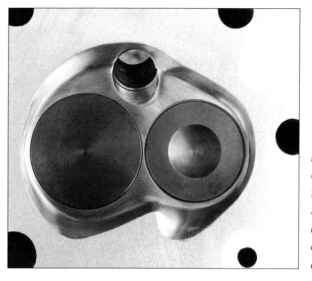

Fig. 11.3. A currently well-developed chamber for the A-Series engine from Swiftune. It has changed dramatically from those early heavily shrouded designs.

A-Series Heads

You recall that my first experiences modifying cylinder heads were with the Weslake-designed A-Series heads for Mini Coopers and the like. As poor flowing as these heads were, though, I learned a valuable lesson about not taking things for granted.

Throughout the 1960s the hot ticket for induction on the A-Series engine was a big side-draft 2-barrel Weber carb. These things really snorted (and that's not a figure of speech). About the late 1960s, the Dell'Orto side-draft carb, which is a Weber look-alike design, began to filter into the UK. The innards looked a lot more sophisticated than its Weber coun-

terpart, and for a given venturi size, these big Dell'Ortos flowed more air. I reasoned that, since it bolted right in the same place as a Weber, a back-to-back dyno test would be about as simple as tests come.

However, before I could get on Tecalamit's dyno in Plymouth, England, I happened to talk to ace Mini racer Richard Longman. Just a week or two before, Richard had used the Tecalamite dyno to test fuel injection and Dell'Orto carburetion versus the Weber on a race engine similar to the one I was going to test. He reported that, on his engine, the Dell'Orto lost 8 of the engine's original 128 hp, and when the change to fuel injection

Fig. 11.4. In-cylinder sensors were historically very expensive but TFX has managed to drastically reduce cost while increasing accuracy and reliability.

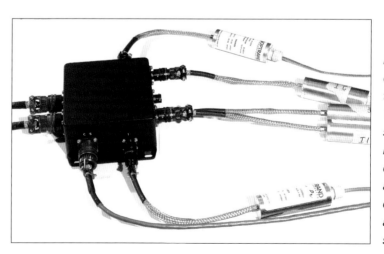

Fig. 11.5. The data acquisition box for the TFX system is small and can be used in the dyno cell and as part of an on-board data acquisition system.

was made, 10 disappeared. Frustrated over why, Richard put the injector nozzles into the Weber carb bodies. Guess what? That engine still lost 10 hp compared to using the carb's own fuel-delivery system.

Although I didn't know why, I thought that the reduced output with the carb/fuel-injection change might be a peculiarity of a Longman-spec engine, so I went ahead and did my own dyno tests. The results mirrored the Longman tests. I now had a burning question that defied an immediate answer: Why did delivering a more finely atomized fuel spray cause the engine to drop so much power? The Weber carb was less effective at atomizing the fuel. In fact, fuel came out of the auxiliary venturi (booster venturi) in globs, rather than anything that resembled a spray. Yet that A-Series engine loved it; and to this day, I have never figured out why globs work and even a moderately good spray does not.

The Chrysler Avenger Saga

In 1970, Chrysler UK unveiled an interesting car, the Avenger. And somehow or other, I got involved with the factory, doing development work as an outside contractor. The Avenger was, from the ground up, basically an all-new machine, and came in two- and four-door forms. John Clarke designed the engine and, fortunately for me, he was one of the numerous genius minds I have managed to surround myself with over the years. John had designed an engine intended to be as environmentally friendly as possible, short of having a catalytic converter. The combustion chamber on this engine was, for a modern engine at least, unconventional. It was formed by the piston stopping about 1/4 inch

short of the top of the bore. The head itself had no chamber; it was flat. It was, in fact, a quenchless chamber.

The intake ports on this head, which were on the same side as the exhaust ports, were very strong on flow. I was supplied one of these cars for my research. It was a two-door GT with 7 miles on it. Later that year, Chrysler brought out a hopped-up version of this car, equipped with twin side-draft Webers and a ported head. This, together with some suspension upgrades and styling mods, was introduced as the Avenger Tiger. It was destined to go head to head with Ford's Lotus Cortina. Although it matched the Lotus Cortina for handling, braking, and cornering, it lacked the power to out drag it.

Anyway, back to the Avenger GT that I had to work with. To get a good part-throttle burn and clean exhaust from the intake charge, the twin 1½-inch Strombergs were heated. This was achieved by having the intake manifold bolted to

the exhaust manifold. Between the two was a 1/16-inch-thick plate with a hole in it. Through this hole the exhaust flame physically played onto the underside of the intake, forming a very hot spot. This, at part throttle, was more than sufficiently hot for vaporizing all of the fuel at any sane street or highway driving speeds.

Okay, this might sound like stock boring stuff, but now we come to the point of the matter. My first discovery was that if the hot spot was semi-eliminated, by replacing the 1/16-inch-thick plate with a hole in it by similar plates with no holes, the power dropped from 78 rear-wheel hp to 74, even though the charge temperature dropped by some 40 degrees. With a quenchless chamber, I had vaguely suspected this might be the case.

This in turn suggested that this type of chamber needed to have a fair amount of vaporized fuel and the rest delivered in really well atomized form. How I figured out the ideal setup for

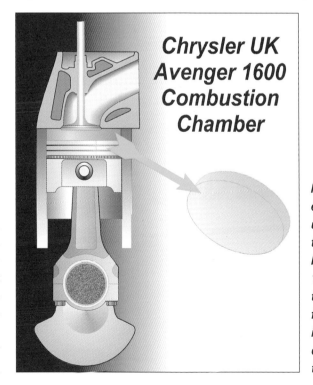

Chrysler UK Avenger 1600 Combustion Chamber

Fig. 11.6. Chrysler's Avenger engine was somewhat unorthodox; the combustion chamber was formed by a piston stopping about 1/4 inch from the deck of the block, topped off with a flat chamberless head. The intake port was a sound design and could be ported to give very good flow.

the intake and optimal output for the engine is what I next explain.

This was the year (1972) I had planned on drag racing the car at Santa Pod Raceway, England, in a class that can best be described as "improved street stock." This class allowed the head to be ported. Any intake and carb combination that was available off the dealer's shelf could also be used. A race exhaust system was permitted. The cam, valvetrain, and everything else below the block deck face had to remain stock.

The factory offered a twin side-draft 40 DCOE Weber kit for this car, which Chrysler's race team manager, the late Des O'Dell, gave to me to test. Knowing that this engine liked fine fuel atomization and that the Dell'Orto DHLA carb delivered much finer fuel atomization, I tried a set, along with the Webers, on the chassis dyno. The difference between the finer fuel atomization of the Dell'Ortos and the more blob-like delivery of the Webers produced a night-and-day difference on the dyno.

I wrote a story about the test involving these two brands of carb and Weber's UK boss apparently went ballistic—told people I did not know what I was talking about, the tests were rigged, etc. He sounded one step shy of putting out a hit contract on me!

The first drag race I did with the Avenger was somewhat amusing. I turned up at the track with this car, viewed by 99 percent of racers at the time as a genuine grocery getter, and the jokes were rampant. Yep, I was the guy to laugh at, before the racing started. After easily putting everyone on the trailer, there weren't even any smiles as far as I could see. Even 1,600-cc four-valve-per-cylinder Cosworth BDA Escorts went down to my two-valve 1,500-cc pushrod, all-iron-engine Avenger.

I continued to develop this engine and, by the end of the year, had it running really well by paying close attention to mixture and ignition properties as well as overall airflow. The useful powerband was from 400 to 8,000 rpm (that is not a misprint). This engine had punch everywhere between those two numbers, and it had awesome torque even by today's standards. It also put any VVT Honda to shame for shear drivability.

Clive Richardson, of the UK's *Motoring News*, conducted a road test and it showed this car capable of 0 to 60 mph in just less than 6 seconds and 0 to 100 mph in 17 seconds. Another test done by *Motor Magazine* at the Lindley proving ground just outside Coventry, England, showed how strong the Avenger's super-wide powerband was. When compared to the figures delivered by a Ford Cosworth BDA Escort, the "through the gears" acceleration was significantly better (more than 1 second faster to 60, and 3 seconds faster to 100). Also the high-gear 20 to 40, 30 to 50, and 40 to 60 times were so much faster than the Cosworth that *Motor Magazine* did not publish them. The Avenger pulled hard from a little faster than 10 mph in high gear. The Cosworth Escort did not pull down low enough to even do the 20 to 40 high-gear test.

After the story came out, I asked why the "in gear" numbers had not been published. The answer I got was, "If the guys at Cosworth read this they will already be embarrassed enough that a two-valve pushrod engine was faster through the gears; do you want to embarrass them further?" I did not answer that, but I really wish those numbers had been published because this engine was

Fig. 11.7. I so often have people tell me what I can't do. In this instance it was win a drag race championship with a Chrysler Avenger. I was also told sedans don't have what it takes to do flame burnouts!

Fig. 11.8. A spectator took this snapshot from the stands with a long lens. After being boxed in at the start at P4 (there were two 350 Z28s and a 3.4-liter injected BMW in front of my 1,600-cc Avenger) I was relegated to last into turn-one. This is on lap five and I have just taken the class lead from the previous year's champ, Bill Sydenham. Having a better understanding of the combustion dynamics gave me a clear 30-hp advantage.

not about outright peak numbers, but rather a huge power-band width and superb drivability.

So what produced the Avenger engine's steam-engine-like low-speed torque, along with its race winning top end? It was not small intake valves as some testers suggested. It was not a reconfiguration of the engine's big bore/short stroke to a small bore/long stroke. Nor was it countless other erroneous tales of moves that are supposed to produce a torquey engine.

The real-world factors that made this engine successful were as follows. First, the head flowed air very well, especially at low lift. And I used as much swirl as I could find, although it was still only about average in that respect. Second, its valves used almost the entire cylinder diameter. Because this was a short-stroke engine, the bore was big for a 1,500-cc unit, and that meant the valves were too. Third, and a very important factor on the list, the engine's ports were the appropriate size. Great attention was given to the twin 2-barrel side-draft Dell'Orto 40 DHLA carb's auxiliary venturis, to ensure a uniformly

fine fuel atomization. Also the independent runner induction (one barrel per cylinder) and a well-spec'd exhaust system (in terms of lengths, diameters, etc.) provided exceptional induction and exhaust.

This total package produced, even at very low RPM, a highly combustible mixture in the engine's quenchless chamber. Frosting on the cake came from a diligent calibration of the mechanical and vacuum advance delivered by the distributor. If I had to isolate one factor that contributed to this engine's wide-ranging performance, it has to be its obviously superior in-cylinder mixture dynamics.

Sifting Through the Data

Let's take stock of where we are. The first engine we looked at, the Mini's A-Series, liked big lumps of fuel while the second, the Avenger engine, liked really small droplets. What this suggests is that there is not a clear-cut route to producing the best approach to optimum in-cylinder combustion dynamics.

At this point, you might wonder if the Chrysler Avenger's quenchless-chamber engine was something

of an enigma. Were we fixing some inherent shortcomings, such as the quenchless combustion chamber, to show results that were very positive on this engine but less likely to show on more conventional engines? Well, that could be. But if this engine was, so to speak, acting as a magnifying glass on combustion dynamics, it is still a good tool with which to work. However, later on, it was found that this seemingly odd-ball engine was not so far from a mainstream case as might have been first believed.

British Touring Car Championship Year

After a dazzling show of speed (beating cars of twice the displacement) during the last few races of the previous year, Chrysler's race boss, Des O'Dell, put his support behind the Vizard three-man team. He gave us a car and all the factory parts we needed to build a BTCC car, which is a championship for a manufacturer's title and is contested on an international level. It's a bit like having NASCAR Cup Car racing with every major world manufacturer competing. We were up against twin-cam engines of Alfa Romeo, Lancia, Renault, and Toyota as well as the big bucks of Ford Motor Company, General Motors, and the like.

How did we do? We came out of the gate fast. By about the fourth race, our 2-buck, all-iron, pushrod-powered grocery getter was by far better than the competition's cost-no-object, twin-cam sports specials. Did we win any races? Hell, no!

Our competition's engines barely made 7,500 rpm. Our first engine of the year had a shift point of 8,800! By the middle of the season we were turning this pushrod engine to 10,500 and, between two corners at Brands Hatch, to 11,000 rpm. What that meant was during our test sessions (i.e., the race) we broke about one each of every part that could break. Sure, we had the fix by the following race, but that did not exactly help our cause that day.

Also we were running the races as part-timers. From Monday to Thursday, 8 am to 6 pm, we all had full-time jobs. From 7 pm until 1 or 2 am in the morning and Thursday through Sunday evenings, we either worked on the car or raced. Our budget for the year was less than what most teams spent per race. By the end of the year our team had managed a second place plus a couple of thirds, a class pole, and maybe half a dozen fastest laps. During six races the car had broken in a new engine in practice to put it on the grid on either the last row or the second to last row.

Sounds bad at this point, but we were learning and getting better all the time. The good part is that before the end of the first lap my Avenger was either first or second! I said the car was fast, and fast

is exactly what I meant. So where did all this speed come from? Just as before, no one thing in general, but I can say that cylinder head flow was important. Low-lift flow (very important) was significant, along with cam design (critical), exhaust (big priority), and mixture characteristics and combustion dynamics (of great importance). Let's start with mixture characteristics.

Weber Revamp

The homologated (that means the ones the as-manufactured car is supposed to have) carbs of the year for the Avenger being run were a pair of side-draft 40-mm Weber DCOEs. These came equipped with 30-mm main venturis. The rules allowed a change of main venturis for any design we wanted, but the hole could be no larger than 30 mm. Also the auxiliary (booster) venturi was free. This gave me scope to make new auxiliary venturis based on what I had learned from the Dell'Orto. The result was an average of about 5 ft-lbs of additional torque throughout the entire RPM range. Peak power, which

occurred right around 8,000 rpm, was up by about 7 hp. This increased output was better than anything that could be built using off-the-shelf Weber parts. At this point, I concluded that I had achieved about as good a fuel atomization as the engine needed, so I turned to the cylinder head.

At the time, the BTCC rules and regulations called for a stock valve lift, which in this instance was a menial 0.390 inch. This meant intake valve acceleration and flow, especially from low lift, became vitally important. In fact, this is just one more incident where high flow at low lift won the day and did not, as is so often claimed, cost power.

F1 engine manufacturers Cosworth and Judd were my competition in the cylinder head department. I won't go into too much detail here because combustion dynamics is the subject but, suffice it to say, the low-lift flow on my head was about 30 percent more at 0.050 than the Cosworth head while the full-lift flow was identical. Although there is more to it than just low-lift flow, it's

Fig. 11.10. There are always horses-for-courses. As impressive as this Pierce Weber setup is for a small-block Chevy, the 40 DCOE Weber variant was far from matching the 40 DHLA Dell'Ortos on the quench-less chamber of a 1,600-cc Chrysler Avenger engine.

worth noting that my Avenger head, on this 1,600-cc engine, made 11 hp more than the Cosworth modified head!

Critical Port Finish

Probably because of its quenchless chamber and the need for a homogeneous and well-atomized fuel mix, the Avenger's intake port size and finish was critical. In this instance I used a port that was a full 1/4 inch smaller in diameter than the ones used in the Cosworth or Judd heads. Also, unlike the fine finish of my competition's heads, my ports were rough by virtue of a 40- and 60-grit emery roll finish. This reduced the tendency of the fuel to coagulate and form rivulets prior to entering the cylinder. Notice I say it "reduced" the tendency; it did not cure it by any means—just made it a lot better. (See Chapter 4 for more info about wet flow and how to minimize it.)

Finally: The Chambers

After all the discussion on the carb's air/fuel mixture preparation capabilities, let's examine the port size and finish and the valve flow characteristics. The scene is set for us to look at the combustion chambers. The Avenger's open chamber looked nauseatingly simple and I felt, since emissions were of no concern, it must be possible to do a better job in terms of power.

As it happens, the rules specified such things as valve size, compression ratio, etc., but did not specify combustion chamber shape. So I started by finding the heaviest pistons (there was a minimum-weight limit and factory-original pistons had to be used) and bringing them

down to weight by machining the piston crown. This allowed the top ring to be nearer the piston crown, thereby cutting the ring land crevice volume. That little space is way more influential than you may suspect.

Along with the piston mod, I also investigated the chamber form for flow efficiency. On the flow bench, I found that better flow, especially at low lift, could be had by forming a shallow chamber around the intake and exhaust valves. This necessitated machining the top of the block to get back to the 9.9:1 (as I remember) CR called for. This move was done a step at a time from one build to another.

We were essentially building, for race and R&D combined, about one-and-a-half engines per race. Each time a build or rebuild was done the chamber volume in the head was increased. And as the chamber increased in volume, the block volume was reduced by machining the block deck. Each time we did this the package more closely approached a conventional chamber with squish.

At each new spec, 0.020-inch more material had to come off the top of the block to bring the CR back up to 9.9:1, and each time we

saw more power. When the situation got to where the piston was 0.080 down the bore and producing the best results to date, I decided that it looked worthwhile to go whole hog and put the entire combustion chamber into the head and deck the block for a tight quench, rather than possibly do four more builds to get there. The results on the dyno were just shy of startling. If all had followed previous form, I would have expected about 6 hp more from this combo; instead it was 8 fewer!

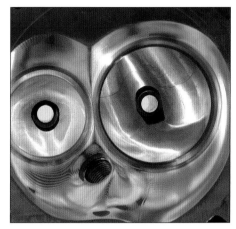

Fig. 11.11. There is more to the combustion chamber than that which resides in the cylinder head. Not only is it necessary to take care of business prior to mixture arrival at the cylinder but also after the charge is trapped within the cylinder.

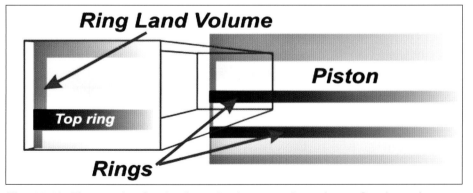

Fig. 11.12. The top ring land volume is also a crevice volume. Crevice volumes are bad news for power, mileage, and emissions and need to be minimized as much as possible.

More Combustion Curiosities

If the love of big fuel droplets for apparently the best combustion dynamics with the Mini Cooper engines intrigued you, here's another somewhat mystifying combustion-dynamics case concerning, again, a Mini engine. After a successful season with a 1,293-cc Mini Cooper S hill-climber (finished second in championship and only narrowly missed first spot due to a priority problem; driver/owner went off on a honeymoon and missed a round), my client asked if I would build him a blown, bored, stroked, and generally no-holds-barred version of this engine. I did just that—I stretched capacity to 1,442 cc and installed a large Shorrock supercharger. Just so that we did not have to use an intercooler (there was no room), I limited boost to about 12 psi.

Dyno testing was to be on a chassis dyno. The successful engine from the previous year made an even 100 hp at the front wheels. After a huge outlay of cash by the owner, a break-in period, and a change of oil and plugs to a race-grade type, the engine was given its first wrestling match with the dyno. This resulted in only 85 hp in spite of the 12 pounds of boost going into this big A-Series engine. This was embarrassing to say the least. The owner was standing right there watching and here my partner Mike Lane and I were, with a car that sounded for all the world like it could break the unlimited land speed record, yet it was way down on even a conservative estimate of what it should make.

Mike and I dove into a search for all the likely causes of this awesome-noise-but-no-power deal. We diligently checked ignition timing, valve

lash, ignition box, etc. All were okay. At several points along the way we made dyno runs but with the same results—about 85 hp. Finally, we got all the way down to pulling the front end off the engine to check cam timing. It was right where we thought it should be.

During re-assembly, the engine was inadvertently flooded. With the engine virtually cold, it may not have fired up too well on those super-cold-grade plugs. If they were also wet it certainly wasn't going to be that happy from a cold start. So we pulled the wet Champion race plugs and installed an equivalent heat range of dry Autolite race plugs.

When fired up, the engine sounded no more or no less wicked than before but the dyno numbers were—at 142 hp—nothing short of a techno shock. Although a pleasant surprise, it was very much a case of "What in the world is going on here?" This was such a surprise that the Champions were re-installed and re-tested. Same killer sound—just 85 hp!

I have to tell you that in just about every other Mini application the Champion plugs were as good as, or better than, anything we could find but here was an anomaly. This engine apparently did not like anything with Champion written on it. So with no further ado we went on, with the Autolite plugs installed, to finely tune the big carb on the engine and get the timing right on the money.

After three hours, we had the ignition and carb dialed in, and this engine ended up pumping out 170-plus-hp at the wheels. I had hoped for about 185, but that's dyno testing for you—it's a lens to focus on reality. This may not always be as

gratifying as fantasy but, regardless of positive or negative results, you do get to learn a lot more about what it takes to win races. And even though it was less than what I had hoped for, this Mini won our driver the class championship.

Failure Highlighting?

So why am I highlighting these negative results? Simple. I want to emphasize that the subject we are dealing with here is anything but simple. I had no idea why power dropped in the instances I have just mentioned and here, with more than 45 years and tens of thousands of dyno tests later, and I still don't have an answer.

In the Chrysler Avenger instance the results, in terms of quench clearance, were about 180 degrees opposed to all the other tests I have been involved with. This Avenger engine liked to have the piston stop 0.120 inch shy of the head face (0.080 down the hole plus a 0.040 head gasket) for best results. For just about every other engine I have tested like

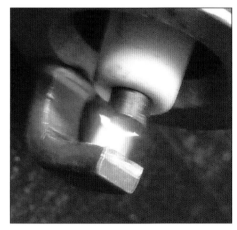

Fig. 11.13. This spark form can be expected in a cylinder with low-mixture motion. In this instance, the required arc length in order to extend from one electrode to the other is about the width of the plug gap.

this, that piston-to-quench surface gap is about the worst in terms of low-detonation resistance and poor combustion. It really begs the question of whether or not we can give an engine too much or too aggressive a quench action. The answer is—yes!

Take a look at Figure 11.13, which shows a spark jumping a gap in a chamber with low mixture motion. You can see that the length of the spark is barely more than the plug gap width. If the mixture motion is high, the spark becomes distended because it cannot take a direct route from one electrode to the other. The result is the spark has to break down a longer path through the mixture to strike an arc. In other words, it's just like the plug gap has become bigger. If the ignition system is able to fire the plug, the distended spark produced starts off a larger and more aggressive flame kernel. This is more effective because it lights off the charge faster and more effectively. If the spark is not of high enough voltage to strike an arc, a misfire results and power drops.

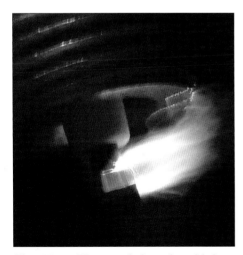

Fig. 11.14. The spark form in a high-swirl combustion chamber. Note that the length of the arc is about 1/2 inch. If the ignition cannot fire a 1/2-inch gap, the cylinder fails to produce.

Atomization Optimization

It is easy to jump to the conclusion that the better the atomization, the better the power output. If only it were that easy! In reality it is far more accurate (but still not 100-percent true) to say: The better the fuel is finely atomized (and/or vaporized), the better the brake specific fuel consumption (BSFC) is. This number should not, as is so often the case (even with pro engine builders) be confused as an indicator of the mixture ratio. It is only roughly connected to the mixture and is in no way a measurement of mixture ratio. In other words, it's only a consequence of the ratio.

At this point the question is: "Can the fuel be atomized and vaporized too much?" Let me set the scene. It's about 1977 and I am just starting testing on some of the trick carbs built by Tucson's premier carb builder/designer, Dave Braswell. The year before, at the 1976 SEMA show, I got to talk with Holley's then–chief engineer Mike Urich. In our conversation I was amazed to find that, as far as Mike knew, Holley had done no official research on the effects of booster design on fuel atomization. I mentioned this somewhat surprising tidbit of info to Dave Braswell and he immediately volunteered assistance and carbs to do some testing on what

we perceived as a typical street-tuned small-block Chevy. Here is how things unfolded.

The tests involved two carbs; each was about 750 to 800 cfm. One had high-gain fine-fuel-spray dog-leg-style boosters, and the other had typical low-gain coarser-spraying straight-leg boosters.

The engine was run with three intake manifold types. The first was the stock exhaust, heated, and consequently hot-running intake. The second was an aftermarket two-plane aluminum intake with the heat crossover blocked off. The last was a Victor Jr. intake, which, as an air-gap-style intake, was even more significantly cooler running.

On the stock intake, which was also the hottest by far, the tricked-up Braswell carb with its small fuel droplets lagged behind the nearer stock carb by 8 hp (on a nominal 360-horse engine), but the fine-fuel spray delivered by the trick booster carb produced, by a small margin, the best BSFC both at wide-open throttle and part-throttle cruise. On the heat-blocked aftermarket two-plane intake, the carbs were very

Fig. 11.15. Here are some typical Holley boosters.

Fig. 11.16. Since the Holley carb is used on more race engines than probably all other brands put together, I am going to use it as an example of fuel atomization versus booster (auxiliary venturi) style.

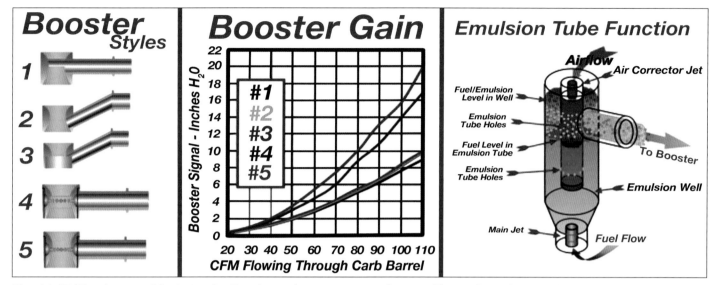

Fig. 11.17. The degree of fuel atomization depends on numerous factors. The main tools to work with here are the booster's gain, the air corrector size, and the hole pattern on the emulsion tube of the carb.

close in terms of output, but we are still considering a relatively hot-running manifold here.

The BSFC with the fine-fuel-droplet booster carb was as much as 8 percent better, especially at part throttle. On the cool-running Victor Jr., the finely atomizing booster-equipped carb was unbeatable everywhere in the RPM range. It made about 12 hp more, and the brake specifics were all better (lower) numbers by a substantial margin.

So what does this tell us? The results indicate that there is an optimum fuel-droplet size that balances the need for some vaporization against the need to not evaporate too much fuel and spoil the engine's volumetric efficiency (VE). Hot-running engines can offset the negatives of big fuel droplets from the boosters but cold ones cannot. Cold intakes need the ratio of the fuel droplet's surface-area-to-volume ratio increased (which is just what happens as the fuel droplets get smaller), so that the loss of the heat as a vaporization source is compensated for by increases in the fuel's evaporative surface area.

Atomization in Practice

In the early 1990s I became involved with booster development with the Carb Shop in California. The plan was to develop a Super Booster that not only gave a big signal but also did not obstruct the airflow of the main venturi to any greater extent than a regular high-performance booster. If a high-gain booster can be used it means that, for any given application, a bigger carb can be used for more top end before drivability and low-speed output suffer.

Well, the program produced some trick-looking high-gain boosters, which found their way (unknown to me) into the carb(s) of a front-running NASCAR Cup Car team. On the dyno in the crisp December days just before Christmas in Mooresville, North Carolina (the ancestral home of all Cup Car teams), these boosters paid off in the team's Daytona 500 engines to the tune of about 10 hp. So, with great expectations, the team headed off in early January for the Daytona 500 in Florida.

It was hotter than usual that January in a normally hot Florida.

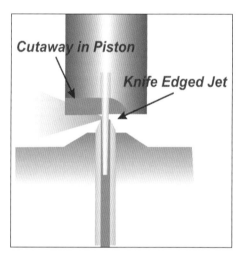

Fig. 11.18. The simple high fuel atomization mods I did to the Constant Vacuum Strombergs as fitted to the Chrysler Avenger GT. As simple as these mods were, they netted no less than 12 hp to this 1,600-cc engine output—mostly in terms of added torque.

With the new carb, the car was well off the pace. In frustration, the team replaced the trick booster carb with the old one, and the car immediately ran on the money. The lesson here is that you can absolutely guarantee that too much of a seemingly good thing is—not so good. The percentage of fuel atomizing prior to entering the cylinder was such that any gains in better combustion were overridden by the drop in VE caused by the added fuel vaporization taking place within the intake manifold.

So when is a high-gain booster any good to a race car engine? Rarely, if ever, as things stood for a typical Cup Car engine of the early 1990s—but let's move on.

Thermal Barriers

In the early 1990s, I was heavily involved in thermal barriers. It's something I have looked at on and off since my Formula Ford days in the late 1960s. We found a temporary 2 hp (it barely lasted a race) by using high-temp exhaust paint on the pistons (Sperex, I believe). In this case, a relatively extensive study was made of the effect of thermal barriers in race intake manifolds.

Using a single 4-barrel carb on a single-plane intake, the effects of various boosters with the intake were explored both with the intake runners raw (uncoated) and then with them coated with a thermal barrier. The booster that worked best with the raw runners was of the stepped dog-leg variety shown in Figure 11.17. When the manifold was coated and used in conjunction with this booster, the power figures were within about a horsepower or so of unchanged.

So what's the deal here? With the raw ports and mixture temps measured on the number-2 runner we saw, from a carb intake temp of 84 degrees F, a drop to 55 degrees F due to the evaporation of a portion of the fuel. By dividing the plenum front to back and using one end of the engine to drive the other (and no fuel to the front float bowl), we found that the air at number-2, without any fuel, picked up (allowing for a few corrections) about 10 degrees of manifold heat (more at low RPM and less at high). With the coated manifold, the engine's number-2 intake runner temp was between 5 and 8 degrees less.

So the thermal barrier was doing what it was supposed to do, which was keep heat out of the intake charge. What was not happening here was any evidence of any increased power due to the cooler charge. When the charge temperature was measured on a functioning number-2 cylinder, the drop in temperature from the carb to the head/manifold interface of the number-2 runner was only barely changed; and if everything had been working as before, it should have been at least 5 degrees cooler. This indicated that the cooler-running intake was not allowing as much fuel to vaporize and, therefore, the added wet fuel arriving at the cylinder was compromising the combustion process.

At this point, we installed high-gain annular discharge boosters along with appropriate (bigger) air correctors. With the same air/fuel ratio, the better atomization restored the percentage of vaporized fuel entering the cylinder. The temperature at the number-2 runner with an air/fuel mixture passing through dropped to 49 degrees F.

The dyno also showed some meaningful gains at this point. Essentially, the cooler-running, more finely atomized charge had the effect of moving the entire torque curve in an upward direction. On a nominal 450-hp engine, the torque at 3,000 rpm rose by 11 ft-lbs (6.3 hp) and by 7 ft-lbs at 6,200 rpm (8.3 hp).

Swirl and Quench

Swirl (and in the case of a four-valve engine, tumble) and quench both introduce mixture motion to the charge trapped in the cylinder. At the beginning of this chapter, I discussed the combustion speeds seen within a typical running engine and pointed out they were probably a lot slower than might be expected. This is where swirl, tumble, and quench begin to play a vital part. Just how vital is shown by a test I did many years ago that, looking back, I wish I had done on a more comprehensive level. But hindsight is always 20/20, so here is what I did learn. The test

Fig. 11.19. This thermal barrier coating added power for this race-winning head I ported for a 2-liter Mitsubishi engine, and it also extended its life from about 20 passes to more than 100.

engine was the almost inevitable small-block Chevy. This was just a mule engine and had a relatively short cam, cast pistons, a 9.025-inch-deck-height block giving about a 0.060-inch quench (a little on the wide side of optimal), and an 8.6:1 CR.

Flow testing the head on the flow bench, I found I could block off about 1/8 inch of the port on one side (cylinder-center side) and have good swirl, but doing the same on the other side (cylinder-wall side) produced poor swirl.

In each instance, the flow was about the same. I ran the tests with an exhaust-heated intake manifold with the heat on, to minimize any effect of any possible changes in wet-flow characteristics. On the 305 test engine, the torque output at 2,250 rpm (that was as low as I could go on the dyno) increased 30 ft-lbs with the higher-swirl port. As RPM rose, the two torque curves got closer. But in this instance, the low-swirl port con-figuration never got to be as much as the high-swirl. From this, you can see that at low RPM mixture motion is important.

It is also of interest that at low RPM (2,250) the best timing was as much as 5 degrees less with the high-swirl port/chamber than the low-swirl one. At peak RPM, the total timing was not that much different, with 30 degrees for the high-swirl and 32 degrees for the low-swirl.

As RPM increases, the situation can change. First, if an engine has a fuel system that is delivering some-what larger fuel droplets than might be optimal, high swirl can centrifuge, or spin, the fuel onto the cylinder wall, thus depriving the main body of the charge of fuel. That places even more fuel in the crevice volume and a leaner-than-supposed mixture during the bulk of the combustion cycle. Neither scenario is good for output or fuel economy.

The lesson here is that higher swirl values in high-RPM engines need to be accompanied by good mixture preparation. When RPM numbers and piston speed get to those typically seen in race engines, the charge is substantially agitated, so the need to add mixture motion becomes less of an issue. However, my experience is that at least a small amount of swirl is a positive, even in a 10,000-rpm 500-ci Pro Stock engine. I can't say if that carries over to a multi-valve F1-style engine. My first thought is probably not; but prob-ably not many of you are designing and building them, so it's not some-thing I am going to worry about.

For a multi-valve engine, the natural tendency is for the charge to tumble as it enters the cylinder.

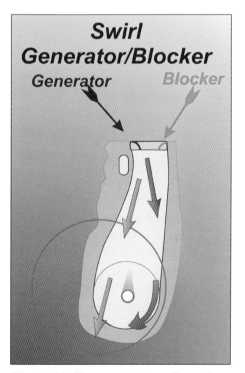

Fig. 11.20. The port test configuration for the high-swirl/low-swirl dyno test in Figure 11.21.

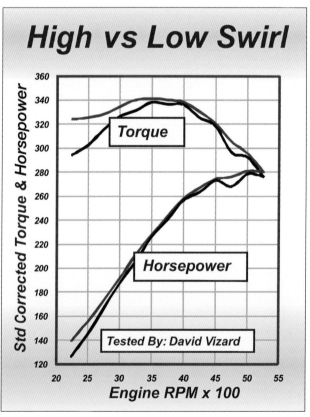

Fig. 11.21. Here is how the output curves fell with high swirl (red curves) versus almost no swirl (black curves).

This is okay, but there is a difference in the way port-induced mixture motion reacts as the piston comes up the bore. By compressing a rotating charge into a combustion space of less diameter/area than the bore (as is usually the case), due to the law of conservation of angular momentum, the swirl can actually increase in value. In contrast, the higher the compression goes, the more the tumble motion is suppressed. At CRs of 11:1 or more, any tumble that existed when the piston was at the bottom of the stroke is largely gone. This is one of the reasons I worked so diligently to generate meaningful swirl on the PolyQuad chamber head described in Chapter 10.

More Thermal Management

From the discussion above, it has become evident that thermal barrier coatings may have more to offer than might initially have been thought. But I have not finished this subject yet. I have worked with many of the leading companies, such as Swain Tech, Tech Line Coatings, and Polydyne Coatings over the years, but since about 2002, I spent a lot of time working with Calico Coatings. It has a great nearby facility and I can go to discuss whatever experiments I am into at that time. Without exception,

the company has been ready to help in such tests and that has allowed me to move along on coating tests at a rate that was otherwise not possible. That is not to say those other companies have not contributed here. As this is being written, I am involved in some interesting experiments with Tech Line Coatings.

On the subject of in-cylinder combustion dynamics, we can say that for a given fuel, ambient weather conditions, and a host of other factors, there is a certain ratio of wet-to-vaporized fuel that is optimum for best output. Based on everything we have discussed to date, we can say that keeping the fuel in suitably small droplets, allowing only a given percentage to vaporize, and avoiding wet-flow streams as far as possible is a major factor toward increased power from an engine (other than a Mini).

But before we wind up, there's one more point to make. All the measurements of the intake charge temperatures were done at the intake-manifold to cylinder-head interface. But heated or not, the fact is the intake manifold is not usually the greatest source of heat input into the charge.

A case comes to mind here, which occurred about 1990 during some tests I did for Cosworth with a 2,000-cc BDP Midget sprint

car engine. I had reason to turn off the dyno cell lights for a photo of the nearly white-hot exhausts seen during a run on this 280- to 281-hp injected engine.

Being in the dyno cell with an engine turning 8,500-plus rpm can be a little unnerving, but as I walked past the deafening intake I realized that I could see, down the intake stacks, the intake valves glowing very dull red. At this point, it had not occurred to me just how hot the intake valves could get. But consider this: Because the intake valves are of greater area than the exhaust they pick up, during the combustion cycle at least, the intake produces more BTUs of heat than the exhaust. And where do they dump a whole load of this heat? You guessed it—they put it right into the intake charge.

This results in one positive and one negative. First the positive: The fuel is further vaporized before entering the cylinder, yet by how much I have little idea. The negative: The intake charge is heated and that is not so good. So I considered what the tradeoff was between these possibly competing factors. Sometime later we pulled the head on a duplicate engine and coated only the intake valves. A week later the results were in.

First, a look down the intake stacks in a darkened cell revealed that the valves were no longer visibly glowing. I fully realize that this is hardly a scientific way to measure the valve temperature, but observation was all I had. The fact they were no longer visibly glowing meant, at a good estimate, they were probably a hundred degrees or so cooler. Second, power figures were up from the low-280s to the mid-280s with the coated valves.

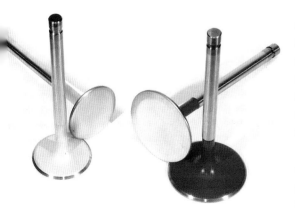

Fig. 11.22. If you have to pick one single element of the induction/exhaust of the head, coat the valves. Here, you see the Calico Coatings treatment to the intake and exhaust valves of one of my 5.0 Mustang racers. The biggest power influence is the face of the intake valve because it cuts heat going into the intake charge.

We can see an increase in power with high-pressure fuel injection and line-of-sight ports exiting into an open area of a combustion chamber and when there is no chamber wall directly in the path of the entering charge. Are the wet-flow dynamics of a typical two-valve V-8 head likely to deliver similar results? Or do we need to see greater fuel shredding at the seat and/or greater heat input to vaporize more of the charge, by this or other means, in order to get the benefits of cooler intake valves? That, along with crevice volumes, is what we examine next.

Small Crevice Volume– Big Consequences

In most instances, crevice volumes, such as the one between the top ring land and cylinder bore wall (see Figure 11.26), look insignificant, and that is why this power-robbing element of the combustion chamber is so easily overlooked. Crevice volumes are the stealthy thieves of those few horsepower that can so often make the difference between you winning the race or not. However, before we investigate the disproportionately negative effect crevice volumes can

have, I need to establish exactly what defines a crevice volume.

The worst crevice volume is that contained within the piston's top ring land. But this, is not the only crevice volume that we have to contend with. A combustion chamber with a sharp corner between the floor of the chamber and the chamber wall is not so good.

Some years ago, I watched a combustion cycle filmed through the wall of a quartz-cylinder engine. It was quite surprising to see that though there was about 1/8-inch radius between the chamber floor and wall, the charge that was immediately in that radius did not burn until much later in the cycle than did the bulk mixture adjacent to it. What this told me is that the floor-to-wall radius in any combustion chamber needs to be as large as possible.

There are also crevices between the edge of the valves and the combustion chamber or cylinder walls. These are the worst on a parallel-valve head, such as we see used in most small-block Chevys, Fords, and Chryslers (but not the new Hemi). Although we need to keep these crevices in mind, the one we need to focus on the most is the top ring land volume.

At this point, you may be thinking that the ring land volume is so small compared to the volume of the rest of the cylinder that it cannot possibly have much influence on anything. At first, it may seem that way, but the opposite is actually closer to the truth.

For an example, consider the cylinder volume of a 350-ci small-block Chevy: 717 cc. To this, we must add the total combustion chamber volume. Assuming a 10:1 CR, this is 89.5 cc. The ring land volume of a typical off-the-shelf high-performance piston for this is right around 2 cc. At the bottom of the compression stroke, the crevice volume within the piston top ring land represents just 0.25 percent of the whole. That's 1/4 of 1 percent!

Now let's take the piston to the top of the bore. Here the volume is now 89.5 cc, and the 2 cc in the top ring land represents not just 1/4 of 1 percent but 2.4 percent. In simple terms, this means that almost 2.5 percent of the inhaled charge now resides in the top ring land crevice volume.

At this point, someone doubting the importance of the crevice volume contained in the top ring land might just start to concede that

RPM	2000	2500	3000	3500	4000	4500	5000	5500	6000	6500
Torque #1	317.8	333.1	375.0	404.8	427.8	430.2	414.6	392.1	361.3	294.1
Torque #2	324.5	339.1	377.6	410.5	432.9	432.9	419.8	398.6	367.4	302.5
Tq. Difference	6.7	6.0	2.6	5.7	5.1	2.7	5.2	6.5	6.1	8.4
HP #1	121.0	158.6	214.2	269.8	325.8	368.6	394.7	410.6	421.8	364.0
HP #2	123.6	161.4	215.7	273.6	329.7	370.9	399.7	417.4	419.7	374.4
HP Difference	2.6	2.8	1.5	3.8	3.9	2.3	5.0	6.8	6.9	10.4
Test #1 is low set ring Test #2 is high set ring										

Fig. 11.23. The power difference between a high set ring (0.150 down from deck) and a low set ring (0.375 down from deck). All this indicates is that crevice volumes are far more influential than their small stature might suggest. To get results this concise, each combination was run seven times with the best and worst thrown out, and the remaining results were averaged.

it's important to minimize the ring land volume. But it is still less than 2.5 percent. You might say "this is insignificant, so let's not fixate on it." But combustion factors in this example are about to change for the worse, as I continue to explain.

As the piston comes up the bore, the ring land volume does not tend to fill with a combustible mixture of fuel and air, but rather a very fuel rich mixture. Any wet flow of fuel that was on the bore walls at the start of the pistons travel cycle up the bore is scraped off by the piston rings. The motion of the piston up the bore and the motion of air and fuel into the ring land volume, as compression takes place, tends to push everything into it rather than letting anything out. By the time the piston has reached the top of the bore, probably half of the ring land volume is raw fuel. As the piston approaches TDC, spark initiates the combustion phase.

Now take a look at Figure 11.24. This is a computer-enhanced version of the photos taken through the transparent walls of a research engine. This was hardly a high-performance engine, but what we learn from it is directly applicable. Using what we see here, we can look at what happens to the mass of burned mixture compared to the volume. First the spark hits at 45-degrees BTDC. Note how the "mass fraction burned" (red curve) progresses very slowly at first. In fact 40 degrees after the spark has fired only about 5 percent of the charge mass has burned.

But take a look at the flame volume in the chamber at TDC. You can see that a lot more than 5 percent of volume has burned. What is happening here is that as the mixture burns, it expands and pushes the remaining unburned volume into a smaller space. This means we have the same type of scenario as we had when the piston was coming up the bore on the compression stroke. As the cylinder pressure rose, a greater amount of charge mass ended up in the top ring land volume. At TDC only 10 percent of the mass has burned, but the burned mixture volume takes up between 60 and 70 percent. Assuming it was all a homogeneous mixture in the cylinder, at TDC, we then have something on the order of 6 percent of the charge now in the ring land volume. That is 2,400 percent more than what was in it when the piston was at BDC!

The mass burned versus the volume burned does not catch up until about 20 degrees after TDC. At this point, the mixture that was compressed into the ring land volume starts to come back out and burn. Also the fuel that was trapped there is released as the piston accelerates down the bore. The mixture that burns is doing so too late in the cycle to contribute a proportionate share of the total energy released. If the entire 6 percent of the mixture that could be contained in the ring land volume were to be burned, it would only contribute about 2 percent of the resulting total energy.

Gas-Ported Pistons

So far we have looked only at regular-style pistons as opposed to race pistons with gas porting to the back of the top ring. Gas porting of pistons does not seem to have caught on in Europe, so for the benefit of those readers, check out Figure 11.25 showing the two common types of gas porting.

The idea behind gas porting is to seal the ring against the bore more effectively. Gas porting does work, but it also increases the crevice volume. So we have to make a thoughtful tradeoff when designing pistons.

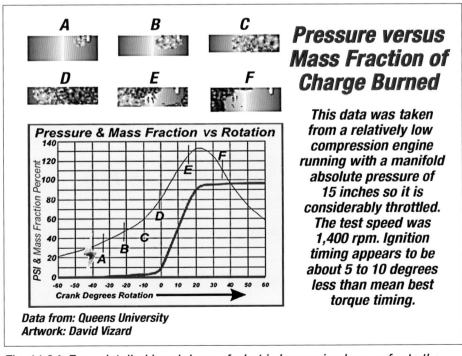

Fig. 11.24. For a detailed breakdown of what is happening here, refer to the text on this page.

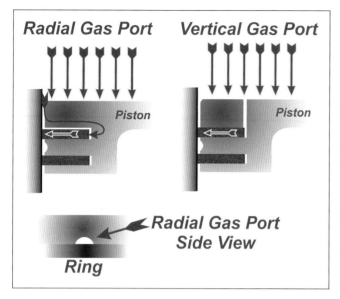

Fig. 11.25. The two common types of gas porting to aid top ring seal. The radial gas ports are the most popular, especially for endurance race engines; they have a significantly less tendency to clog and show less ring/bore wear than the vertical gas ports.

For what it's worth, I favor radial gas ports because they never plug up with carbon deposits.

Piston Dishes

At this juncture, I should point out that as much as, or more than, half the combustion-chamber area resides in the piston. If the piston is to have anything of a cutout other than for the valves, it seems most logical to have the dish located as near as possible, right under the spark plug. As obvious as that may seem, things don't always work out that way and often it's down to dyno testing to see what works.

A test showed that the A-Series Mini Cooper engine preferred a valve cutout combined with the piston chamber that was no more than a plain slot—about 0.080 inch deep right across the piston. This worked better than conventional valve cut-outs and a bowl under the plug, to the tune of 4 hp within 135 hp. Working with Sealed Power many years ago, I had the idea that a dished Chevy piston should have a sloping dish with the bulk of the dish right under the spark plug. This would, in effect,

put more of the charge mass in closer proximity to the plug. It seemed such an obvious move but the 400-horse mule lost more than 10 hp with this style of piston. This shows again that things are not always as they seem when it comes to simple answers for chamber dynamics.

Testing Theory

So far we have mostly looked at the potential power loss from the prime crevice volume. The dyno is now the reference point. First let's consider the eradication of the top ring land volume. During the mid 1970s, the primary topic in the auto-

motive world was the problem emissions were causing in terms of power and fuel economy. In the late 1960s, Sealed Power came out with the Head Land ring. This was a top compression ring that eliminated the top ring land volume. Sales of this ring were really lackluster until the promises of lower emissions prompted a semi-revival in interest. See Figure 11.26.

About 1977, I had the opportunity of doing a back-to-back test between conventional Sealed Power top rings and Sealed Power Head Land rings. My co-conspirators on this test managed to borrow a three-gas analyzer, so we could look at some of the emissions with each style of ring. I have long mislaid the test results, but they were significant enough to stick in my mind. We saw a drop of at least 30 percent of unburned hydrocarbons and a drop of at least 20 percent in carbon monoxide. Since the rings primarily targeted emissions, that was good.

For power production, things were less clear cut. The bottom line here was that low-speed output went up. At about 1,800 rpm (that was as low as the dyno pulled down the test mule), torque was up by a solid 3 percent. At about 3,500 rpm, both styles of top ring were even, and at 5,000

Head Land Ring

This style of top ring has zero ring land crevice volume.

Fig. 11.26. The Sealed Power Head Land ring. Note that it gives a crevice-free piston top. The problems here for a high-output engine are ring mass and the encroachment of valve cutouts on the ring.

rpm the Head Land ring torque was down about 2½ percent. As it happens, we had a simple blow-by gauge hooked up to the crankcase, and this showed that above about 4,000 rpm the Head Land ring was losing its ability to effectively seal. I talked to my friend and then Sealed Power's chief engineer, Cal DeBruin, and he confirmed what we suspected. The mass of the ring and its large face was difficult to control at higher RPM and resulted in an increase in blow-by.

As conclusive as that may seem, it was not the end of the story. Enter Dale Fox, who worked with Smokey Yunick on and off from around 1968 until a few years before he passed in 2000. During 1969 and 1970 Dale worked full time for Smokey, and did a lot of whatever engine building Smokey could not personally find the time for.

Here is how it went for the second round of our look at Head Land rings. For the tests, the forged pistons used Sealed Power's recommended clearances, which turned out to be about 0.005 to 0.006 inch. The width of a Head Land ring meant that to accommodate any rocking of the piston in the bore, the face against the cylinder wall had to be a barrel shape. Dale and Smokey liked the concept of the Head Land ring and, although their first round of testing showed pretty similar results to those I ran, they stuck with the concept. What they did was to see if they could cut piston clearances to a minimum, and thereby reduce the rocking of the piston in an effort to help seal everything. Their efforts paid off; they managed to get the ring to work much further up the RPM range. Remember, back then most endurance engines did not turn much in excess of 7,500 rpm.

So Far, What Have We Proved?

At this point we can say that eliminating the top ring groove crevice has proved that output can benefit. Other than minimizing clearances as Dale Fox and Smokey Yunick did, it is not quite obvious how we can implement the Head Land ring principle in an extreme high-RPM engine. Maybe, if the ring was made of titanium, weighing no more than a conventional steel ring, it would work up to a much higher RPM. Yes, I realize that someone is going to say that titanium is the most seize-able material on the planet and barely stops short of welding itself to ice when it's rubbed against it.

The good news, if anyone is interested, is that I know how to make titanium into a better bearing material than phosphor bronze. This has allowed the production of Ti wrist pins (gudgeon pins if you live in England) that have no coating, are about twice as seize-resistant as tool steel pins, and have a Rockwell hardness of about 76. But I digress; so far I have not been in a position to do anything with respect to a Ti ring, but there are some moves employing more conventional approaches toward the reduction of the top ring land volume.

Sometime in 1978, I was at lunch with Pro Stock and engine building legend Bill "Grumpy" Jenkins, and the conversation turned to the subject of the top ring's position in relation to the crown of the piston. Grumpy told me of the differences he had seen on a Pro-Stock-style, small-block Chevy. After my experience with the Head Land ring, I put a back-to-back test of a low-set top ring versus a high-set at the top of a long to-do list.

The problem was I needed to get a piston manufacturer to make two sets of pistons, for free and for no other reason than to establish what the difference might be. This opportunity came about when Moe Mills decided to leave Arias Pistons and, with a partner, start Ross Racing Pistons. Here, Moe made me two sets of pistons with valve cutouts minimized for the 280-degree (off-the-seat-duration) cam that was to be used.

The valve cutout depth is an important factor for an inclined-valve engine such as a small-block Chevy because the cutout can easily intersect with the ring groove. To get that top ring up as far as possible, it was necessary to make sure the intake valve pocket was no deeper than needed. The low-set top ring was 0.375 down from the piston crown while the high-set one was 0.150. This gave crevice volumes of 1.36 and 0.55cc, respectively, for a reduction of 55 percent in crevice volume. Remember, we are only looking at a reduction of 0.81 cc, and you may well ask just how much a small change like that can possibly make.

The CR for the test engine was a solid 10.5:1. In this test, the pistons had a skirt profile that was intended to minimize piston-to-wall clearance. At the open end of the pistons, the clearance was only 0.001, which is relatively close for a forged piston. The clearance at the pin was 0.0035.

Also I need to make it clear that when I run tests I go to a lot of trouble to calibrate the carb right on, so there is a minimum of excess fuel. That is no more than whatever the engine wants for power optimization of the air/fuel ratio.

Additionally the carb had high-gain boosters (Braswell carb) that delivered good atomization and the heads were a relatively small port

(165 cc) variety (ported factory 186 castings). All this should add up to a better-than-average quality of mixture arriving at the cylinders (i.e., minimum of wet flow versus airborne fuel flow). The tests were run after these pertinent parameters were taken care of. The numbers in Figure 11.23 are from an average of seven runs, with the best and worst tests thrown out in each case and the rest averaged.

This is a test done as diligently as possible with the equipment available. The situation for the "before" test was as good as it gets, with the engine showing very good brake-specific fuel consumption. This indicates that the combustion process was already good. That probably meant the minimum of wet fuel entering the cylinders and, consequently, the minimum raw fuel into the ring land volume. Even with this best-case scenario, the power trend was decidedly upward.

Talking to various piston manufacturers has indicated that similar tests done on all-out race engines with a much higher CR have often shown bigger percentage gains. This makes sense; as more charge is driven into the ring land volume the higher the cylinder pressures

go. From this, we can reasonably conclude that what is shown in Figure 11.23 is about the minimum increase that can be expected. In round numbers, we are looking at an average of 1.5 percent for some additional cleanup on an already good combustion process.

This is a pretty good result, because all the theory on how a nearly unprecedented amount of charge can end up in the ring land volume has not as yet accounted for one important aspect: The reason the top of the piston is smaller is that this is where the most heat is and the top thus expands more. What may be a 2-cc-volume cold may only be a 1-cc-volume hot. So, with the volume even smaller than we calculate it to be, we can see that a crevice volume that is even very small has a disproportionate effect on the combustion process.

Where from Here?

Other than setting the ring up as high as possible or getting a ring company to re-investigate the Head Land ring, what else can we do to rid the combustion space of the top

ring land volume? About 20 years ago, Cosworth made a move to do just that. The company made the top land larger than normal, and then grooved it. The idea was that, during break-in and eventual WOT operation, the piston would touch the bore and wear the peaks from the grooving, so that the piston almost exactly fit the bore, thus eliminating most of the top ring land volume.

I remember talking to Cosworth's piston designer (the late Geoff Roper) about this and the fact they were just starting to do this for Cup Car pistons. That move might just have been the start of Cosworth's downslide in Cup Car piston sales! I forget what Cosworth called the grooving, but these days we commonly refer to them as "anti-detonation" grooves. How they help suppress detonation has not been convincingly explained to me, so I am still waiting on that one! I have never done a back-to-back test for power increase either, but they have now been around for more than 20 years. I think the jury is still out on the advantages of anti-detonation grooves.

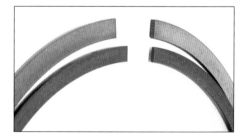

Fig. 11.27. The trend over the years has been for piston rings to become thinner and have less radial depth. Also, duty cycle permitting, the ring pack as a whole has moved toward the piston crown.

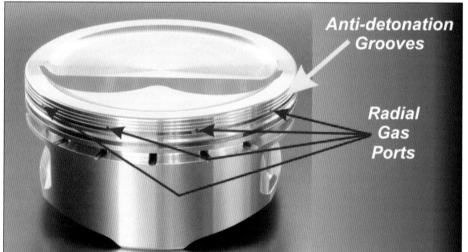

Fig. 11.28. This JE piston features many of the design parameters we have discussed as being pertinent to the combustion dynamics exhibited in a high-performance engine.

One aspect that creeps in here is the way increasing the cylinder pressure, either from compression or the combustion process, drives the charge into the top ring land volume. If you think about this, igniting the charge from the middle of the cylinder is the worst way to do this. If the charge burn is propagated from all around the circumference of the cylinder, the highest pressures occur long after the charge in close proximity to the ring land volume burns. Granted, this sounds like a good way to go, but firing the charge from all around the outside looks difficult to accomplish. It's difficult, yes, but not impossible.

About 1995, I met a guy in California who had designed plug electrodes into a head gasket. The gasket had about 6 points around the circumference that fired the charge. Fel-Pro apparently liked the idea—at least initially—because it acquired the rights to it. I never saw any test data, but I heard it worked pretty well. Unfortunately production was not practical; the heads had to be removed to change the plugs!

Conclusions

In this chapter, several things have become more clear. First, we talked about a lot of factors that influence combustion dynamics before even arriving at the combustion chamber. From this, it is evident that what happens inside the cylinder can be greatly influenced by how the intake charge is prepared prior to its arrival at the cylinder. Also the thermal barrier cases put forward here are examples from maybe a dozen or so tests. All were similar in their intent, and all show that the so-called Dyno Test Rule Number-1, concerning making only one change at a time and so often touted by do-it-yourself performance magazines, is seriously flawed.

So, What Are the Rules?

From the foregoing, we can draw a reliably tentative conclusion about combustion dynamics. Namely that applying any universal rules can all too often turn around and bite your rear end. Just to keep my feet on the ground, I have a policy: All lessons learned, no matter how certain or obvious they may seem, should be regularly re-appraised for anomalies that may actually reveal something that was overlooked or misinterpreted.

What can be said is that paying attention to port velocity to give good swirl pays off, especially at low speed. But above about 8,000 rpm or so, swirl becomes academic or indeed may, under some circumstances, prove to be a disadvantage. Keeping the combustion chambers compact and as crevice-free as possible is a decided plus. Placing the plug in a high-mixture-motion area is also a plus. To this, we can also add that under most circumstances holding the quench tight is also good, especially for engines that are required to deliver over a wide range with, say, about 8,000 rpm as a max.

Raising the CR increases torque, and consequently power, throughout the RPM range. Because raising the CR increases thermal efficiency, it brings about an increase in fuel economy. If a longer-duration cam is installed, raising the CR at the same time can be worth considerably more than these two moves done separately.

When the CR is raised, peak combustion pressures are increased. A rule for typical production engines is that combustion pressures are equal to the CR times 100. This tells us that, from a 10:1 engine, we expect to see about 1,000 psi of peak combustion pressure. For a well developed, high-performance engine, combustion pressures can be as much as the CR times 120.

MAXIMIZING COMPRESSION RATIO

Though not readily appreciated, understanding and optimizing an engine's compression and compression ratio is a valuable tool toward maximizing performance.

A four-stroke (or four-cycle) engine is so called because, in the process of producing power, the piston passes up and down the bore four times. These strokes or events are the induction, compression, power, and exhaust. As you may suppose, the effective function of all are important for producing a high-output engine. Of the four, the compression stroke has far less obvious but more reaching implications on an engine's optimal spec and its subsequent success as a power producer.

Obviously, the principal idea of the compression stroke is to compress the intake charge as effectively as possible, and to do so with minimal leakage. We need to remember that as we continue, because there are two principal factors associated with the compression ratio. The first is the calculated ratio, which we refer to as the geometric or static ratio. The second and equally important factor is how effectively, and to what degree, the physical components of the engine compress the charge into the combustion space. In essence, it's a measure of how effectively theoretical compression ratio is translated into real-world pre-combustion cylinder pressure. This is commonly known as the dynamic compression ratio and is influenced by such things as ring and valve seal

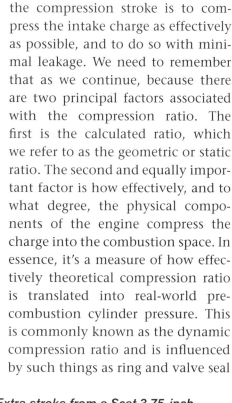

Fig. 12.1. Extra stroke from a Scat 3.75-inch stroker crank upped this 350 to 383 cubes and allowed a 13:1 CR to be achieved without compromising the combustion chamber of the un-ported Canfield heads. This high CR, in conjunction with a 300/304-degree Comp Cams solid flat-tappet cam, made 560 hp possible from what was essentially a low-cost "bolt it together" engine.

Four-Stroke Function

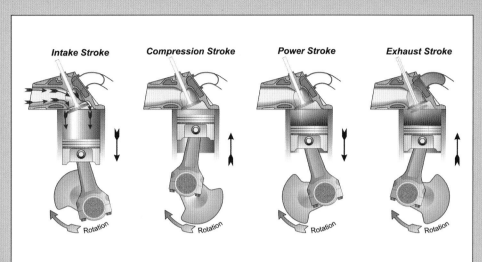

Intake Stroke **Compression Stroke** **Power Stroke** **Exhaust Stroke**

In a four-stroke engine, we have the intake, compression, power, and exhaust strokes. On the intake stroke a fresh air/fuel charge is pulled past the open intake valve as the piston moves down the bore.

At around BDC, the intake closes and the piston motion moving up the bore starts the compression stroke. At some point just before the piston reaches the top of the compression stroke at TDC, the spark plug fires. At this point, there is a small delay in the combustion before it really gets underway (hence the firing a little before TDC). As the piston goes past TDC, the combustion event burns the charge and the heat generated causes the contents of the cylinder to rapidly rise in pressure.

This pressure pushes the piston down the bore on the power stroke. As the piston approaches the end of the power stroke, the exhaust valve starts to open. Initially the gases, still at relatively high pressure, vent themselves out through the progressively opening exhaust valve.

By the time the piston starts to move up the bore, the exhaust valve is already well off its seat. After this initial cylinder "blow down," the piston's motion up the bore pushes out the remaining spent charges through the exhaust valve.

At the top of the exhaust stroke, the intake begins to open and the whole sequence of events starts over again.

---

and, to the greatest degree, valve opening/closing events.

Now you may well have heard the term compression ratio (CR) many times but may not know exactly what defines it and how it's calculated. If so, you need to refer to sidebar "Compression Ratio Definition" on page 146.

More on the Strokes

It may look like we are treading a well-worn path here, but it's worth taking a quick look at the four strokes, because each of the other three is intimately tied to the compression stroke. Every one of these strokes must accomplish its goal effectively for an engine to be able to produce a high output.

Let's start with the intake stroke. The more efficiently the cylinder is filled on the induction stroke, the more RPM the engine can turn before it "runs out of breath." The better the intake filling is, the higher the pressure achieved on the compression stroke. This, along with as high a compression ratio as the fuel permits, means significantly higher pressures on the power stroke.

On to the compression stroke. The higher the compression ratio, the higher the resultant combustion pressure. Not only that, but the charge burns faster, thus necessitat-

ing less advance for an optimal burn event. A higher CR also reduces the amount of residual exhaust remaining in the chamber at the beginning of the intake stroke. This reduces unwanted intake dilution by the exhaust. These are the most obvious power-enhancing factors, but they are not the biggest influencing factors. There are other less obvious but more influential implications that I cover later, when we look at the CR and compression factors in detail.

Next is the power stroke. Every bit of power the engine develops is made on this stroke. We need to make sure everything that happens before, during, and after this stroke

---

Compression Ratio Definition

The CR is the ratio of the volume above the piston at BDC (left) compared to the volume at TDC (right). The formula for finding the compression ratio is:

$$CR = \frac{(V + C)}{C}$$

Where:

V = the swept volume of the cylinder (i.e., the cylinder's displacement in cubic centimeters, or cc)

C = the total combustion-chamber volume (in cc) when the piston is at TDC

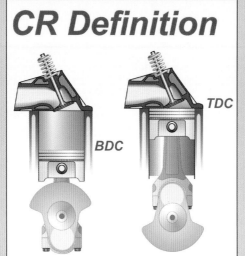

CR Definition

BDC

TDC

An example might look like this:

Assume the volume above the piston at BDC is 110 cc, with 100 cc being the displacement volume (V) due to piston motion, and 10 cc of the total combustion space (C) remaining at TDC. When the contents of the cylinder at BDC are squeezed into the 10 cc remaining at TDC, the charge occupies 1/11 of the space; so the CR is 11:1.

$$\frac{(100 + 10)}{10} = 11$$

To find out what total combustion chamber cc is required for the CR, you subtract 1 from that ratio and divide the result into the displacement volume of the cylinder.

Measuring Chamber Volume

The basic essentials to cc'ing heads (and pistons if they have a dish) are seen here. This includes a 100-cc burette and a stand to hold it. Also a Plexiglas plate is required which, for most domestic V-8 heads, requires some eyebrow cutouts to clear the valves. Comp Cams has an inexpensive kit with all the parts you need. Use windshield washer fluid because it is easy to see. Also the alcohol in it minimizes rust and helps reduce surface tension.

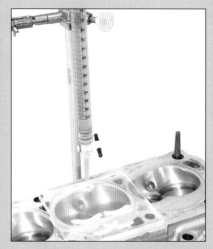

Finally, the exhaust stroke. Here, we need to make sure that cylinder emptying is done without undue pumping losses. Any pressure remaining in the cylinder while the piston is on the way up the bore is negative power. As far as exhaust stroke efficiency is concerned, having a higher CR can lead to significantly reduced exhaust pumping losses.

Thermodynamics Made Easy

It is easy to understand that increasing the CR raises cylinder pressures, thus causing torque output throughout the RPM range to simply follow suit. What is less obvious is that the increase in output from the higher CR comes about largely due to an increase in thermal efficiency. Thermal efficiency is a measure of how effectively the engine converts the heat-generating potential of the

either enhances it or at the very least has minimal negative impact on it. That means sealing the cylinder in the first place, making sure it does not leak throughout the power stroke, and ensuring that its sealing ability is not at the expense of high ring-to-cylinder-wall friction.

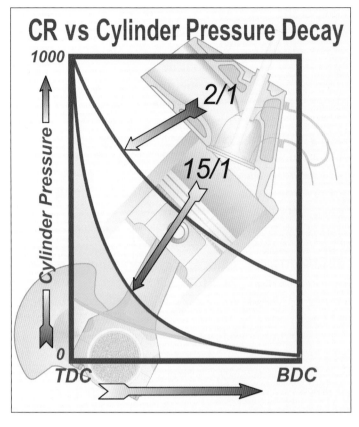

CR vs Cylinder Pressure Decay

Fig. 12.2. If a 2:1 and a 15:1 cylinder start at the same pressure, the 15:1 cylinder's pressure decays at a far higher rate. So it delivers the power to the crank mostly before 90 degrees after TDC is reached. Unless supercharged, a 2:1 cylinder only achieves about 200 psi. The difference in power between the two ratios is represented by the shaded green area.

% Thermal Efficiency $E = 1 - \left(\dfrac{1}{R^{K-1}}\right)$

In this formula, R is the compression ratio (CR) and K is the coefficient of adiabatic expansion for air which is nominally 1.4.

Fig. 12.3. This formula for the thermal efficiency of the Otto cycle may not look like much, but when all its implications are applied, it can be responsible for about 200 hp of the total produced by a 500-ci Pro Stock engine.

New Compression Ratio

Original Compression Ratio	8/1	9/1	10/1	11/1	12/1	13/1	14/1	15/1	16/1
8/1	0	2.0	3.7	5.2	6.5	7.6	8.7	9.7	10.5
9/1		0	1.7	3.2	4.5	5.7	6.7	7.7	8.5
10/1			0	1.5	2.8	4.0	5.0	6.0	6.8
11/1				0	1.3	2.5	3.5	4.5	5.3
12/1					0	1.2	2.2	3.2	4.0
13/1						0	1.0	2.0	2.9
14/1							0	0.9	1.8
15/1								0	0.9

Fig. 12.4. To find out what a higher CR may be worth, locate the existing ratio in the left-hand column. Follow across until you reach the appropriate column with the new CR at the top. The figure in the intersecting box represents about the minimum-percent increase to expect.

fuel, when burned with an appropriate amount of air, into mechanical power.

To more clearly appreciate how the thermal efficiency is improved, we need to consider the opposite side of the CR coin. This is the expansion ratio (ER), which describes what occurs as the piston moves down the bore on the power stroke rather than what happens as it moves up on the compression stroke.

Take a look at Figure 12.2 and then let's go through the characteristic difference (computed taking into account typical heat losses) between a high-compression cylinder and a low-compression cylinder. For a moment, imagine that both the 15:1 and the 2:1 cylinders start off at TDC with 1,000 psi. As the piston of each cylinder moves down the bore, the drop in pressure follows a distinctly different line. The 15:1 cylinder drops pressure much faster than its 2:1 counterpart because of its more rapid change in volume. It only has to go down the bore a short way for the original volume to have doubled, whereas the 2:1 cylinder must travel to the bottom of the bore to double its original volume.

At the bottom of the stroke, the 15:1 cylinder has dropped to about 25 psi above atmospheric pressure, whereas the 2:1 cylinder is still at some 260 psi. In simple terms, the high-compression cylinder, when the exhaust valve opens at BDC, is only dumping 2.5 percent of its original pressure while the 2:1 cylinder is dumping 26 percent!

Up to this point, we have assumed that both cylinders start with 1,000 psi. But the best that the 2:1 cylinder really generates is about 200 psi. That produces the lower curve (light blue line) in Figure 12.2. The 2:1 and

15:1 cylinders both draw in about the same amount of fuel and air. But we can see that the 15:1 cylinder has more area under the curve by an amount equal to the green shaded area. Adding the green shaded area under the curve amounts to nearly doubling the power output from the same amount of fuel and air. That means, from the same heating value of fuel, we have doubled the thermal efficiency, and in so doing extracted twice the power.

You can now see why a high-compression cylinder produces better power and fuel economy. It is not solely because the charge is squeezed harder and the resulting combustion pressure is increased, but also because the higher expansion ratio allows more energy to be extracted from the original high-pressure charge.

Simple Theoretical Power Gains

Figure 12.3 can be used to calculate the theoretical power gains seen from raising the CR, and Figure 12.4 saves you the effort of calculating those gains. This formula does not take into account the inevitable heat losses, and to allow for this the value of K is commonly reduced from 1.4 to 1.3. Using this value, we find that changing nothing else but the compression output pretty much follows the trend dictated by the formula until about 14:1. From there on up, some heat is absorbed by chemical reactions brought about by the high temperatures and pressures generated. This heat is subsequently delivered back to the cycle, but it's too late in the expansion event to serve any useful purpose.

Because of this, many books tell you that trying to utilize CR past about 14:1 is a fruitless exercise. But this only applies if no other changes are made to the engine. If the side benefits of ultra-high compression are taken advantage of, the situation takes a complete about-face.

Dynamic Compression

In the real world we normally find that theoretical increases are not usually seen in practice because of losses which, to simplify already complex theory, we have ignored. For high-performance engines, part of what has been overlooked by the simple thermal efficiency equation (Figure 12.3) works to produce results far better than theorized. In other words, all the numbers in Figure 12.4 are on the low side. For instance, a mildly modified 9:1 350 small-block Chevy makes about 380 ft-lbs of torque. Based solely on our thermal efficiency formula, raising the compression to 12:1 should bump that figure to 397 ft-lbs.

In practice that number is usu-ally exceeded and the bigger the cam, the bigger the gain. To understand how much more can be had, let's look at the effect the cam has on the situation.

At lower RPM, the static CR is never realized because our thermal efficiency formula assumes that the intake valve closes exactly at BDC prior to the start of the compression stroke. This does not happen in reality.

At low RPM, port velocity and pressure waves are too weak to produce any cylinder ramming. Couple this to the fact that even a short cam of some 250 degrees of off-the-seat timing does not close the valve until about 50 degrees after BDC. Figure 12.5 shows the typical extent of piston motion back up the bore before the intake closes for three cams.

Because of the delayed intake closure, there is considerable piston motion up the bore from BDC before

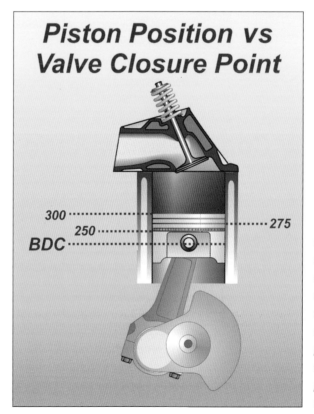

Fig. 12.5. Because the intake valve does not close at BDC, the increase in static compression delivers a far more effective increase in dynamic compression. Here are some typical intake valve closing points for three different cam-duration figures.

Angle Milling for Compression

In 1955, when General Motors introduced the small-block Chevy, the head featured a wedge chamber, and eventually this became the most common chamber shape for a two-valve-per-cylinder engine. Chevrolet adopted a 23-degree valve angle, which means the valve is 23 degrees from the cylinder bore axis. While that may have been okay for the small-chamber engines of the day with 8:1 or 9:1 compression ratios, it does present a problem when using big valves in unshrouded chambers. In this situation, we cannot make the chamber small enough to get a high compression ratio. This leaves us with using a high piston dome, which is not good for burn characteristics, or doing something else.

Well, that something else is angle milling. The heads are set up so that milling takes much more off the spark plug side of the head than the intake manifold side. This results in a much smaller chamber volume than would be the case if the head had just been flat milled. Also, as the valve lift progresses, the valve head is moved farther away from the cylinder wall, and therefore is slightly less shrouded. Another small advantage is the valve pockets, which for a given valve-to-piston clearance are shallower.

Most production heads won't angle mill much more than 1 to 1½ degrees or so, while some aftermarket heads have sufficient material in just the required places to allow an angle cut of as much as 4 degrees. At this extreme level of angle milling, you need to know what you are doing or you can easily ruin a set of heads.

In these photos, I am about to start porting a set of heads for a drag car. The head is a 23-degree Dart Platinum Pro 1. I had my friend Bill Rose do the angle milling work as he is very experienced in this area. He has gained this experience from building 2-barrel-class V-8s that are limited to stock ports and a flat-top piston. With these restrictions it is a case of "he who has the most compression probably wins."

The Dart heads shown here have been milled so the valve angle is at 19.75 degrees. A finished chamber volume of 45 cc, allows me to make the 16:1 compression ratio with just a small dome in the region of 0.075 inch on the piston. Follow along with the photos as I go through what is involved.

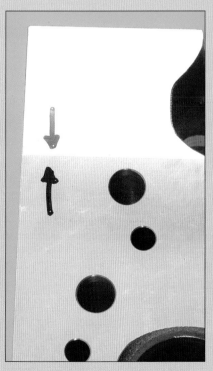

On a small-block Chevy (and other similar style heads), it is not necessary to angle mill across the entire original head face. The extensions on either end that are normally sealing the lifter valley can be left as original. The change in angle can be seen at the arrows. Sealing the lifter valley is done using silicone sealer at this spot.

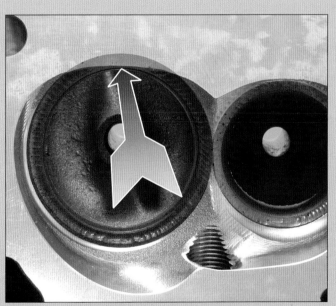

Other than deck thickness another limitation to the amount that can be angle milled is the valve seat. Here, the arrow shows the approximate limit for an uncut seat insert.

Angle Milling for Compression *CONTINUED*

Here is a finished valve seat. Note that it is only just cleaned up. Also note the dramatic reduction in chamber volume. With a volume as small as this, a flat-top piston 0.005 out of the bore would deliver a 15:1 CR in a 350.

Once the head has been angle milled, none of the bolt holes align correctly. This is remedied by re-drilling the bolt holes in the correct position and at the right angle.

Rolling a 23-degree head to 19.75 degrees means that the chamber tends to move away from the spark-plug-side cylinder wall. Here, you see the position of the cylinder wall scribed on the head. Most of the metal between the two arrows can be removed to further reduce shrouding compared to a 23-degree head.

the intake actually closes. This, at low rpm, pushes some of the mixture back into the intake manifold. This means the volumetric efficiency (breathing efficiency), and thus the effective displacement of the cylinder, is well below 100 percent. In other words, a 100-cc cylinder with a static CR of 10:1 may only trap 75 cc of air. This means the dynamic CR, at about 8.5:1, has dropped well below the static CR of 10:1. The bigger the cam, the more this effect comes into play.

The following example shows just how much influence the delayed intake closure has on the dynamic CR. Let us take three different-duration cams, all having a 108 lobe centerline angle (LCA), and all timed-in at 4 degrees advanced. Along with this, let's say our static CR measures 12:1. With a 250-degree duration cam, the dynamic CR is in the mid to low 11s. For a cam of some 275-degrees duration, the dynamic CR drops to around the mid 10s.

Because of the piston, rod, and crank geometry, the piston tends to move much more slowly around BDC. This works in our favor for shorter cams, but the piston quickly moves out of this sweet spot, so when we get much past about 280 degrees, we had better have a decent dynamic CR. To give you an idea of the extent to which this occurs, our 300-degree race cam used with a static CR of

12:1 has a dynamic CR of only about 8.3:1. This snippet of info should bring home the importance of having sufficient CR for a big cam. If it doesn't, maybe the dyno test results in Figure 12.6 will.

These are some tests I did with the 2-liter Ford Pinto series of cams I designed for Kent Cams in England some years ago. I realize that very few of you drive Pintos but the 2-liter version of this engine, because of its geometry, reacts just about the same as a typical small-block Chevy; so the results do directly apply. From these results we see that, with a 9:1 CR, a 265-degree cam produced (the gray curves of Figure 12.6) some decent results from low RPM on up.

As expected, it started to drop torque by the time 5,000 rpm was being approached and power peaked just shy of 140 hp. This cam was then substituted for a 285-degree cam.

On the same 9:1 CR (blue curves of Figure 12.6) this bigger cam dropped 38 ft-lbs of torque at 1,750 rpm. That amounts to a 32-percent reduction. The extra duration did not start to pay off until 3,750 rpm. From there on up the bigger cam paid off by delivering an increase in peak torque of 4 ft-lbs and almost 26 hp.

At this point, the head was milled to bump the CR to almost 12:1. The results of this move are shown by the green curves in Figure 12.6. As you can see, this increase in compression regained almost all the low-speed torque that was lost. On top of this the big-cam/high-compression combo produced an increase of 15 ft-lbs and 33 hp. Projecting that result

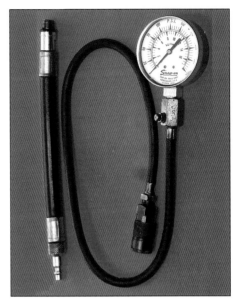

Fig. 12.7. A typical compression tester. Preferably with the engine warm, the procedure is to open the throttle a little and crank the motor. Keep cranking and check to see what pressure is registered on the eighth compression stroke.

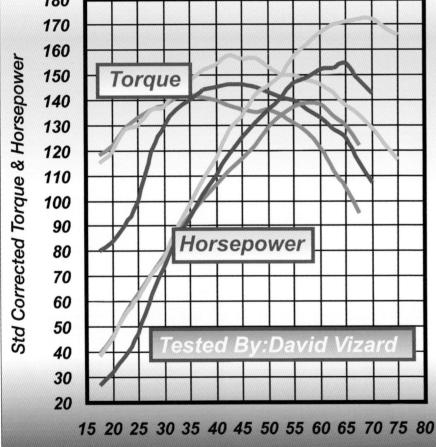

Fig. 12.6. When used in conjunction with a bigger cam, increased compression can work wonders for the entire curve. When a 265-degree cam (gray curve) was substituted for a 285-degree cam (blue curve), a substantial drop in low-speed output was seen. Raising the CR from 9:1 to 12:1 recovered almost all the lost low end and gave a further big increase in top-end output.

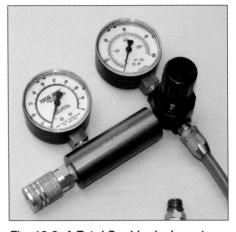

Fig. 12.8. A Total Seal leak-down tester. An air supply of a little more than 100 psi is required to use this. The percent of leak down is the measure of the calibration pressure (100 psi) versus the pressure the cylinder can sustain after leakage has taken its toll.

to equate to a 350-ci engine, the numbers look more like 40-plus ft-lbs extra and 95 hp. Are these numbers realistic? Sure they are. I have seen a 100-plus-hp increase from a 355-ci small-block Chevy with 25 degrees more cam duration, 0.100 more lift, and 2 points more compression.

When we go back to the basics, the big increases seen with a combo of more compression and cam are easier to understand. If you check the numbers in Figure 12.4, you see that the biggest gains from a compression increase happen when moving from a low compression to a higher one. Going from 8:1 to 10:1 is worth a theoretical 3.7 percent while raising the compression the same two points from 11:1 to 13:1 is only worth 2.5 percent. This means the bigger the cam, the more responsive it is to an increase in CR, especially in the lower-RPM range.

Compression Pressure

By now, some of you are wondering whether the engine you have just built has enough compression for the cam you chose. Assuming your engine has good ring and valve seal, a simple way to determine whether this is the case is to check cylinder compression pressures. With the ring package and bore prep procedure I use, my own engines are almost always near zero leakage and I discuss how to achieve that on page 154. If the cylinders are sealing well, I look for 190 psi as a lower limit, with preferably 200 psi as a target when using 93-octane fuel. For every octane number less than 93 the compression pressure needs to be about 5 psi less, to avoid detonation under normal circumstances.

How effective a compression test may be, for determining whether or not the cam you are using is accompanied by adequate compression, hinges to a certain extent on how well the rings and valves seal. The best way to establish that is to do a leak-down test. This requires a leak-down tester and a source of compressed air at about 100 to 110 psi.

Just how much leak-down is acceptable is open to debate. With the rings and bore prep that I use, I expect no more than 1 percent and something close to zero is what I normally see. But the average street engine is rarely that good, so if your cylinders check out at 7 percent or less, you are okay. With such a cylinder, let the compression gauge go eight pumps and use that as a reading to determine your cam/compression compatibility. If the ring seal shows 10-percent leak-down, that's borderline for a high-performance engine and compression readings

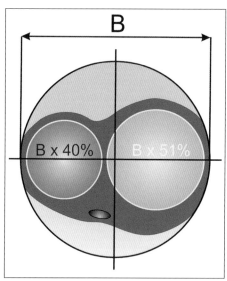

Fig. 12.9. For engines with a CR between about 9.5:1 and 12:1, the relative sizes of the valves for best output fall about as shown here. However, as the CR is increased, the bias toward increased intake size at the expense of exhaust size starts to have a measurable influence.

Fig. 12.10. A derivative of one of Ford's most successful race heads ever—the D3. A 350-inch drag race engine with 15:1 compression is capable of 900-plus hp from a single 4-barrel configuration. The point to note here is that all the exhaust from such an output still goes through a 1.6-inch exhaust valve just as we see on a typical street 350. But the intake is almost 2¼ inches in diameter, so the size bias is much more toward the intake than is seen on a low-compression engine.

Fig. 12.11. This Chrysler Hemi head (2003-on) has two spark plugs and two quench pads. This, along with an excellent port and valve layout giving near-zero valve shrouding, results in a head capable of high output without resorting to an overly long duration cam.

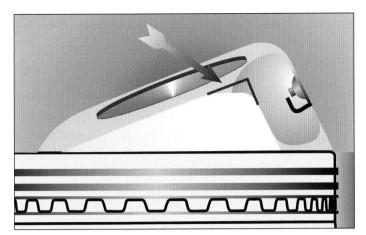

Fig. 12.12. If the dome intrudes too far into the combustion chamber, it inhibits flame travel. Out of the box, many pistons are shaped like the line indicated by the arrow. This needs to be removed as shown to promote more effective combustion.

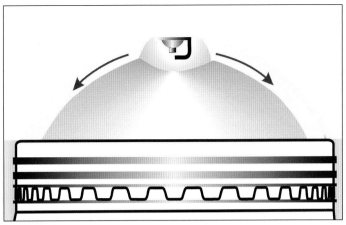

Fig. 12.13. Here is why a high-compression ratio in a hemi configuration can fail. With a high dome, the combustion chamber ends up resembling the skin of an orange. This has about as bad a surface-area-to-volume ratio as can be had and effectively quenches flame travel.

are going to be artificially low. If the leakage is 15 percent or more, maybe you should consider new rings to be a performance-enhancing move, as much as a reconditioning one.

Intake- to Exhaust-Valve Ratios

The controlling factors influencing the best intake/exhaust ratio for maximum output has been much debated for the past half-century. (Of course, this assumes all the available space for valves is used.) For the most part, it has left the reader little or no wiser. The often-touted 75-percent rule is usually accepted without further question. In reality, the value is far from fixed. The optimum intake/exhaust ratio could range from as little as 1:1 (for a low-CR supercharged engine) to as much as 1:0.6 (for a very-high-CR NA engine).

What is usually not appreciated is that the CR is, for the most part, the controlling factor. Because the high-compression cylinder delivers energy to the crank much earlier in the power stroke, there are implica-

tions we can take advantage of. The most obvious is the exhaust valve opening can be made earlier, and it can be held open longer. This can be done for an improved high-RPM output without significantly impacting the engine's low-speed output. The rule here is that the higher the compression ratio goes, the smaller the

exhaust valve needed to get the job done. This in turn leaves more room for a larger intake.

When we are forced to use a lower compression, such as in the case of a supercharged engine, the exhaust valve needs to be left on the seat until later in the power stroke to avoid unnecessarily dumping usable

Fig. 12.14. A stroker crank, such as this lightweight Scat big-block 1/4-inch example, not only adds inches for more torque and horsepower but also makes it easier to achieve a higher C/R without compromising chamber shape.

Fig. 12.15. Big-block Chevys thrive on high compression, but remember that the full benefits of a high CR can be lost if the piston crown shape is not conducive to effective combustion. Here we see Silv-O-Lite's new Icon high-power big-block forging. Note how the area around the spark plug location (arrow) has been formed to promote flame travel.

cylinder pressure. Because it has to open later, there is less time to dump the exhaust, especially in the blow-

Fig. 12.16. If your target CR can be achieved with a dished piston, such as the JE item shown here, so much the better. Going this route usually guarantees an unimpeded flame travel.

down phase, so a larger valve must be used at the expense of the intake. That 75-percent exhaust flow rule mentioned earlier works for engines in the 10:1 to 13:1 range, but by the time we get to 16:1 plus, the optimum is to have the exhaust flow at about 65 percent of the intake.

Maximizing High-Ratio Results

By now, it is pretty clear that making the most of the potential that can be had from high compression is a goal worth pursuing. But as the ratios sought get higher, problems can begin to arise. Probably the most commonly seen of these is due to the final combustion-chamber shape achieved when all the stops have been pulled out.

The problem here is, as ratios much above about 10:1 are required, the only way to further minimize the volume after maximizing head milling is to have a raised-crown piston. To a point this is okay, but if the crown intrudes into the chamber too far it can, as previously mentioned, severely compromise the flame travel, resulting in a very ineffective combustion process. How much can be lost? Suffice it to say, I have seen 100 hp disappear because of a piston crown intruding about 1/8 inch too much.

The rule here is, unless you know what combination of chamber and crown form works or are prepared to do the necessary R&D, don't go overboard on crown intrusion into the chamber. For typical small-block V-8s from Chevrolet, Chrysler, or Ford, a good guideline is to use no more than about 0.100- to maybe 0.125-inch crown height in your quest for a high CR.

If you are forced to stick with conventional heads patterned after the OE-style head, big-block

Fig. 12.17. If strong torque figures per cubic inch from a big-block Chevy are to be realized, the combustion event needs to be a priority. This means attending to wet flow, chamber and piston form, valve events, and ignition. (For full details of what is required here get a copy of my book, **How to Build Max-Performance Chevy Big-Blocks on a Budget**.)

Chevys can be something of a law unto themselves. Compared to a regular parallel-valve engine, the chamber is somewhat less than conventional. A big-block Chevy tolerates a substantially raised crown before the tradeoff starts to cancel out potential gains. The key is to make sure the raised section of the crown does not too closely shroud the spark plug.

Fig. 12.18. Note the minimal raised crown on this Calico-coated Lunati piston (left). It was used in a 441-ci small-block Chevy to achieve a 13:1 CR in conjunction with this chamber form (also coated) in conventional 23-degree heads (right). On 100-octane fuel, it delivered 600 ft-lbs and more than 700 hp, and was street drivable.

If achieving the CR sought results in an overly intrusive crown, there is an alternative solution. Instead of trying to reduce the capacity of the combustion chamber, try increasing the capacity of the cylinder. Either a bore or stroke increase does this. For instance, if you were looking to achieve, say, 10.5:1 with a 454, it would take a maximum head milling job plus a piston intrusion approaching 1/2 inch. The head-milling job is going to mean a lot of possibly expensive manifold machining to re-align the ports. An easier and only minimally more expensive way is to install one of Scat's cast-steel 4¼-inch stroker cranks.

This and a 0.100 overbore delivers 505 inches and also allows you to achieve a 10.5:1 ratio with a very acceptable crown height of about 0.150. The same kind of move can be beneficially applied to small-blocks. Using an inexpensive stroker crank in a 350 Chevy not only delivers extra cubes, but also allows a 10.5:1 CR to be achieved with flat-top pistons and regular un-milled 68-cc heads.

Quench Clearance

The quench clearance is the distance the deck of the piston is from the cylinder head face at TDC. Loose (wide) quench clearances can actually promote detonation. The worst to have for most conventional-style wedge-head V-8s is about 0.100 to 0.125 inch. Reducing this clearance (by block milling or using a taller piston) can actually stave off detonation by a substantial amount. How tight the quench can be made depends on how flexible the block

Fig. 12.19. Getting an LS6 Chevy to produce 750 hp and still retain some semblance of street drivability does not happen by chance. Success was achieved by diligent attention to maximizing component airflow and tuned lengths of the intake and exhaust.

Fig. 12.20. Top-notch ring seal starts with an equally top grade bore and hone job. Always have the bores honed with a deck plate and finish recommended by the ring manufacturer.

and bottom-end assembly is and how much thermal expansion has to be allowed for. With good steel rods and crank, the net clearance can usually be taken down to 0.030. With a typical Fel-Pro gasket of 0.040-inch thickness, this means the pistons come out of the block by 0.010.

If quench is so good at suppressing detonation and allowing the use of higher CRs for more power and better mileage, why doesn't the factory make it tight to start with? In a nutshell, the answer is emissions. Tight quench areas cause unburned hydrocarbon emissions to increase. High-compression ratios bring about a dramatic increase in oxides of nitrogen, which are the primary cause of smog. Should we worry about this for our street machines? No; some high-flow cats and a well-calibrated fuel delivery system keep emissions adequately in check.

Containing the Pressure

Having a high-compression ratio brings about greater demands on cylinder sealing. The higher the pressures involved, the more attention you

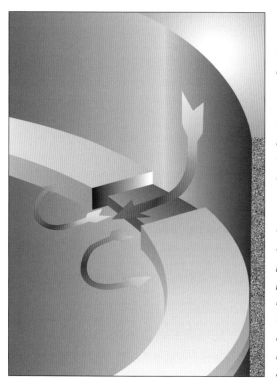

Fig. 12.21. My extensive testing has shown Total Seal rings can produce virtually zero leak-down and can continue to do so for as much as 100,000 miles. Here is how they work. First, the gap for the lower ring is on the opposite side of the bore where it is sealed off by the upper ring. Gas pressure, routed from the top side of the piston, passes down and through the gap as shown, or through the radial gas ports if the piston has them. This pressurizes the back side of the ring, ensuring firm contact with the cylinder wall. Because upper and lower ring are both virtually in contact with the bore, no leakage route exists.

Fig. 12.22. Gas porting is a technique whereby compression and combustion pressure is routed to the back side of the ring, thus pressing it more firmly against the cylinder bore wall. Piston deck located ports such as shown here work well for a drag race engine but plug up too easily for an endurance engine.

must pay to details. The first part of the equation for sealing the cylinder is to make sure your machine shop hones the block correctly. This should involve using a deck plate to simulate the distortion brought about by the stresses of head bolt tightening.

Then make sure your machine shop is aware of the type of piston ring material being used, so they can apply an appropriate finish.

Next, give the bores a good rubdown with a new Scotch Brite–type pad and plenty of Gunk engine cleaner. After that, scrub (with a stiff brush) the bores with a strong liquid detergent and rinse them with hot water.

When you are sure they are clean and grit free, immediately spray the machined surfaces with WD-40 to prevent rust.

With the bores ready, let's look at the rings that are to ride on them. With modern oils, ring wear is hardly the problem it used to be; so use the thinnest practical rings. Many older-style V-8 pistons are still in wide production. The majority of these pistons still have 5/64 compression rings. There is no good reason for using these wider rings. The 1/16- or even 0.043-inch-wide rings are what you should go for.

Be aware that the wider the ring gaps are, the greater the loss of cylinder pressure and, consequently, power. Add to this an increase in blow-by into the crankcase. This contaminates the oil faster and necessitates more frequent oil changes. If you stick with conventional rings, gap them to the minimum recommended by the manufacturer. If you can afford them, go with Total Seal rings because they really do deliver near-100-percent sealing and, equally important, they maintain it over a substantially longer period than even the best regular-type rings.

I mentioned the term "gas porting" earlier, but I am not quite finished with it yet. Gas porting is a technique to back up the top ring with combustion chamber pressure, so that the ring is more firmly pressed against the bore. There are two types of gas ports: those that pass down through the crown of the piston (see Figure 12.22) and those that are located radially, intersecting the top surface of the top ring groove.

The radial-style gas ports are common for long-distance race engines. The current trend is to use radial gas ports because they seem to be as effective, but do not unduly accelerate ring and bore wear at TDC. With a good race blend or street synthetic oil, bore wear at TDC is not really an issue. I have just completed a 1,000-mile endurance test with the new Joe Gibbs Racing race oil and the rings of the gas-ported JE pistons in my Cup Car engine wore less than 0.0003 off the surface. This amount of wear led to the ring gap getting bigger by only about 0.0010. An oil analysis at the 100- and 1,000-mile point indicated that most of the wear took place in the first 100 miles. This indicates that the ring and oil combination could be good for as much as 10,000 race miles.

SOURCE GUIDE

Air Flow Research
28611 W. Industry Drive
Valencia, CA 91355
877-892-8844
www.airflowresearch.com

Audie Technology
23 N. Trooper
Trooper, PA 19403
610-630-5895
www.audietechnology.com

Brodix Inc.
301 Maple, P.O. Box 1347
Mena, AR 71953
479-394-1075
www.brodix.com

Calico Coatings
6400 Denver Industrial Park Road
Denver, NC 28037
704-483-2202
www.calicocoatings.com

Dart Machinery, Inc.
353 Oliver Street
Troy, MI 48084
248-362-1188
www.dartheads.com

Design Dreams
513-403-3165
Email: Design_Dreams@cinci.rr.com

Dr. J's Performance
436 Montgomery Street
Orange, CA 92868
714-943-3404
www.j-performance.com

Edelbrock Corp.
2700 California Street, P.O. Box 3500
Torrance, CA 90503-3907
310-781-2222
www.edelbrock.com

EngineQuest
4050 Wentworth Avenue
Chicago, IL 60609
773-624-6111
www.aaeq.net

Ferrea Racing Components
2600 N.W. 55 Court, Suite #234
Ft. Lauderdale, FL 33309
888-733-2505
www.ferrea.com

Motion Software, Inc.
Anahiem, CA
714-231-3801
www.motionsoftware.com

Performance Trends
P.O. Box 530164
Livonia, MI 48153
248-473-9230
www.performancetrends.com

Racing Head Service
3416 Democrat Road
Memphis, TN 38118
877-776-4323
www.racingheadservice.com

Tech Line Coatings
26844 Adams
Murrieta, CA 92562
972-775-6130
www.techlinecoatings.com

Trick Flow Specialties
285 West Avenue
Tallmadge, OH 44278
330-630-1555
www.trickflow.com

Ultra Pro Machining
6350 Brookshire Boulevard
Charlotte, NC 28216
704-392-9955
www.ultrapromachining.net

Notes

Notes